Laws, Mind, and Free Will

Life and Mind: Philosophical Issues in Biology and Psychology
Kim Sterelny and Robert A. Wilson, editors

Laws, Mind, and Free Will

Steven Horst

The MIT Press
Cambridge, Massachusetts
London, England

For information about quantity discounts, email special_sales@mitpress.mit.edu

Set in Stone Sans and Stone Serif by Toppan Best-set Premedia Limited. Printed and bound in the United States of America.

Library of Congress Cataloging-in-Publication Data

Horst, Steven W., 1960–
Laws, mind, and free will / Steven Horst.
    p.   cm.—(Life and mind)
"A Bradford book."
Includes bibliographical references and index.
ISBN 978-0-262-01525-7 (hardcover : alk. paper)
1. Free will and determinism. 2. Philosophy of mind. 3. Law (Philosophy) I. Title.
BJ1468.5.H64   2011
123'.5—dc22

2010026310

10 9 8 7 6 5 4 3 2 1

to all my teachers, living and departed

Contents

Preface

It is customary to acknowledge in a preface that whatever is of value in the book is largely a product of the contributions of others. In this case, at least, such an acknowledgment is more than a mere formality. This book is, in fact, a kind of by-blow of an entirely different project, one that was originally envisioned as a critique of naturalism in philosophy of mind. The main line of argumentation in that project, which focused on notions of reduction and reductionism in philosophy of science and philosophy of mind, is contained in another book, *Beyond Reduction* (Horst 2007). Both that book and this one are products of a philosophical realization that overtook me in the midst of that project and shook me out of my residually Empiricist slumbers. I hope in this preface to give due credit to the several people who acted as beacons guiding me out of the neo-Empiricist night in which all ravens are black.

My original conception of the naturalism project would have resulted in a book that took a position much like the one David Chalmers took in his 1996 book *The Conscious Mind*, only with a Kantian rather than a dualist twist, and with a great deal more philosophy of science, particularly with respect to questions about the nature of explanation in the physical sciences and the sciences of the mind. At that time, my implicit prejudices, outside the domain of the mind, were Empiricist and reductionist: I took the view that laws were basically empirical generalizations, and that inter-theoretic reductions were the norm outside of the sciences of the mind, and hence that the "explanatory gaps" encountered with respect to consciousness, intentionality, and normativity were unique and sexy problems. One thing I set out to do, and which I had seldom seen done, was to look closely at the kinds of explanations one finds in the sciences of the mind, and see what explanatory virtues they might possess, even though they fall short of reductive explanations.

I discovered, when I began to talk to the philosophers of science, that my reductionist assumptions were naive and outdated. Not only has contemporary philosophy of science rejected the notion that inter-theoretic reducibility is a kind of *a priori* test of the legitimacy of a special science such as psychology; it has also revealed, through case studies, that such reductions are in fact quite rare. I think it was Paul Humphreys who first whacked me over the head with this realization, and Bas van Fraassen who tattooed it into my brain during a sabbatical spent in part at Princeton in 1997–98 with the help of a National Endowment for the Humanities Fellowship (for which I am duly grateful both to the NEH and to Princeton, and particularly to the late Margaret Wilson, who was my sponsor there). My Wesleyan colleague Joseph Rouse also deserves credit here for setting me on the right path, as do Michael Silberstein and William Bechtel, with whom I have discussed such topics and sparred in colloquia in recent years.

Besides the reductionist vision of inter-theoretic relations, the other mainstay of the Positivist-Empiricist philosophy of science that was a kind of orthodoxy through much of the twentieth century was its view of laws as universally quantified claims (perhaps modally strengthened) that range over real-world objects and events. I had, for I do not recall how long, felt this view was somewhat problematic, in that I held laws and theories to involve idealized claims. As I developed my views on this topic, people started telling me that I sounded like Nancy Cartwright. (Well, at least that my ideas sounded like hers.) And so, in the course of working on the naturalism project, I began reading Cartwright's work, and found that there was a great deal we agreed upon, a great deal that she had argued in ways I would have been incapable of arguing, but also a great deal about her views that I found unclear or disagreed with. But, at very least, she had already developed the kind of arguments against the Empiricist view of laws that I wished to avail myself of, and reading her work helped force me to recognize that I needed to replace my view of laws with a more adequate one. (There are, of course, a number of ironies along the way here. It was van Fraassen who set me on a course that led to my rejecting Empiricism; indeed, by the time I seriously engaged Cartwright's views I had come to the conclusion that those views were insufficiently distanced from the Empiricists she was attacking.)

A much more modest treatment of laws was a part of the initial draft of the naturalism project, initially titled "Mind and the World of Nature" (a title on which I claim dibs as a possible future book for the educated public). But eventually it became clear that the main line of that project was about reduction, not laws. Yet it also became clear that the material on laws was of interest for independent reasons in philosophy of psychology and in philosophy of mind. And so I spun it off into an independent book of its own. My recollection is that the core of parts I and II of this book took shape in a great creative whirlwind of perhaps a month's time, and that the initial drafts of most of the chapters in those parts were written each in a single sitting. (They have each gone through six or seven subsequent drafts, and several more chapters have been added.)

I was initially ambivalent as to whether to combine the purely philosophical arguments set forth in parts I and II with the case studies presented in part III. On the one hand, I wish to establish the importance of both the details of the sciences of cognition and up-to-date philosophy of science for those doing philosophy of psychology; on this score, case studies seemed almost obligatory. On the other hand, the audience interested in case studies is almost completely different from that interested in "the vindication of psychology," not to mention free will. In the end, I decided to include case studies, but to put them at the end.

Michael Silberstein, Eric Schliesser, Joseph Rouse, Brian Fay, and Elise Springer read drafts of the chapters that now make up part I. Silberstein has also done heroic duty in reading subsequent drafts and suggesting improvements. Eric Schwitzgebel and his seminar at U.C. Riverside ploughed through the ponderous 900-page predecessor manuscript, as did Carol Slater. Louise Antony commented on some cognate material at a meeting of the Society for Philosophy and Psychology. And William Bechtel, John Bickle, Michael Silberstein, Paul Churchland, Peter Godfrey-Smith, and Cory Wright interacted with some of the topics at a series of colloquia on the topic of what contemporary philosophy of mind can learn from contemporary philosophy of science. I have learned a great deal from these and a number of other people. (I shall mention in addition Ernan McMullin, to whom I give major credit for inspiring me, years ago, to take the roles of both mathematization and idealization in science seriously.) Special thanks also to Doretta Wildes, who proofread the manuscript with the exception of this sentence, saving me from some silly blunders and reminding me (ever so gently) how much I had forgotten about the proper use of hyphens. Of course, the blame for mistakes, logical lapses, and incomprehensible philosophical gaffes is entirely my own.

Middletown, Connecticut
Feast of the Holy Innocents (December 28), 2008

I Laws and the Mind: Philosophical Issues

1 Laws and the Mind

Since the seventeenth century, our understanding of the natural world has been one of phenomena that behave in accordance with natural laws. While other elements of the early modern scientific worldview (i.e., that of the seventeenth and eighteenth centuries) may be rejected or at least held in question—including the metaphor of the world as a great machine, the narrowly mechanist assumption that all physical interactions must be contact interactions, and the idea that matter might actually be *obeying* rules laid down by its Divine Author—the notion of natural law has continued to play a pivotal role in actual scientific practice, in our philosophical interpretations of science, and in our metaphysics.

The history of philosophy since early modernity has been, in no small measure, an attempt to understand the things that are most central to our self-image as human beings against the backdrop of our best understanding of the natural sciences. This project, of course, has its fingers in many philosophical pies, including ethics, the metaphysics of freedom, the mind-body problem, and naturalized epistemology. In philosophy of psychology, one way it presents itself is as a set of problems about psychological and psychophysical laws. On the one hand, when one looks at the sciences of the mind, one might well come to doubt that they really possess anything as exact as natural laws at all, and to think that they possess only rough generalizations. On the other hand, to the extent that we are committed to the truth of physical *or* psychological laws, we would seem to be committed to denying the reality of free will. If the mind and the world are entirely governed by natural laws, there seems to be no room left for free will to operate.

This book seeks to address, and to work a form of philosophical therapy on, the apparent dissonance between the picture of the natural world arising from the sciences and our understanding of ourselves as agents who think and act. It is crucial here to distinguish between the sciences themselves and their philosophical interpretations in the form of metanarratives in philosophy of science. The intuition that there is a principled difference between the generalizations one finds in the sciences of the mind and those one finds in physics and other natural sciences is based in part on considerations of the sciences themselves, such as the nature of the generalizations one finds in disciplines such as psychology and psychophysics. But it is also driven in large measure by a philosophical thesis about the nature of laws: that laws make universal claims about how objects actually behave. This interpretation of laws was the mainstream view of laws among Positivist and Logical Empiricist philosophers of science through much of the twentieth century. But it is not without alternatives, and indeed the Empiricist orthodoxy has suffered significant setbacks in recent philosophy of science. It is therefore incumbent on us to see whether familiar problems in philosophy of psychology can endure the great sea changes that have transpired in philosophy of science generally, or whether they are artifacts of an outmoded Empiricist view of science. The apparent conflict between laws and freedom is driven almost entirely by a particular philosophical understanding of laws, and is largely independent of the details of particular laws in psychology or physics. Here it is largely the philosophical issues that will prove telling, and again the crucial question is whether, on the best interpretation of the nature of laws, such problems actually arise.

This chapter presents a general overview of the problems and of how I intend to dissolve them. Let us begin by considering these problems in order.

1.1 Strict Laws and *Ceteris Paribus* Laws—Philosophical Problems

The first fundamental question would seem to be whether there are any psychological laws. In physics, we find an amazing variety of phenomena explained by a few simple equations. The laws can be verified with considerable rigor, the values of the physical constants can be determined with an almost arbitrary degree of accuracy, and the laws and models can be used to predict real-world behavior to such an extent that one can, say, send a spaceship to Mars. Our understanding of the mind presents a very different picture. There is a very great deal about the mind that we do not understand at all. What we do think we understand tends to come in the form of isolated insights and local models, and these models are often *informal* ones that lack the mathematical rigor of physical laws (and hence the preconditions for accurate prediction and confirmation).

Moreover, there are important philosophical views about the mind that are, to varying degrees, in tension with the idea that there are strict psychological laws. If there is libertarian free will, then at least some aspects of our psychology are radically anomic (that is, not governed by laws). If the soul is a non-material substance, it is not clear that we should expect its internal operations to be governed by laws (especially if we assume that it is a simple substance, one for which there are no component parts to interact in a lawlike way), and its interactions with matter have to be of an altogether different kind than interactions between two bits of matter. But one need not be a dualist to believe in free will. The assumption that we at least sometimes act freely is bound up in a much broader humanistic understanding of ourselves, one that is relevant to questions of ethics and responsibility as well as metaphysics. How to reconcile the humanistic assumption that we are free agents with our best understanding of the world of nature is, thus, an urgent question, regardless of one's assumptions about the metaphysical nature of the self.

There are, however, psychological and psychophysical generalizations of various sorts, and it seems reasonable that at least some of these should be regarded as laws. Some of these generalizations are, indeed, employed as laws in the models of various human sciences. Economics, for example, models economies as statistical generalizations over populations of idealized rational decision makers whose actions are (or tend to be) functions of their beliefs and desires. Psychophysics, a discipline that began to acquire experimental and mathematical rigor in the late nineteenth century, has produced robust laws describing the relations between the intensities of stimuli and percepts. And neuroscience is mapping the neural correlates of various types of psychological states, and finding relationships that are robust in ways that it is tempting to treat as lawlike.

If we are content to use the word 'laws' in these cases, there is still an issue lurking in the wings for the philosopher of psychology. Generalizations cast at the level of belief and desire, and even the psychophysical laws stemming from the work of Ernst Heinrich Weber and Gustav Theodor Fechner, seem to differ in important ways from, say, the inverse-square law or Coulomb's law. The most familiar physical laws seem to apply exactly, always and everywhere, and to be scale invariant. The psychological and psychophysical laws, however, seem fraught with conditions and exceptions. Even a classical economist, when pressed, will usually admit that real human beings are not ideally rational decision-theoretic agents. Generalizations about how people behave as a consequence of their beliefs and desires are not particularly good for predicting how an individual will

behave on a particular occasion, even if one assumes (and this is controversial) that the ways individual behavior diverges from the models will
cancel out statistically over sufficiently large populations. And the psychophysical laws hold only against a host of background assumptions about
the organism—for example, that we are dealing with a normally sighted
subject who has not been staring at a light or a single saturated color, and
who does not suffer from macular degeneration. And the list of qualifying
conditions is long and potentially unbounded.

Philosophers of psychology have recognized a problem here for several
decades. It is often framed as follows: Physical laws are "strict" or "universal
and exceptionless," whereas human sciences (e.g. economics, psychology,
even psychophysics) have only *"ceteris paribus"* laws (i.e. generalizations
that are hedged by the caveat "other things being equal.") In itself this
characterization may seem only an observation about a particular special
science, or about the human sciences in general, and not a problem. It
leads to a problem, however, when combined with several additional
philosophical theses. The first of these is the claim that having strict laws
is some sort of defining characteristic of "real" sciences. One might take
such a view on *a priori* grounds, as the Logical Positivists did in their reasoning about "the logic of science," which they viewed as serving as a kind
of norm for the actual practice of science. Or one might take it on the basis
of observation of the status of the more developed sciences. One characteristic of mature sciences (one might think) is that they employ strict and
exceptionless laws; thus, if psychology (or any other human science) is to
become a mature science, it too must be framed in terms of strict and
exceptionless laws, and the fact that it does not do so at present is at best
an indication of its immature state and at worst an indication that it
cannot be made scientific (at least in anything close to its present form).

Another worry is metaphysical. Some philosophers take the view that
we may distinguish "natural" kinds from other *soi-disant* "kinds" (really
artifacts of human interests) as follows: A kind is a *natural* kind just in case
there are strict and exceptionless natural laws that apply to it. Artificial
kinds may indeed submit to useful generalizations; otherwise they would
have been of no use in the first place. But the difference between classifica-
tions that provide only a rough grip on the world and those that reveal
how things of a certain sort always behave is itself an indication that in
the latter we have hit on something real and fundamental, rather than an
artifact of our own interpretation or interests. And as a consequence, one
is inclined to view the real—the "really real," if you will, or the fundamental—as the nomic, the law-governed.

Of course, if you combine this view with the view discussed above—that psychology does not have strict laws—you are faced with a problem for psychology. It is perhaps most usefully and charitably framed as a dilemma: Unless strict laws can be found for psychology, psychological kinds will turn out to not be real in some privileged sense. And thus a lack of strict laws becomes not merely an interesting observation about psychology, but a call to the bucket brigade to help put out a dangerous philosophical fire and "vindicate" psychology, and likewise other sciences of the mind and indeed the human sciences generally.

Much philosophical discussion of these matters has accepted the general assumptions (a) that there is a difference between strict and exceptionless physical laws and *ceteris paribus* laws in psychology and other human sciences and (b) that the real is the nomic, yet has tried to dissipate the sense that there is a crisis for philosophy of psychology. Jerry Fodor (1974), for example, has argued that the messiness of psychological generalizations is not only explained but predicted by the fact that psychological kinds are functionally individuated kinds which are multiply realizable. The multiple-realization model of functional kinds, according to Fodor, underwrites both the ontological legitimacy of psychological kinds and the prediction that they should not have strict laws. I think this analysis yields some good insights for the philosopher of psychology, and indeed does so better when fleshed out with real examples than it does as pure philosophy of psychology. However, Fodor's response is only as good as the terms in which it is cast, and these terms have turned out to be problematic.

The whole distinction between strict laws and *ceteris paribus* laws is embedded in a set of deeper assumptions about the nature and the logical structure of laws. In particular, it assumes that laws are (true) universally quantified statements ranging over the real-world behavior of objects. This familiar interpretation of laws was made explicit by various Positivist and Logical Empiricist writers in the twentieth century. However, it came under withering attack in the last decades of that century. Nancy Cartwright, in particular, has pointed out that if we were to construe the laws of physics this way, they would turn out to be false. I would strengthen her case to say that most of the laws would have no true substitution instances— that is, that nothing ever behaves exactly as the gravitation law describes it. If this is the case, it is hard to see how psychological laws could fare worse. Cartwright seems to change her views, however, on the implications of this. Should we conclude that the laws are false? Or perhaps that they are true, but are not to be interpreted as universally quantified claims over objects and events? And if the latter, what characterization of laws should we put into the place left vacant by abandoning the Positivist view of laws?

On this last question, Cartwright offers two suggestions, neither of which I ultimately consider satisfying. (See chapter 4.) However, I offer (in chapter 6) my own account of laws as idealized claims that pick out potential partial causal contributions to real-world behavior. This account shares with Cartwright's the virtue of dissolving the supposed problem for philosophy of psychology by rejecting the opposition between strict laws and *ceteris paribus* laws. It also yields more positive fruit: An investigation of the different types of idealization that may be at work in different laws and models both reveals the deep unity between physical and psychological laws and explains why the latter are, in intelligible and principled ways, messier than the former, in the sense of being less susceptible to integration with one another into a single "super-model" of the mind, and in terms of a greater rift between modeling and prediction.

In the case of physical laws, we are blessed to have a small number of fundamental forces, which are mutually independent. Given that we are dealing with more than one basic variable, this is a best-case scenario for getting a good fit between the theoretical goal of revealing deep invariants and the more practical goal of predicting real-world kinematics. Independent forces are factorable; they can be evaluated separately and then summed through vector algebra. Computational problems may arise from chaotic systems, but we are still in the best sort of scenario nature presents us with. With mind and brain, on the other hand, we are dealing with a complicated feedback system. When we model one part of it, we necessarily idealize away from facts about other parts that may matter crucially *in vivo* in modulating the behavior of the system we are studying. This kind of nonlinear, dynamic system is more complex than a system with only independent physical forces, and this kind of complexity makes the relationship between model and prediction much more tenuous.

My account of laws and modeling represents a view that I call Cognitive Pluralism. It is cognitivist in that it traces features of our scientific models to the cognitive process of modeling features of the world. Our models of the world, including our scientific models, are not simply reflections of how things are in their own right; they are idealized representations of particular features of the world, features taken in isolation, and represented in a particular representational system. It is pluralist in suggesting that the *de facto* plurality of models, and the apparent impossibility of integrating them all into a single "super-model" that allows us to explain everything at once, may be principled and abiding features of our science, rather than symptoms of science's immature state. The cognitivism and the pluralism are related in the following way: I suggest that the reason for a principled plurality of models may lie in facts about *how* the mind models the world. If the mind necessarily understands the world piecemeal, through idealized models employing diverse representational systems, this may itself present significant barriers to the unification of the sciences. Models may be separate, inconsistent, or incommensurable, not because of anything about the world, but because of how the mind is constrained to understand it. At the very least, the alternative assumption that we *can* integrate our insights about the world into a single "God's-eye view" involves a significant empirical assumption about the nature of our minds—an assumption that seems improbable once one begins to consider it carefully.

1.2   Laws and Freedom

I contend in chapters 7–9 that my analysis of laws also resolves other problems for philosophy of psychology and its relation to other philosophical problematics, namely problems presented by claims for libertarian free will. Such claims might have been thought to conflict with the very notion that there *are* psychological *laws* on the ground that laws are universal and thus imply a kind of determinism incompatible with freedom.

My analysis of laws, however, shows that one can embrace the truth of individual laws, or indeed any set of such laws, without any implication of determinism, because the idealization conditions of each law are essentially open-ended. That is, no law includes a clause that says, in effect, "and this is the entire story about the universe." A gravitational law does not claim, for example, that dynamics is closed under gravitation. Nor does our commitment to gravitational laws plus strong, weak, and electromagnetic laws imply that the universe is closed under those forces. The truth of those laws is compatible both with the discovery of additional laws and with the possibility of genuinely anomic events, including voluntary spontaneity. Likewise, psychological laws, as idealized laws, do not claim to govern all possible behavior, but only to extract a partial list of real invariants in psychodynamics. In no way are further lawful invariants or voluntary anomic spontaneity excluded.

1.3   Are There Really Psychological and Psychophysical *Laws*? Case Studies

Parts I and II of this book take up the philosophical issues about psychological and psychological laws that have just been discussed. The kind of general and principled philosophical case developed in their chapters may or may not prove persuasive to the reader. However, philosophy of psychology would be ill served if it were discussed only at this highly abstract level, without looking at the particulars of real psychological and psychophysical generalizations. The final three chapters, which make up part III, look more concretely at three types of such generalizations: laws of what Fechner called "outer" psychophysics, relating stimuli to percepts (chapter 10), computational neuroscience's network models of the dynamics of cortical systems involved in vision (chapter 11), and generalizations cast at the level of the common-sense inventory of mental states(such as beliefs, desires, perceptions, decisions, and actions) and relating two mental states (chapter 12). Both the "entities" and the "laws" turn out to look very different in these three cases, and to involve distinct philosophical issues.

In outer psychophysics, one finds things that look very much like natural laws in their form and perhaps in their robustness, even though they are implicitly hedged by a much larger number of background assumptions than are the most familiar physical laws. Chapter 10 takes this as an opportunity to flesh out more details of the general idealization account, and to explain how outer psychophysics is related to projects of localization and formal modeling.

The models of mechanisms accounting for psychophysical transformations examined in chapter 10 share many features with familiar models from the physical sciences. They involve laws relating quantitative data, and they provide explanations in terms of straightforward circuit-like mechanisms involving only feedforward causation. Chapter 11 examines the explanation of further psychophysical effects through "later" neural processes in the lateral geniculate nucleus and in the visual cortex, using a family of models developed by Stephen Grossberg and his associates at Boston University over the past three decades. These indeed rely on formal modeling techniques, but ones in which algebraic equations of the sort involved in laws play a far smaller role. They also involve complicated feedback processes. And this, I argue, results in a kind of idealization not found in basic physics, in outer psychophysics, or in the modeling of early vision. Mechanisms standing in a feedforward chain can, like independent causal forces, be factored, because the operation and the output of the earlier mechanism are independent of the operation of the mechanism standing later in the causal chain. As a result, one may model each system separately and then recombine them, using the outputs of the earlier mechanism as inputs to the later mechanism. But when two systems are related by a feedback loop, this is not possible. To model either system in isolation—to idealize away from the contributions of the other in modulating its behavior—is distorting. Separate models of interconnected areas of the cortex, therefore, are idealized in ways that separate models of, say, gravitation and electromagnetism are not, because the latter are independent forces, whereas the processes modeled in the former case are, in real life, radically interdependent. This difference in the types of idealization employed in different modeling contexts results in very different kinds of gulfs between abstract models and real-world behavior.

Chapter 12 explores both common-sense belief-desire psychology and various attempts to regiment such psychology into more exact models, such as decision theory, Freudian psychology, cognitive/computational psychology, and explorations of knowledge representation in artificial intelligence (semantic networks, frames, scripts). Common-sense belief-desire psychology, I argue, does employ models of the mind, but these models lack many of the benchmark features of scientific models, including methodological and formal exactitude. It is, I believe, dangerously misleading to use scientific theory as a paradigm for understanding such processes as acquiring grammar or understanding other minds. However, the shortcomings of common-sense psychology by no means prohibit the development of truly scientific theories that either invoke belief-desire explanations in a more rigorous way or postulate other inner representational structures to explain features of belief-desire reasoning. Models of the sort explored in cognitive psychology and artificial intelligence seldom have laws in the form of algebraic equations, and often lack any quantitative element at all. However, computer programs and data structures are themselves an alternative form of formally exact modeling.

1.4   Modularity and Cognitive Pluralism

The case studies in part II also develop themes that support the general Cognitive Pluralist account developed in part I. The case studies, particularly those in chapters 11 and 12, all proceed by supposing that mind and brain have a number of distinct modules that represent particular parts or features of the world. The modules explored in chapter 11 plausibly are products of natural selection and are innate or at least strongly biased toward particular functions. Those explored in chapter 12 are acquired through learning and must be viewed as "soft modules"—partially autonomous structures that employ proprietary representational systems for their problem domains yet are acquired and fine-tuned through learning. This supports the claims, made in chapter 6, that scientific modeling is but a specially regimented case of a more ecumenical phenomenon of mental modeling and that the abiding plurality of scientific models is a consequence of a basic design principle of human cognitive architecture.

1.5 Rhetorical Slant

This book has several rhetorical objectives. One of these is directed primarily at fellow specialists in philosophy of mind. There is a division among philosophers of mind on the question of whether philosophy of mind should be pursued as a largely autonomous discipline concerned primarily with the metaphysics of mind or should be pursued in close conjunction with recent work in the sciences of cognition and philosophy of science. I fall in the second camp, and I hope that this book will help to show the importance of taking both the sciences of the mind and recent philosophy of science into account when pursuing issues in philosophy of mind and philosophy of psychology. To the extent that philosophers of mind are engaged with philosophy of science, their discussions are often mired in philosophical views of science made popular by the Logical Positivists and the Empiricists—views that have been fairly decisively rejected within philosophy of science in the past several decades. For the purposes of this book, the most of important of these views is the Empiricist interpretation of the nature of laws. It is my claim that some problems in philosophy of mind and in philosophy of psychology are artifacts of an outmoded philosophy of science, and that they dissolve if one adopts more adequate and more up-to-date views.

The second rhetorical thrust is aimed both at fellow specialists and at the educated public. Since early modernity, people have worried that there is a kind of dissonance between the view of the world presented by modern science and the things about our own self-image that we hold most near and dear, such as the role of our mental states in determining behavior and the freedom of the will. On some philosophical views, the very reality of consciousness, beliefs, and desires seems to be threatened. Fodor (1990) puts the point eloquently: "If it isn't literally true that my wanting is causally responsible for my reaching . . . then practically everything I believe about anything is false and it's the end of the world." Likewise, we tend to assume that a commitment to the truth of laws involves a commitment to determinism, and hence to a denial of free will, and with it the abandonment of any moral evaluations that make sense only on the assumption that we at least sometimes act freely. Accepting modern science is sometimes seen as implying that we must move "beyond freedom and dignity" (Skinner 1971) to a more mechanistic understanding of ourselves. This, too, is a view that many find quite threatening, as is evidenced by the number of works that attempt to argue that determinism ought not, on closer examination, to feel so threatening after all (e.g. Dennett 1984 and Flanagan 2002).

While I applaud attempts by convinced determinists to salvage human dignity and at least some types of (non-libertarian) freedom, I think they have bought too quickly into the assumption that a commitment to scientific laws implies a commitment to determinism. If my view of laws is correct, no such implication follows. There may be other reasons to be a determinist, and determinism may turn out to be true in the end, but we cannot get determinism out of scientific laws alone. And hence those who feel they have reason to believe in libertarian free will are free to embrace scientific laws without fear that doing so will compromise their commitment to freedom. This falls short of any sort of proof that we are, in fact, free. But it works a kind of philosophical therapy on a widespread but flawed way of coming to the conclusion that freedom is not compatible with what modern science tells us about ourselves and the world we live in.

1.6   How to Read this Book

The book is written for several audiences with different interests. Its principal theme is that questions of philosophy of mind are often best approached in close conjunction with explorations of the best that is offered by both the sciences of cognition and contemporary philosophy of science. Indeed, its main argument is that certain philosophical problems about the mind, such as the status of mental states and the possibility of human freedom in a world with natural laws, are attributable to unfortunate and outdated views in philosophy of science that can cause us to misunderstand what the sciences actually tell us about the mind and the world of nature. The primary goal of the book is to work therapy on these problems by applying a more adequate philosophical interpretation of natural laws.

Part I should be of general interest to readers concerned with issues in philosophy of mind. It also provides the background for parts II and III. Parts II and III, however, are largely independent of one another, and not every reader who is interested in the issues discussed in one of them will be equally interested in those discussed in the other. Part II deals with free will, part III with a more detailed examination of how laws and other types of rigorous models are found in particular sciences of the mind. In part III, I occasionally make a brief return to issues of freedom; but the main argument in part II does not depend on those passages, and in other respects these two parts of the book are parallel and independent continuations of part I. Readers who are interested in free will but indifferent to case studies in philosophy of cognitive science will probably be more interested in the chapters of part II; readers who after finishing part I are still bothered by the question of whether there really are laws or rigorous models in the cognitive sciences may wish to read part III before returning to the material on free will in part II.

2 Laws, Vindication, and Ontology

For several decades it is has been commonplace in philosophy of the human sciences to claim that those sciences differ from the physical sciences in the types of laws they employ. Typically, the claim is that the natural sciences employ laws that are "strict and exceptionless," while the human sciences have only "*ceteris paribus*" laws. This claim involves both an informal insight and a particular logical machinery for casting that insight in more precise terms. The informal insight might be stated as follows: Physical laws, such as those of gravitation and electromagnetism, can be formulated exactly and apply always and everywhere. The "laws" one finds in economics and psychology, by contrast, are little better than rough generalizations. Insofar as they deserve to be called laws at all—a claim that some philosophers of social science, including Giovanni Battista Vico, E. H. Weber, and Peter Winch (1958), have found dubious—they must be regarded as lacking the universal and exceptionless character that paradigmatic cases of laws in the physical sciences are believed to have. This informal insight is then cast in terms of a contrast between "strict" laws and "*ceteris paribus*" laws—that is, nomic claims hedged by a clause that says "other things being equal." Both types of laws are traditionally cashed out in terms of first-order logic. Strict laws are interpreted as universally quantified claims ranging over objects or events. In the famous Logical Empiricist example, the supposed "law" that "all swans are white" is cashed out as the quantified conditional claim

$\varphi: \forall x(Sx \supset Wx),$

where the predicate letter S expresses "is a swan," the predicate letter W expresses "is white," and $\forall x$ is the universally quantified "for every x."

Suppose, however, that we consider claims from psychology instead. There are several distinctly different types of lawlike claims about minds. Let us begin with an example from belief-desire psychology, as examples of this kind also affect other social sciences that are based on analyses cast in belief-desire language. Suppose we take it to be a psychological generalization that people pursue the things they desire. At some level, this claim seems a truism. But now suppose we cast it as a universally quantified claim:

ψ: $\forall a \forall b$ ($Dab \supset Pab$),

where Dab = "a desires b" and Pab = "a pursues b." Even if one were inclined to accept as true the dubious claim that all swans are white, one would no doubt balk at this logically regimented formulation of our psychological truism, for it is all too apparent that people do not always pursue everything they desire. Sometimes they have two incompatible desires, sometimes other things get in the way of pursuing a desire, sometimes moral or social inhibitions lead them to reject its pursuit, and so on. Whatever one may think of the original truism, the quantified claim ψ is clearly false. But perhaps there is a true claim in its vicinity. After all, we have motivated its falsity by listing conditions C: $\{c_1, c_2, \ldots, c_n\}$ under which it fails to hold. If such a list can be fully enumerated, we may be left with a true claim of the form

ψ^*: Not-C $\supset \psi$,

or, equivalently,

ψ^*: Not-C $\supset \forall a \forall b$ ($Dab \supset Pab$).

One might thus hope to come out with a first-order claim that is at least materially true and which contains a genuinely nomic element in the quantified material conditional after the first "horseshoe" ($\supset$). Indeed, the logical form of a strict law ψ is embedded within ψ^*. And so the latter claims, in essence, "other things being equal, ψ" (in Latin, "*ceteris paribus*, ψ").[1]

Here we seem to have an important difference between laws in physics and laws in belief-desire psychology—a difference both in scope and in logical form. Nor is the problem restricted to belief-desire psychology. Even the parts of psychology (broadly understood as the scientific study of the mind) that have the best claims to experimental and mathematical rigor seem to share this feature. Consider the Weber-Fechner laws, a paradigm of psychophysical respectability. They claim that the intensity of a percept is a logarithmic function of the intensity of the stimulus. Such laws are well established by repeated experiments, are robust across many subjects, and take the form of a mathematical equation. In short, they have many of the hallmarks of respectable scientific results. But it simply is not true that the intensity of the percept is always related to that of the stimulus in the manner that they predict. In fact, in a number of well-understood cases such predictions break down. For example, if you stare at a light before looking at a test sample, you will see only the afterimage of the light. There are interesting optical illusions that take place within and at boundaries between objects with distinctive illumination gradients, and so on. (See chapters 10 and 11 for more details.) Other well-confirmed psychophysical results also have well-known boundary conditions. For example, with color vision, staring at one color ("saturating" on it) before looking at a test image will change how the test image is seen. And of course color-blind people will perform differently on such tests—one always assumes a "normally sighted subject" even though one knows there is considerable variety within the human population. Even the most respectable of psychological laws—those of perceptual psychophysics—seem to share this *ceteris paribus* character.

So far, however, we have at most identified a putative difference between psychology and the physical sciences. Though this putative difference has been viewed as problematic for psychology, we have yet to see why this should be so.

2.1 Davidson's Anomalous Monism

The view that there is a principled difference between the laws of the physical and the social sciences has led independent lives in different contexts. It is, for example, a central canon of the "interpretivist" (or *Verstehen*) tradition of philosophy of social science, which stems from the work of Vico and Weber in the nineteenth century. In recent analytic philosophy of psychology and philosophy of mind (our main concern here), this view has emerged in large measure out of discussions of Donald Davidson's (1970/1980) thesis of anomalous monism. Anomalous monism was developed as a resolution to an apparently unstable triad of views that Davidson endorses. Louise Antony (1989, pp. 160, 161) summarizes these views as follows:

Principle of Causal Interaction (henceforth CI)—"At least some mental events interact causally with physical events."

Principle of the Nomological Character of Causation (NCC)—"Where there is causality, there must be a law." (Davidson 1970/1980, p. 208)

Principle of the Anomalism of the Mental ("PAM")—"There are no strict deterministic laws on the basis of which mental events can be predicted and explained." (Davidson 1970/1980, p. 208)

Taken together, these three principles seem to result in a contradiction. If causality requires causal laws and if mental states enter into causal interactions, it would seem to follow that there must be laws governing mental-physical and/or mental-mental interactions. But this is what is denied by the principle of the anomalism of the mental.

Davidson's solution to the paradox presented by these three theses is to treat laws as intensional contexts and to embrace a token-identity theory of mental events. Davidson's view is monistic in that it claims that there are no objects over and above the physical objects; each mental state or event is token-identical with some physical state or event. However, Davidson is also committed to the thesis that our physical and psychological vocabularies are used to type events as physical or as mental (a dualism, if not of properties, at least of modes of description), and laws employ these descriptions intensionally, and so one cannot substitute different modes of description *salva veritate*. Thus, each mental event-token is also a physical event-token, but only under its physical description does it enter into strict laws that undergird the causal relations that bind mental states to other mental states or to physical states.

Antony (1989, p. 163) suggests that we might reformulate PAM, or that we might understand it as entailing the Principle of Non-Generalizability.

Principle of Non-Generalizability ("PNG"): There are no strict deterministic laws formulable in the vocabulary of psychology.

This seems both correct and consistent with most subsequent interpretations of Davidson. However, we may follow Jaegwon Kim (2003 p. 115) in distinguishing two different theses about anomalism that might be included under this general heading: psychophysical anomalism, which denies that there are strict laws relating mental states to physical states (including brain states), and psychological anomalism, which denies that there are strict laws governing causal relationships between pairs of mental states. The former are the main target of Davidson's essays "The material mind" (1973/1980) and "Psychology as philosophy" (1974). However, Davidson (1970/1980, p. 224) also includes psychological anomalism in "Mental Events," on the grounds that "the mental does not . . . constitute a closed system" and that "too much happens to affect the mental that is not itself a systematic part of the mental." Davidson does allow that there are psychological generalizations that may be cast in the same logical form as laws, but denies that they are strict laws. His "strict deterministic" laws are in large measure contrasted with statistical laws of the sorts often found in the social sciences, though subsequent writers—e.g. Lepore and Loewer (1987)—have often taken them to be properly contrasted with *ceteris paribus* laws too.

Davidson's anomalous monism was received with some incredulity in the late 1960s, the heyday of reductive physicalism. Since then, however, it has spawned a powerful movement of nonreductive physicalisms, which combine ontological materialism with property dualism and supervenience claims. It has also, somewhat less directly, opened up a new problematic in philosophy of psychology and philosophy of mind, which I shall designate "the Davidsonian Problematic" (not because Davidson himself viewed anything about anomalous monism as problematic, but because it is a problematic—that is, a set of problems—whose historical roots are intertwined with Davidson's early work).

2.2   The Davidsonian Problematic

Davidson's anomalous monism touches on both philosophy of psychology and philosophy of mind. In philosophy of psychology, it makes claims about the kinds of generalizations one finds in psychology and in psychophysics. And in particular, it makes a sharp contrast between these and the strict laws one finds in physics. This pulls Davidson's claims into the orbit of much older problems—debated from Weber through the Logical Positivists—about the nature and status of the special sciences. In particular, it re-introduces old questions about whether psychology and the other human sciences are perhaps second-rate sciences, or even non-sciences, because of ways in which their form, their methods, and the form of knowledge they yield fall short of the standards set by physics. In particular, are strict laws a hallmark of legitimate and mature sciences? If they are, can psychology be a legitimate and mature science? I shall call the set of problems found here *vindication problems*.

Davidson's claims also intersect with very old and robust conversations in philosophy of mind about the metaphysical nature of mental states and events. Anomalous monism is in tension with some present-day views about ontological legitimacy and natural kinds that align the "really real" with the reducible, the causal, or the nomic. I shall call these *ontological problems*.

2.3 The Vindication Problems

Davidson's anomalous monism was itself conceived as a way of showing that psychological events have one of the principal features deemed necessary for a scientific psychology—they enter into causal relationships—and hence as a step toward "vindicating" psychology against criticisms that it deals only in interpretative *Verstehen* (Weber 1834) or in normative relationships (Dray 1957). However, doing so by treating psychological events as anomalous arguably invites kindred criticisms in a revised form. If we interpret the word 'anomalous' strictly, as implying that there are no psychological or psychophysical laws, it runs afoul of the assumption that real sciences deal in laws. If we interpret it as meaning that psychology lacks "strict laws" but has "*ceteris paribus* laws," the situation is little better, as the methodological purist might insist that respectable sciences deal only in strict laws, or, at very least, that the physical sciences do so, and we are thus left with a need to explain the distinctive character of psychological and psychophysical laws and whether the ways in which they differ from physical laws matter for psychology's methodological and epistemic credentials. And the move of interpreting laws as intensional contexts while asserting token identity may lead to an epiphenomenalism that itself impugns the status of psychological generalizations as scientific claims, as it can be argued that only strict laws are closely connected with causation.

2.3.1 Methodological Purism

The very distinction between the *ceteris paribus* laws of psychology and the strict laws of physics invites the interpretation that psychology suffers in the comparison. Many philosophers have been tempted by the view that "real" sciences trade in strict laws, whether on the basis of aprioristic Positivist views of "the logic of science" or by inductive generalization from reconstructions of the physical sciences as having this form. This concern would have been particularly acute in the 1960s, when Davidson first developed his anomalous monism, as much of philosophy of science was then still stumbling about in the Positivist night in which all ravens were black. And it would have been exacerbated by Davidson's own view that psychology (or psychology and other sciences that depend on it, including sociology and economics) was uniquely anomalous because it alone among the sciences was concerned with interpreting its subject matter (the actions of agents) as rational as well as causal, and hence suffered a unique problem due to indeterminacy of interpretation. The force of the contrast has been called into some question by subsequent work in philosophy of science that has argued that other special sciences, including biology, lack strict laws, and even that they are lacking in physics. (See particularly Cartwright 1983.) However, the lingering force of the concern can be seen in a number of recent articles that attempt to show that what appear to be *ceteris paribus* laws turn out to be strict laws after all (Smith 2002; Earman et al. 2002; Woodward 2002).

We may pose an argument against the credentials of psychology in the following manner.

V1: Strict laws are a necessary feature of legitimate (pure, mature, first-rate) sciences.

V2: Psychology (necessarily) lacks strict laws.

Therefore,

V3: Psychology is (and cannot be) a legitimate (pure, mature, first-rate) science.

Of course, V1 ultimately requires justification in the form of some pro-syllogism having V1 as its conclusion, whether an aprioristic argument about the logic of science or an argument based on observations of features of paradigmatic sciences such as physics. For example:

P1: Characteristic features of the paradigmatic sciences are necessary features of legitimate (pure, mature, first-rate) sciences.

P2: The physical sciences are paradigmatic sciences.

P3: Strict laws are a characteristic feature of the physical sciences.

Therefore,

V1: Strict laws are a necessary feature of legitimate (pure, mature, first-rate) sciences.

Such argumentation sets clear agenda for the defender of scientific legitimacy for psychology. The defender may respond by arguing one or more of the following:

R1: Psychology has strict laws.

R2: Contrary to P1, one cannot legitimately make normative inferences from the features of one science to those of another. (Or, for the case from the logic of science: contrary to the Positivists, one cannot (or ought not) set *a priori* norms for scientific legitimacy.)

R3: There are paradigmatic sciences (biology? physics itself?) that also lack strict laws, and hence strict laws are not a characteristic feature of paradigmatic sciences.

R4: Strict laws are not a necessary feature for scientific legitimacy.

R5: The entire reconstruction of real scientific laws in terms of "strict" and "*ceteris paribus*" laws is flawed.

Responses R1 and R3–R5 will be discussed in subsequent chapters. R2 will not receive extended discussion here, though it should be noted that both aprioristic arguments from the logic of science and normative arguments about one scientific domain based on features of another have largely lost their following in philosophy of science.

2.3.2 The Specter of Epiphenomenalism

Davidson's approach is not situated purely in the methodology and the logic of science. It also brings in metaphysical concerns, and these raise additional worries for psychology. In particular, a number of writers have charged that anomalous monism entails epiphenomenalism, the view that mental states *as such* (or perhaps mental properties) are causally impotent (Honderich 1982; Kim 1993; for a contrary view, see Lepore and Loewer 1987). At one level, this might seem problematic only for the metaphysicians and not for philosophers of psychology or philosophers of science. And yet, on at least some views of scientific explanation, and indeed of scientific laws, it is essential that laws have a causal character. Yet if we hold, with Davidson, that there are no (strict) psychological laws, and that (strict) laws are the locus of causal attributions, we seem to be left with the view that there is no mental causation either. Moreover, there seems to be no work for a psychological law to do. Since all events are physical events, and are fully determined by how the physical laws act on earlier states, there is no causal work left to do, even if the lack of psycho-physical laws means that the resultant physical state underdetermines its corresponding mental state. While we may be left with psychological and psychophysical generalizations that serve some sort of utility, they are not to be taken as assertions of causal regularities. There are indeed causal regularities involving mental tokens—but these are all captured under the physical descriptions of those tokens rather than their mentalistic descriptions. According to Davidson, there are no causal laws cast in the psychological vocabulary. Whether or not the lack of causal laws in the psychological vocabulary presents a problem for the status of psychology as a science will then depend on what view one takes of the nature of scientific laws generally.

Some forms of Empiricism, including the Humean form, regard laws only as reporting empirical generalizations. On this view, psychology still has to weather the problem of its generalizations' not being exceptionless, but the problem of epiphenomenalism does not arise, as laws are not, in general, viewed as expressing causal relations, and hence the fact that psychological laws do not underwrite mental causation does not differentiate them from physical laws. If, however, one takes the view that laws involve attributions of a more robust notion of causation, psychological laws are once again on the ropes because of the following argument:

Epi1: Laws express causal regularities.

Epi2: Psychological and psychophysical generalizations do not express causal regularities.

Therefore,

Epi 3: Psychological and psychophysical generalizations are not laws.

Epi4: It is a necessary feature of legitimate (pure, mature, first-rate) sciences that they trade in laws (i.e., expressions of causal regularities).

Therefore,

Epi5: Psychology is not (and cannot be) a legitimate (pure, mature, first-rate) science.

Again, agenda are set for the would-be "vindicator" of scientific psychology, who might pursue one or more of the following strategies in reply:

R6: Psychology and psychophysics do (contra Davidson) contain (true) causal generalizations.

R7: Laws do not (always) express causal generalizations.

R8: Possession of causal laws is not a necessary feature of legitimate (pure, mature, first-rate) sciences.

2.4 The Ontological Problems

The Davidsonian Problematic also poses issues for the philosophy of mind, and more particularly for the ontology of mental states and events. Or, rather, it does so if one makes any of a number of assumptions that many contemporary physicalists are inclined to make. Divorcing psychological generalizations—and hence psychological kinds—from causation and from strict laws has metaphysical consequences if one ties ontological status (for example, "natural kinds") to reducibility, causation, or appearance in laws.

2.4.1   Reductionism

While non-reductive materialism has enjoyed a resurgence in the wake of Davidson's anomalous monism, both reductionism and the broader view that there is a forced choice between reductionism and eliminativism are still very prominent forces in philosophy of mind. Davidson's psycho-physical anomalism is generally taken to imply a rejection of reductionism. It surely implies a rejection of what is sometimes called "nomological" reduction, as it repudiates strict laws binding mental states to brain states (or any other kinds of physical states). As a consequence, reductive materialists have taken Davidson's position as a serious challenge to their own.

What causes philosophers concern here is not so much the question of whether Davidson's account or the reductionists' account is the correct account. The deeper worry is that a failure of reducibility somehow threatens the ontological legitimacy—the reality—of irreducible mental states. As Fodor puts it (1987 p. 98), "It's hard to see . . . how one can be a Realist about intentionality without also being, to some extent, a Reductionist." While Fodor himself rejects reductionism (or at least type physicalism), both reductionists and non-physicalists tend to see non-reductive physicalism as leaving no place for the mental: The real consists (they say) of things belonging to ontologically fundamental kinds and things that can be constructed out of them. If the mental is neither fundamental (as the nonreductive physicalist holds *qua* physicalist) nor reducible (as he holds *qua* nonreductivist), there is no room left on the boat, and it must be cast overboard along with other such unsuccessful theoretical posits as phlogiston and the heavenly spheres.

2.4.2   The Real and the Causal

Other philosophers, notably Kim (1993), have assigned causation a special role in ontology. Kim identifies the natural with the causal, and, as he is a naturalist, this amounts to restricting a privileged space in ontology for things that have causal powers. (This makes Kim a curious kind of materialist, as it would count a God who created the world—a causal relation—as a natural object.[2]) On this view, the charge that anomalous monism entails epiphenomenalism has serious metaphysical consequences. Although each token object picked out by the mental vocabulary might retain its ontological legitimacy because it is also a physical object or event, the status of mental kinds is called into real question, as there are no causal relations typical of psychological kinds.

2.4.3   Natural Kinds and Laws

Many philosophers have linked laws themselves to a kind of ontological legitimacy, particularly that of "natural kinds." In essence, they hold that the real is the nomic. Philosophers in this camp differ in their attitudes toward things about which there are no laws—say, mutton chops. Some bite the ontological bullet and claim that there literally are no such things. Others (Fodor among them) admit the reality of such kinds—conventional kinds, perhaps—but reserve a special honorific for kinds that "carve nature at the joints," calling them "natural kinds." On this view, the ontological status of psychological kinds may be in peril as well as their status as *natural* kinds. If the "laws" that carve nature at the joints in the required way must be strict laws, then psychological kinds are unreal or at least non-natural. (Fodor says that *ceteris paribus* laws are good enough for natural kinds. But he is motivated to argue this position because he perceives the threat of the argument to the opposite conclusion.)

2.5   Assessment of the Davidsonian Problematic

In short, many problems seem to arise if one takes the view that psychology employs a different and weaker type of law than the physical sciences. On the one hand, there are vindication problems in philosophy of psychology, concerning the status of psychology as a science. On the other hand, there are ontological problems in philosophy of mind, concerning the status of psychological states. All these problems arise against a set of background assumptions about laws in general, and about the character of laws in physics and in psychology in particular; hence they are, in a sense, parts of a single problematic: Make these assumptions about the laws, and these problems arise. For want of a better name, I call this set of problems "the Davidsonian Problematic." I do so in spite of the fact that Davidson did not himself seem to consider this constellation of views to be a problem—indeed, he viewed it as a solution to some pre-existing problems in philosophy of psychology. However, as anomalous monism has been a major contributor to the revival of interest in the status of psychological generalizations in philosophy of psychology, it is perhaps not unfair to link these problems with Davidson on historical grounds.

The following chapters seek to address these problems by undermining the assumptions of the problematic. In particular, the supposed difference between laws in physics and laws in psychology depends on a particular characterization of the laws of physics as universally quantified claims ranging over objects and events. This characterization is not tenable, and without it the opposition between laws in physics and in psychology is in jeopardy—as is the whole Davidsonian Problematic—until we provide a better account of laws.

3 The Received Solution in Computational Psychology

Many in philosophy of psychology and cognitive science would regard the Davidsonian Problematic as having already been satisfactorily resolved. Among philosophers of mind influenced by functionalism and the computer metaphor, at least, there is a kind of received solution (RS), advocated by Fodor and others, that seeks to show that the contrast between the laws of physics and those of psychology need not imperil either the status of psychological laws or the legitimacy of psychological kinds. (See especially Fodor 1974.)

The core of the RS is that psychological kinds are functional kinds that are multiply realizable in different kinds of physical media. The messiness of psychological laws is a direct consequence of the multiple realizability of psychological kinds; however, both the legitimacy of those laws and the exceptions to them are ultimately underwritten by properties of the real izing system. This view is often presented at a highly abstract level, but I shall try to show that it gains even greater plausibility when applied to concrete examples. One of the appeals of the RS is that it accepts two of the main assumptions of the challenge—that there is a difference between the *ceteris paribus* laws of psychology and the strict and exceptionless laws of (basic) physics, and that genuine natural kinds are those to which laws apply—while denying the implication that the laws of psychology are thereby rendered problematic. However, adopting these assumptions also prevents advocates of the RS from exploring any deeper sort of critique that calls these assumptions into question.

3.1 The Messiness of Laws Involving Functional Kinds

The RS seeks to maintain the legitimacy of generalizations such as "People avoid things they believe will harm them" by treating belief and other psychological kinds as functional kinds. Functional kinds figure not only

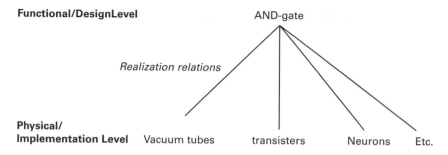

Figure 3.1
Multiple realization of a functional kind through alternative physical realizations.

in psychology, but also in many other special sciences, including biology, neuroscience, and computer science. In computational approaches to the mind, analogies to computer programs and circuits enjoy particular pride of place. A simple example of a functional kind is a basic gating circuit, such as an AND-gate. An AND-gate is a circuit in which the output will be set to its ON state just in case all of the inputs are set to their ON states. One can make AND-gates out of an indefinitely large variety of physical configurations. Such gating circuits are the basic building blocks of digital computers. There are also neural circuits in human and animal brains, made of proteins and driven by electrochemical reactions, that function as AND-gates. Functional kinds such as the AND-gate are thus said to be *multiply realizable*. (See figure 3.1.)

When we discuss the behavior of an AND-gate, or any other functional kind, we are describing how it behaves when the system is working properly. We are, in Dennett's (1987) terminology, describing it from the "design stance." Under these conditions (often specified vaguely if specified at all), the functional-level description is sufficient for describing and predicting the behavior of the circuit. Of course, there are many conditions that can cause such circuits to malfunction. Immerse your computer in water and it will no longer perform as advertised. Likewise, if you significantly increase or decrease the amounts of crucial neurotransmitters in a human brain, its "circuitry" will cease to perform in its wonted and customary ways. The functional-level description will hold good only so long as the circuitry in question is kept within a particular range of parameters— only so long as it is what Cartwright (1999) calls a "nomological machine."

Note, however, that the conditions that will cause one AND-gate to malfunction may not do the same to another. The circuits in my computer's motherboard will probably not be affected by a difference of a few sodium molecules, whereas too much or too little sodium in my nerve synapses may disrupt their normal function. My neurons thrive in an aqueous solution, but the motherboard of my Macintosh would cease to function if immersed in a watery environment like the inside of my cranium. And likewise for any pair of realizing systems. Just when this physical system will really behave like an AND-gate is a resultant property stemming from the realizing system, and no generalization cast at its functional level will get at these differences. In order to get at the functional-level description, we must idealize away from these differences, even though they sometimes matter *in vivo*.

Take another example: Most computers have adder circuits, which are used to perform mathematical operations. But not all adder circuits represent numbers in the same way. Some use a 32-bit digital string, others a 64-bit string. The difference does not matter so long as neither the addends nor the sum exceed $2^{32} - 1$, but with larger numbers the circuits behave differently. This difference is not to be discovered at the level of abstraction at which the circuits are described as adders, but is resultant from differences at a lower functional level, and ultimately at a physical level.

In another domain, consider how psychological generalizations may go awry in "exceptional" circumstances. The description we give of how a person acts as a rational decision maker breaks down when his brain has too great an amount of alcohol or some other psychotropic drug introduced, or when there is an endogenous biochemical imbalance such as severe depression. (One might well debate whether rational decision making is even common among most human beings, but for present purposes a few clear examples of situations in which it breaks down will suffice.) It is arguable that the regularities that drive such differences will not show up at the level of belief-desire psychology. Insofar as there are good generalizations at the level of belief-desire psychology, they, like the functional description of simple circuits in computers or brains, hold good only under a particular range of conditions, and the range is never exhaustively specified in advance.

In none of the above-mentioned cases, however, are we justified in inferring that the generalizations characterized by the higher-level generalizations—the functional and psychological laws—are not genuine simply because they are not universal. They are empirically robust under a significant range of conditions, and that robustness is not simply an artifact of interpretation or experiment. But they are not fundamental. Rather, both the regularities and the conditions under which they hold or break down are resultant from more basic regularities. We do not, however, generally take the fact that a property or a law is resultant from other properties and laws to imply that it is not a genuine property or law. And, at least insofar as we are justified in viewing psychological kinds as functional kinds (in the weak sense of having a functional description[1]), there is no reason to call their legitimacy into question on those grounds either.

3.2 Composition Effects

There is also a second way in which the non-exceptionless character of higher-level laws can be attributed to properties of the particular realizing system. Consider this belief-desire-level generalization: "People avoid stimuli that they are afraid of." This generalization certainly seems to capture some sort of truth, perhaps even a bland truism. It is also plainly not exceptionless. The brave woman goes into the burning house to rescue her children, not because she is unafraid, but because some other motive outweighs her fear of the flames. Perhaps there is a second general principle cast in terms of beliefs and desires at work in this example too: "People will act so as to protect the well-being of those they care about deeply." I think our intuition is that both generalizations state truths, even though they both have exceptions.

The multiple-realization account might treat this situation as follows: Each of the belief-desire generalizations is cast at the level of functional description. However, the psychologies of fear and of care, thus described, are realized in an individual through biological mechanisms that also have a "lower" level of description, for example in the vocabulary of neuroscience. Each belief-desire description captures real regularities that can be employed quite effectively in predicting a wide range of human behavior. But neither of them says what will happen when more than one such generalization is in play—for example, when one must face something that one fears in order to protect loved ones. It is possible, of course, that in some cases that there is yet another generalization cast at the level of belief-desire psychology that will cover such cases. (Some people, for example, sometimes act on explicit rules they endorse, and even have second-order rules for how to act when the first-order or *prima facie* rules come into conflict.) But it is also likely that in a great many cases there is no such explanation to be had at the level of belief-desire psychology, only one at the level of the realizing system. The difference between a woman who runs into flames to save her children and one who stands appalled in terror probably is not that one believes "It is better to face my fears than to allow my children to suffer" while the other operates on some opposing principle. Indeed, the woman who does not rush into the house may very well also believe that she should act in spite of her fear, and loathe herself for not acting in accordance with that belief. It is much more likely that the mechanisms underlying fear and compassion interact differently in the two women at a level that is not well described by the belief-desire vocabulary. In such a case, one cannot do a "summation of forces" at the level of belief-desire psychology, and hence the psychodynamics of cases where multiple psychological generalizations are relevant may not be decidable at the level of psychological description alone. As a result, there is a gap between the psychological-level description and prediction because of the variety of ways in which psychological properties are realized in particular individuals at particular times.

Nor is this a peculiarity of psychology. Computer programmers are at pains to make sure that two programs running on the same computer interfere with one another as little as possible. However, all too often, one program will eat up memory or processor time in ways that affect the performance of another. (The problem is especially acute if one program's functions are time-sensitive.) And of course virus programs can be designed specifically for the purpose of interfering with the normal performance of other programs. When these things happen, some or all of the programs in question stop working in the ways the manuals describe.

Does all of this mean that the higher-level generalizations—whether at the psychological level or at the program level—are somehow less than legitimate? It need not. The deleterious effects of a computer virus or a program that monopolizes memory and processor time do not imply that another program is not described well by its flow chart or its user manual. Nor does the fact that compassion can be outweighed by terror (or the fact that this is more likely to happen in me than in my neighbor) mean that there are no robust empirical generalizations to be made at the level of how people can be expected to act toward those they care for. It does imply that there are limits to the scope within which such generalizations can be applied for purposes of prediction of actual behavior, but we already knew that.

3.3   The Received Solution Recast

I shall now attempt to recapitulate the RS in propositional form.

RS1: The physical sciences have strict and exceptionless laws.

RS2: Psychology has only *ceteris paribus* laws.

Psychology, however, is not alone in this boat: any laws cast at the level of functional kinds will share this feature, owing to multiple realizability, and thus RS2 is a consequence of RS3 and RS4.

RS3: Psychological kinds are functional kinds.

RS4: Any science employing multiply realizable functional kinds will have only *ceteris paribus* laws.

One is thus faced with a choice between questioning the legitimacy of all sciences that deal in functional kinds and admitting the legitimacy of *ceteris paribus* laws. The latter seems the more acceptable option on at least two grounds. First, the limited scope of a law does not seem to impugn its having a claim on reporting a real (though not universal or fundamental) invariant in nature. Second, the cost of dismissing all sciences employing functional-level laws would be immense, as these would include not only psychology but also neuroscience and biology. Thus we have RS5.

RS5: Scientific laws must be empirically robust and non-accidental, but need not be exceptionless or fundamental.

Several terms in RS5 require more comment. A generalization may be disqualified from being a legitimate law of nature if its truth is accidental. For example, there is a gastronomic rule about when one may safely eat oysters that is cast in terms of months ending in the letter "r". (I always forget which way it goes, but oysters do not agree with me at any time of year.) This may be an effective way of avoiding food poisoning from bad oysters, but surely does not count as a law of nature, as the connection between the times of year that oysters are harmful to humans and the times of year whose English Julian calendar names end in "r" is accidental. A generalization can also be disqualified from being a law if it is an artifact of interpretation or experimental design. Advocates of the RS assume that psychological generalizations are not accidental:

RS6: Psychological generalizations are non-accidental.

What might ground such an assumption? For most advocates of the RS it is grounded in the further assumption that psychological kinds can be viewed as functional kinds whose properties in each case are resultant from properties of the realizing system, and ultimately from properties that are fundamental rather than resultant or emergent. Thus RS6 is seen as a consequence of the following.

RS7: The fact that organism O conforms to psychological law P is resultant from lower-level facts about O (or perhaps about O and O's environment).

Likewise, even though a psychological law P does not itself say how it interacts with other laws, or when it is enabled by particular realizing systems, these facts are not themselves ultimately mysterious. Rather, they, too, are resultant from properties of the realizing system.

RS8: The facts about when a law P does and does not hold good of an organism O are resultant from lower-level facts about O (or perhaps about O and O's environment).

Finally, the advocate of the RS can accept RS9 and RS10 so long as he or she rejects RS9*.

RS9: Natural kinds are those to which laws apply.

RS10: Psychological kinds are natural kinds.

RS9*: Natural kinds are those to which strict and exceptionless laws apply.

3.4 Evaluation of the Received Solution

The RS seems to have two cardinal virtues. First, it vindicates the methodological and ontological legitimacy of the psychological at the cost of only minimal departures from the assumptions in the Davidsonian Problematic. This is at least a rhetorical virtue in that it engages the challenge to psychology in more or less its own terms. (Whether it is ultimately a virtue will depend, of course, on whether the original problem is well posed.) Second, when one fleshes it out with real examples, it seems intuitively plausible. The function/implementation analysis does seem to explain some types of exceptions to higher-level laws, and in those cases we have strong intuitions that the legitimacy of those laws is retained.

There are, however, several potential problems, limitations, and objections to the RS. First, we have assumed thus far that psychology has laws of some sort, even if they are not exceptionless. But a critic might wish to call into question whether psychology really has any laws at all. In the case of outer psychophysics, there do indeed seem to be laws of a familiar sort, such as Fechner's Law (though we shall examine a challenge to this assumption in chapter 10). Generalizations cast at the level of belief-desire psychology, however, are not cast in the form of equations, and certainly do not have the kind of mathematical rigor of the psychophysical laws, and this at least raises the question of where laws end and rough heuristics begin. And when we come to the "laws" of inner psychophysics—the relations between mental states and brain states—we are faced with things that do not bear much resemblance to the kind of dynamic laws we have been discussing thus far. Indeed, both the materialist and the dualist might have reason to see these as being very different from functional laws. The materialist may well believe that the realizing system will explain the properties of mental states, but is likely to see the relationship as one of identity or emergence (supervenience that is epistemically opaque and mysterious) or as being resultant (supervenient in a way that is epistemically transparent and derivable), and not as laws. The interactionist substance dualist will see the relationship as a causal law but will deny that there is the same level of explanation to be had in terms of the physical properties. The property dualist and the parallelist substance dualist will agree with both of these limitations. The assumption that there are psychological and psychophysical laws thus needs more attention, and these three cases must be treated separately. (This will be the topic of chapters 10–12.)

A second criticism of the RS would come from a critic who denies that mental kinds are functional kinds. Since the RS has shown us how to vindicate psychological kinds only on the assumption that they are functional kinds, this would undercut the argument. But there are at least two ways of denying that mental kinds are functional kinds, and only one of these presents a problem for RS. Some critics of functionalism are really critics of the strong thesis that the nature of mental kinds (such as belief or sensation) is exhausted by their functional description. That is, they deny that functional descriptions provide a conceptual analysis or a set of necessary and sufficient conditions for mental kinds—for example, because some non-functional properties (e.g. subjective feel) might be essential to them. RS has a ready response to this objection. In order for RS to work, it is not necessary to assume that mental kinds be "functional kinds" in this strong sense. All that RS requires is the weaker views (a) that mental kinds that enter into laws have functional descriptions and (b) that it is under these descriptions that they enter into laws.

But one might object to even this weaker sort of functionalism. One of the criticisms of behaviorism that is often presented in textbooks as telling is the failure of behaviorists to ever produce actual reductions or translations of the mentalistic vocabulary into behavior dispositions. In almost exactly the same way, it is often asserted that belief, desire, and other notions can be captured by a kind of function table, but that assertion is never backed up by producing such a table. And so one might well be tempted to think that what is sauce for dispatching the behaviorist gander will do equally well for the functionalist goose. But if functionalism can overcome this challenge, the advocate of the RS has some further work to do: either to justify the functionalist interpretation of mental states or to show how the RS can be applied to cases in which generalizations range over non-functional kinds.

A third objection comes from the critic who is willing to accept the disturbing conclusion that we may lose neuroscience, biology, metallurgy, and electronics along with psychology in the interest of methodological and ontological purity. It is hard to know how to engage such a criticism directly, but I think the advocate of RS should say something like the following: "I will stipulate that we will reserve the term 'laws' for what I was calling 'strict laws', and 'science' for things that have such (strict) laws. But we can make up new terms—'schmaws' for what were previously called "laws'," and 'schmience' for what we previously called 'science'. You can talk about laws and science; I'll talk about schmaws and schmience. But then all the interesting and important work is going to be done in philosophy of schmience and not in philosophy of science."

A fourth sort of objection—the most important, to my mind—uses the results of the RS analysis to call the very terms of discussion into question. One of the ways in which we saw that laws could fail to be exceptionless was when events were of a sort that was covered in multiple laws. In such situations, the individual laws, taken singly, do not determine how the object will behave; we need some further account of how the laws behave in combination. But this is not a situation that occurs only in psychology, or even only in the special sciences. Even in basic physics, multiple forces are normally at work. An object that is subject to gravitation will typically also be subject to strong, weak, and electromagnetic forces. Taken alone, a gravitational law will generally not correctly describe the behavior of objects *in vivo*. This seems, at least potentially, to threaten one of the basic assumptions of the whole discussion so far (that there is an important distinction between "strict and exceptionless" laws and "*ceteris paribus*" laws), and to do so to the detriment of the assumption that even basic physical laws are "strict and exceptionless." This concern, however, requires more attention and development. Its development in the work of Nancy Cartwright will be the topic of the next chapter.

4 Cartwright, Universal Laws, and Fundamentalism

The Davidsonian Problematic for philosophy of psychology is set up in terms of a contrast between two, purportedly different, types of laws: those that are "strict and exceptionless" and those that are hedged by "*ceteris paribus* clauses." This distinction may seem clear enough, but we might do well to ask what it really amounts to and whether a substantive assumption about the nature of laws is lurking under the guise of an innocuous distinction.

It is quite natural to view the *ceteris paribus* clause itself as the distinguishing feature: Whereas strict laws simply take the form "*L*," *ceteris paribus* laws take the form "Other things being equal, *L*," or perhaps "If not (conditions under which things are *not* equal), *L*."[1] The laws themselves, moreover, are supposed to be "universal and exceptionless." And this notion has generally been cashed out in the terms suggested by the Logical Positivists: namely that laws are universally quantified claims in first-order predicate calculus (perhaps augmented by modal machinery to accommodate counterfactuals) ranging over objects and events.

4.1 How the Laws of Physics Lie

In a justly famous series of publications dating back to the late 1970s, Nancy Cartwright has argued that the interpretation of laws received from the Positivists is fundamentally flawed. The basic gist of her articles, and the progression of her themes, is well reflected in the titles of her books: *How the Laws of Physics Lie* (Cartwright 1983), *Nature's Capacities and Their Measurement* (Cartwright 1989), and *The Dappled World* (Cartwright 1999). The frontal assault on the Positivist conception of laws and the covering-law model of explanation begins in *How the Laws of Physics Lie*. An alternative understanding of laws (that they express causal capacities) is developed in *Nature's Capacities and their Measurement*. And *The Dappled*

World emphasizes the theme that individual laws give us partial under-standings of the world that are not ultimately integrated into a single God's-eye view that embraces them all as a common denominator, but remain a dappled collage.

The frontal assault on the Positivist view of laws begins in "Do the Laws of Physics State the Facts?" and "The Truth Doesn't Explain Much" (both reprinted in Cartwright 1983). The former begins as follows:

There is a view about laws of nature that is so deeply entrenched that it does not even have a name of its own. It is the view that laws of nature describe facts about reality. If we think that the facts described by a law obtain, or at least that the facts that obtain are sufficiently like those described in the law, we count the law as true, or true-for-the-nonce, until further facts are discovered. I propose to call this doc-trine the *facticity* view of laws. (The name is due to John Perry.)

It is customary to take the fundamental explanatory laws of physics as the ideal. Maxwell's equations, or Schroedinger's, or the equations of general relativity, are paradigms, paradigms upon which all other laws—laws of chemistry, biology, ther-modynamics, or particle physics—are to be modeled. But this assumption confutes the facticity view of laws. For the fundamental laws of physics do not describe true facts about reality. *Rendered as descriptions of facts, they are false; amended to be true, they lose their fundamental explanatory force.* (Cartwright 1983, p. 54, emphasis added)

The last sentence, which I have emphasized, makes a very strong claim. But exactly what does it mean to say that laws do not state true facts? (Surely there are no false facts for them to state instead?) What Cartwright seems to mean by this is that laws do not "tell what the objects in their domains do" or "describe how things behave" (ibid., p. 55). That is, laws do not yield accurate descriptions or predictions of the actual behavior of objects—of what I shall call their *in vivo* kinematics. (A note on terminol-ogy: I am contrasting 'kinematics' and 'dynamics' so that the former picks out accounts that capture the actual behavior and the latter picks out accounts of underlying causes.) If laws are taken to have the function of describing (or licensing predictions of) the actual behavior of objects, such as the actual flight path of a projectile, they turn out to be false. Thus, if laws are taken to be universally quantified claims about the kinematics of objects and events, the laws are false. Cartwright's main line of argument for this surprising claim stems from an observation about what happens in cases involving the combination of forces:

For bodies, which are both massive and charged, the law of universal gravitation and Coulomb's law (the law that gives the force between two charges) interact to describe the final force. But neither law by itself truly describes how the bodies behave. No charged objects will behave just as the law of universal gravitation says; and any massive objects will constitute a counterexample to Coulomb's law. These two laws are not true; worse, they are not even approximately true. In the interaction between the electrons and the protons of an atom, for example, the Coulomb effect swamps the gravitational one, and the force that actually occurs is very different from that described by the law of gravity. (Cartwright 1983, p. 57)

This is strikingly similar to one of the examples of exceptions to laws in the case of psychology discussed in the preceding chapter: that a generalization describing how people behave when they fear something and a generalization describing how people behave when their loved ones are in danger may each express truths, even though neither of them licenses dependable predictions about what will happen when both fear and concern are at work, and even though they pull toward opposite outcomes. Likewise, a gravitational law and an electromagnetic law may each apply to a situation, and in that case the actual kinematics of the situation are not (fully and accurately) described by either law. This, I think, is all Cartwright means when she says that the laws are false—i.e., if you interpret laws as making claims or entailing predictions about real-world kinematics, then they are false, at least in those instances in which multiple laws are in effect. Indeed, one might strengthen Cartwright's point here: Since most types of physical bodies contain both charged particles and particles with mass, the laws have no true substitution instances (or, at best, they have very few of them, and none involving familiar sorts of macroscopic objects).

Before we evaluate Cartwright's claims, let us pause to appreciate their relevance to the Davidsonian Problematic for philosophy of psychology. The problems there were predicated on the assumption that physical laws are strict and universal whereas psychological laws are hedged by *ceteris paribus* clauses. And the reason for saying that psychological laws are not strict was that sometimes people in fact behave in ways that contradict the supposed psychological generalizations—i.e., their actual behavior is not what the law would describe or predict. But Cartwright points out that the very same thing can be said for fundamental physical laws such as gravitation. If such a gap between law and actual behavior counts as an exception in psychology, it ought to count as an exception in physics too, and hence the physical laws are not exceptionless laws but *ceteris paribus* laws. There is, thus, no longer an opposition here between the strict and exceptionless laws of physics and the *ceteris paribus* laws of psychology, and hence the original problem dissolves or at best turns out to be ill-posed. It is not often that we can be rid of a problem at a stroke; but if Cartwright's analysis of laws holds good, this may be one of them, as Davidson's problem seems to turn out to be an artifact of a particular (and erroneous) interpretation of laws.[2]

4.2 Nature's Capacities and Composition of Forces

It may be necessary to separate Cartwright's point in her early articles from her rhetorical strategy of saying that the laws are false or do not describe the facts. Although Cartwright has never retracted this way of putting things, she has changed her emphasis over the years. Even the point made in her early articles might instead be put as follows: If we take the view that laws are universally quantified claims about the behavior of objects, then they turn out to be materially false. Putting it this way leads to an obvious way of trying to preserve the intuition that laws are true: by interpreting laws as something other than universally quantified claims about the behavior of objects.

On this point, Cartwright's works evidence a certain vacillation. In some places, she seems to favor the view that laws are aimed at describing the (kinematic) facts but are always hedged by *ceteris paribus* clauses; in other places, particularly in her more recent work, she has tended to see laws as expressing the capacities of objects to make causal contributions in real-world kinematics. The first description still seems to be a minimal departure from the covering-law account of explanation Cartwright is attacking; the latter embraces a causal model of explanation. There is reason to think that Cartwright's ambivalence here is explicit and principled. Consider the beginning of "The Truth Doesn't Explain Much":

Scientific theories must tell us both what is true in nature, and how we are to explain it. I shall argue that these are entirely different functions and should be kept distinct. Usually the two are conflated. The second is commonly seen as a by-product of the first. Scientific theories are thought to explain by dint of the descriptions they give of reality. Once the job of describing is done, science can then shut down. That is all there is to do. To describe nature—to tell its laws, the values of its fundamental constants, its mass distributions—is *ipso facto* to lay down how we are to explain it. . . . This is a mistake, I shall argue. (Cartwright 1983, p. 44)

Though I am not sure Cartwright would embrace this interpretation, I would put the point as follows: Laws really serve two different functions. One function is to give explanations of why things behave as they do; the other is to describe how objects behave and to underwrite predictions. But to get the explanatory force of the law, you have to take it singly, as expressing a capacity or causal contribution that is always at work, whether the law is operating alone or in combination with other laws in a given situation. Taken thus, the paradigmatic instances of laws are not hedged by *ceteris paribus* clauses. If the law of gravitation expresses a causal contribution (a force?), it is not affected by whether Coulomb's law is also in play. However, laws are also used in description and prediction. And they yield accurate descriptions and predictions of how things actually behave only under very special circumstances—when other forces are fortuitously not in play, or when we contrive such situations in our experimental set-up, creating what Cartwright calls a "nomological machine" (1999, chapter 3). To get them to be more accurate as generalizations about real-world kinematics, one might screen off the cases in which they would yield false predictions by hedging them with *ceteris paribus* clauses. For example, one treats the law of universal gravitation as saying "If there are no forces other than gravitational force at work, then the kinematics of two bodies will be computable by the inverse square law."[3] But if one does this, one distorts the scope of the law and limits its predictive power. For what the scientist is interested in is not simply what happens when only gravitational force is at work (is there such an occasion?); rather, she is interested in gravitational force in all the cases, regardless of what other forces are in play. Moreover, the gravitation law is by no means irrelevant to the prediction and description of cases in which more than one force is in play, and so setting it off in such a *ceteris paribus* clause limits not only its explanatory power but also its predictive utility. The scientist is not interested in the fact that physical laws are true of "ideal worlds,"[4] but in what they say (and say truly) about the real world.

This, of course, brings up a potential rejoinder. Cartwright's objection to the "facticity" of laws is predicated on the observation that, taken singly, they do not describe real-world behavior. But there have been techniques for factoring and recombining forces through vector algebra at least since Newton. Why can't the older view of laws be saved, at least as modified by the claim that when more than one force is in play one must sum the forces through vector algebra?

Notice first that to make this reply is at least partially to play into Cartwright's hands. It is to agree, in effect, that the laws, as stated by the scientists, express something like a causal contribution, and that only when we combine them into some larger sort of equation involving vector algebra do we get a description of behavior *in vivo*. And this is a significant concession both for Cartwright's purposes and for ours. For her purposes, it concedes that the covering-law model must at least be supplemented by a model that treats laws as expressing causal capacities. For our purposes, it undercuts the move against psychology that treats the "exceptions" to its laws (i.e., the cases in which people do not act as the generalizations, taken singly, predict) as indicating that their status is any different from those of physical laws. If physical laws predict behavior only when the "super equation" encompassing the interactions of *all* forces is written down, or perhaps only when the right heuristic for integrating *this* combination of forces in *that* situation is applied, the same should be true for psychological laws. Such a "super equation" is out of reach for psychology, but it is out of reach for physics too. Again it is hard to see wherein the damning difference is supposed to lie.

However, Cartwright offers several additional replies to the objection that the Empiricist model can be rescued by locating the "facticity" of laws not in individual laws but in a "super law" that covers their combination and interaction (cf. Cartwright 1983, pp. 70–71). The most important of these for our purposes is that "super laws" are not always available and are not necessary for purposes of explanation:

> There are a good number of complex scientific phenomena which we are quite proud to be able to explain. . . . For many of these explanations, super covering laws are not available to us. Sometimes we have every reason to believe that a super law exists. In other cases we have no good empirical reason to suppose even this much. Nevertheless, after we have seen what occurs in a specific case, we are often able to understand how various causes contributed to bring it about. We do explain, even without knowing the super laws. We need a philosophical account of explanations which covers this very common scientific practice, and which shows why these explanations are good ones. (Cartwright 1983, p. 70)

Let us take the second point first. There are perfectly good explanations of singular events that proceed by identifying partial causal contributions separately and do not employ a super law. Cartwright's point here is really about whether we should adopt a covering-law view or a causal-contribution view. But we might turn the point to another purpose: In order to explain singular events, we often do not need a super covering law. A patchwork of separate laws is often enough.

Let us now return to the first point of the paragraph—that sometimes no such "super law" is available. Just what might this mean? I should prefer to put the point in a way that I do not find in Cartwright: Even once you have identified a number of causal contributions to an event, it is not always possible to compute a summation of forces—*and this fact in no way impugns the laws or models used for understanding the individual contributions.* Though Cartwright does not put the point in quite this way, I think she would endorse both parts of this claim. In several places, she outlines cases in which it is not possible to factor or sum forces. One important case is that of what I shall call *interaction effects*. Suppose you know what happens if you mix a given substance with an acid and know what happens when you mix it with a base. You cannot tell what will happen when you mix it with an acid *and* a base just by doing some sort of vector addition on the models for mixing with acids and mixing with bases, because the acid and the base interact with one another in a way that negates their individual abilities to react with the third substance:

When two forces in mechanics are present together, each retains its original capacity. They operate side by side, independently of one another. The resulting effect is a pure combination of the effect that each is trying to produce by itself. The law of vector addition gives precise content to this idea of pure combination. In chemistry, things are different. The acid and the base neutralize each other. Each destroys the chemical powers of the other, and the peculiar chemical effects of both are eliminated. This is not like the stationary particle, held in place by the tug of forces in opposite directions. When an acid and a base mix, their effects do not combine: neither can operate to produce any effects at all. (Cartwright 1989, p. 163)

In chapter 6 I shall introduce a short taxonomy of situations in which models that are good for explanation may not be combinable to produce accurate descriptions of events or license predictions. For now, the basic point is that we cannot rescue the claim that laws in the natural sciences are exceptionless generalizations about real-world events by interpreting it as saying that a summation of operative forces in any given situation will yield an accurate description (or yield an accurate prediction) of real-world behavior, because in some situations this kind of summation of forces is not available.

4.3   The Patchwork of Laws and the Dappled World

The picture of scientific laws that Cartwright presents is directly contrary to the picture favored by twentieth-century Positivists and Empiricists and by seventeenth-century Rationalists—that is, a picture on which Science (singular and capitalized) is seen as being, or at least moving toward, a single account of the world in the form of an axiomatized deductive system. Instead, we have a number of laws and models that say true things about the world when interpreted as statements about causal contributions or capacities. We sometimes, but not always, have ways of integrating two or more of these into a larger picture. But even when we do not have a "super-model" that combines them, we can often use multiple models to gain increasing understanding, and predictive power, in a given situation.

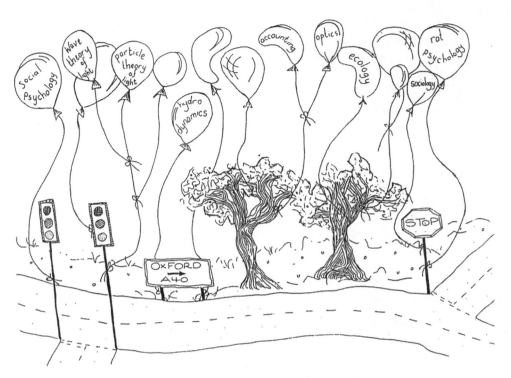

Figure 4.1
Representation of theory pluralism on jacket of Nancy Cartwright's 1999 book *The Dappled World*.

The collection of laws is not an axiomatic system but a patchwork. The world picture is not unified but "dappled." (See figure 4.1.) Whereas the Positivists pursued the goal of "unified science," Cartwright embraces what she calls a "nomological pluralism." While this chapter cannot do justice to the argumentation Cartwright has offered for this view over the course of several books (not to mention that supplied by other proponents of disunified science, including Ian Hacking (1996) and John Dupré (1993)), I would venture to say that Cartwright has presented both a challenge and an alternative to the view that laws are to be interpreted as universally quantified claims ranging over objects and events. So interpreted, they turn out to be false, and to preserve the very plausible intuition that the laws are true we must reconceive them as something other than universal claims about actual events. This is the negative result of Cartwright's corpus. I think we should embrace it. For reasons I shall explain shortly, I am less thoroughly enthusiastic about the positive side of her program—the account she gives of laws and explanation.

But note that the negative result alone is enough to throw the Davidsonian Problematic into disarray. Whether we say (a) physical laws are also *ceteris paribus* laws or (b) that laws are not universally quantified claims about objects and events, we have denied the fundamental assumption on which Davidson's problem was based: that we can distinguish psychological laws from those of the natural sciences on the ground that the former are "*ceteris paribus*" laws while the latter are "universal and exceptionless." Without this distinction, the original problematic is dissolved. There may be other important differences between psychology and physics, but to characterize them we will have to look for a new theoretical framework, and we need not presume that anything like Davidson's problematic will re-emerge there. The philosophical problem would seem to be an artifact of a particular philosophical interpretation of the nature of laws. Since that interpretation is inadequate on more general grounds, the problem is dissolved.

I think that this analysis is both right-headed and conclusive in establishing that there is something wrong with the Davidsonian Problematic itself: that it depends on an untenable understanding of scientific laws. This, of course, does not mean that some of the underlying intuitions— particularly that there are important differences between physical and psychological generalizations—might not be formulated in a more successful way. But at very least we will have to find a new way of putting the questions.

4.4 Looking Beyond Cartwright

While I find Cartwright's critique of Empiricism compelling, I am less satisfied with the positive account she offers as an alternative. And even Cartwright's critique of Empiricism has received mixed reviews. Some view her work as having brought about a paradigm shift in philosophy of science; others claim to find it difficult to see a cogent argument in her critique at all. It is thus problematic to make too much rest on an assumption that Cartwright has succeeded in her attempt to overthrow the Empiricist account of laws.

4.4.1 Cartwright's Critique and Mine
A brief digression on the history of my relationship with Cartwright's work on laws seems in order. Some years ago, I came to be troubled by the

universally quantified character of laws as understood by Empiricism. Foremost in my mind was the following sort of issue: Suppose we take the gravitation law to make (or entail) claims about how objects actually fall— say, that objects of equal mass, dropped from the same height from a state of rest, will accelerate toward the ground in equal ways and will reach the ground at the same time. Now suppose that the two objects in question are pieces of paper of equal mass. One is crumpled tightly into a paper ball, the other folded into a paper airplane. The paper ball falls to the ground much more quickly than the paper airplane, even though they are of equal mass. This example makes it plain to see that real-world behavior does not always conform to the law of gravitation, and if the law is interpreted as saying that it should, then either the law is false or the interpretation is wrong-headed.

When I talked about this with other philosophers, they said things like "Ah, yes, that's what Nancy Cartwright argued." When I read her books, I did indeed see a kindred position, though to this day I am not sure how exactly her critique lines up with my own. I have presented her critique first, out of respect for precedence in publication amounting to almost three decades. However, in the next chapter I shall present an independent critique of the Empiricist account of laws in my own way. I shall leave to the reader to decide whether the critiques are equivalent, or whether mine adds to hers, or whether mine is altogether different. Perhaps one critique will persuade if the other fails to.

4.4.2 Issues with Cartwright's Positive Account

On the question of what alternative to offer to the Empiricist account of laws, I am more certain that there are important differences between my view and Cartwright's. I am not convinced that Cartwright's accounts of laws provide an adequate way of reformulating questions about laws in psychology and physics. Though I think that Cartwright's negative case is persuasive, I am not content simply to embrace her positive account here, for two sorts of reasons. The first are concerned with what I see to be problems in her account, the second with questions to which her account does not seem to present answers. (Most pressingly, we have a sense that there is *some* sort of difference between psychological and physical laws, even if that difference is not captured by the opposition between strict laws and *ceteris paribus* laws, and Cartwright's account does not provide resources for situating those differences.)

Let us begin with the ambiguity or duality in Cartwright's positive account(s) of laws identified earlier. Sometimes she speaks of physical laws as being *ceteris paribus* laws concerned with real-world events; sometimes she speaks of them as expressing causal capacities. I am not fully comfortable with either of these formulations. First, consider the claim that, construed as *ceteris paribus* laws, physical laws are true in the sense of getting the facts (i.e., the actual kinematics) of objects right. But this seems untenable even by Cartwright's own lights. Construed as a *ceteris paribus* law, the gravitational law would say only what would happen in cases when other forces were not at work. But it is not clear that there are any such cases. Other things are *never* equal. So construed thus, the laws would be vacuous. Moreover, truths that apply only in cases where there is no composition of forces at work do not adequately reflect what the scientist is after in stating laws. The scope of the law of gravitation is not confined to cases where only gravitation is in play. It includes cases where other forces are also in play, even though it does not license exact kinematic predictions in such cases. But Cartwright seems to be drawn back to this description of laws, even though she has at hand the alternative of saying that laws express causal capacities.

On the other hand, I am not sure just what "causal capacities" are supposed to amount to. The Empiricist might be tempted to cash such a notion out dispositionally. But a dispositional account would ultimately treat capacity talk as a construction out of event talk, and that is precisely what we cannot do if Cartwright's arguments work at all. The Realist, on the other hand, might be tempted to interpret "laws express causal capacities" as meaning something on the order of "laws commit us to an ontology of forces." This, however, seems to go beyond anything Cartwright explicitly endorses, and indeed she has consistently denied the reality of "component *forces*." There may be some intermediate interpretation that I simply do not see as of yet, but both of the possibilities I do see seem to come at substantial cost.

But perhaps we would do better not to see all this as an ambiguity (in Cartwright) or a forced choice, but as a compelling duality within the nature of laws and models themselves. Laws, as it were, have both a kinematic aspect (i.e., of describing and predicting actual behavior) and a dynamic aspect (i.e., of expressing underlying causes responsible for that behavior). This view would, I think, be agreeable to Cartwright, but it stands in need of a further philosophical development to go beyond this basic intuition of duality. I will attempt such a development in the next two chapters.

My final concern is not about any way in which Cartwright's project fails on its own terms, but rather that it does not provide all one might wish for as a background to discussing laws in psychology and psychophysics. Cartwright's negative project undercuts a view of laws that resulted in the Davidsonian Problematic, and hence we can use Cartwright to dissolve that problematic. But my experience is that dissolving that particular philosophical problem does not necessarily dissolve the intuition that there is an important dissimilarity between physical and psychological laws, and indeed that the former are somehow more general, more rigorous, and more useful for prediction than the latter. Cartwright's interpretation of laws as expressing causal capacities would help us see the commonalities between physics and psychology, but not the differences. We could use an account that could do both. I aim to provide it in chapter 6.

5 Empiricism and Laws

In the preceding chapter, I discussed Nancy Cartwright's critique of the Empiricist account of laws. That critique is an important contribution to the philosophy of science, and if I have interpreted Cartwright correctly I think it contains sound arguments. Nevertheless, Cartwright's arguments against Empiricism have not gained universal acceptance, nor has her alternative account. Indeed, many of her critics claim to have difficulty understanding what she is arguing at all, and many others interpret her in ways significantly different from the interpretations I have suggested. Moreover, while I agree with the general spirit of Cartwright's alternative interpretation of laws as expressing "causal powers," I find some of her statements to echo some of the assumptions of the Empiricists she is criticizing—assumptions that I think we would do better to abandon. And my own preferred formulation of a "causal" account of laws is somewhat different from Cartwright's, employing a cognitivist framework for understanding what laws are in the business of doing.

Consequently, I deem it prudent to develop a critique of Empiricism and an alternative account of laws that are not rooted in Cartwright's ground-breaking work. In this chapter, I shall present an alternative analysis and critique of Empiricism.

5.1 Variations on the Empiricist Account of Laws

In many classic expositions of Logical Empiricism, one sees individual laws treated as universally quantified claims. In some versions these are cast in first-order predicate calculus, but in later versions they tend to be modally strengthened in order to cover counterfactuals and to exclude accidental generalizations. If we take such characterizations at face value, they suggest the interpretation that natural laws, taken individually, are universally quantified claims that are at least materially true, and whose domain ranges over objects and events. I shall assume that such pseudo-scientific laws as "all swans are white" should not guide us in our interpretation of laws, and that we should assume that the Empiricist account is really intended to be applied to bona fide scientific laws such as those of gravitation and magnetism. And so I shall use those laws in my analysis.

Some laws are concerned with the synchronic relations between two variables, such as the temperature and the pressure of a gas. Other laws are concerned with temporally extended processes—processes of change. But there are two ways one might further interpret laws concerned with change over time. On the one hand, such laws might directly make kinematic claims—that is, claims about the actual behavior of objects that interact gravitationally or magnetically. On the other hand, they might directly make dynamic claims—that is, claims about something like forces—and imply kinematic consequences only indirectly. I shall begin with the kinematic interpretation of laws taken one at a time.

5.2 Piecemeal Kinematic Empiricism

On the most natural reading of the quantified interpretation of laws, the law of gravitation makes claims about how objects actually and always behave under the influence of gravitation. It is thus in the business of making a systematic claim about real-world kinematics. This interpretation is central to Humean Empiricism, but is also evidenced in many more recent Empiricist accounts, whether or not their proponents share Hume's skepticism about a realist interpretation of forces.

Interpreted as a kinematic law, the gravitation law would seem to require a universally quantified claim involving (at least) two variables representing objects, two variables representing their masses, two variables representing their antecedent and consequent distances, and either one variable for the time between antecedent and consequent conditions or multiple variables, one for each time (these are notational variants). Thus interpreted, the laws are precisely claims about gravitational kinematics. They might be interpreted as applying to all objects or as restricted to objects with mass.

But thus interpreted, they would be false for a number of reasons. Take the familiar case of bodies falling to the Earth. The law, it is claimed, says that two bodies of equal mass, if dropped from an equal height, will approach the Earth by the same distance over a given interval of time. But suppose that one object is a paper airplane and the other a dense sphere of equal mass. Plainly they do not in fact fall alike. And the reason for this is well understood: other forces, such as wind resistance, operate differently on them, and play a causal role in their trajectories that is independent of that played by gravity. Likewise, if a magnetic field is present, and one object is metallic and the other made of paper, they will behave differently, even in a vacuum. The gravitation law, interpreted as a piecemeal kinematic law, is at best true of bodies and situations in which no other kinematic laws apply. Indeed, since the law of inertia is an independent law, this is quite a serious problem: the gravitation law would be false of any bodies already in motion relative to one another (with the important exception of systems involving stable Keplerian orbits).

And if there are more than two bodies with mass in the system, the two-body equation for any pair of them will fail to predict their kinematics correctly. As initially stated, the gravitation law, thus interpreted, would yield correct descriptions and predictions only in a two-body system involving bodies that do not interact through any non-gravitational mechanisms and start out in a state of rest relative to one another or in stable Keplerian orbits. This last concern can perhaps be remedied to some extent by dividing the law into separate cases for two-body, three-body, and n-body systems. This might suffice for an accurate mathematical description of the kinematics of such systems. However, it would not serve for exact prediction, as the kinematics becomes computationally intractable once the number of bodies exceeds two.

Given this interpretation of laws, it is hard to make a meaningful distinction between laws of physics and the laws found in the sciences of the mind. If psychological laws are also interpreted as universally quantified claims about real-world events, they are false. But so are the physical laws. Indeed, the physical laws, interpreted as kinematic claims, have so few true substitution instances that it is hard to see how psychological laws could fare worse if we are keeping score on the basis of how often they correctly capture the exact kinematic outcomes.

If, on the other hand, psychological laws are interpreted as quantified claims within *ceteris paribus* clauses, their form would indeed differ from the form ascribed to physical laws. But it is not clear that psychological laws would compare unfavorably here. If adding *ceteris paribus* clauses can make the psychological laws yield true universal claims about how people behave, they in fact fare better with respect to truth than universally quantified kinematic laws in physics. Indeed, one might reasonably conclude that the right moral to draw here is that what is needed to save the Empiricist account of physical laws is to add some *ceteris paribus* clauses to them as well.

5.3   Piecemeal Kinematic *Ceteris Paribus* Laws

We have, in effect, already moved from an interpretation of laws that views them as universally quantified claims to an interpretation that views them as universal claims embedded within *ceteris paribus* conditions. Such conditions would, most simply, take the form of material conditionals in which the nomic portion of the claim is the consequent and the antecedent contains either the conditions under which the nomic portion holds true or the negation of the conditions under which it fails to hold true. If this is needed to keep physical laws from being false whenever there are multiple forces at work or whenever there are more than two bodies, then even very low-level laws such as those of gravitation and electromagnetism are *ceteris paribus* laws. Perhaps there are some laws that would not have to be hedged by such conditions, but nonetheless *ceteris paribus* laws would be commonplace in the natural sciences.

On this revised Empiricist account of laws, physical laws and psychological laws are similar in logical form. Both involve quantified statements embedded in *ceteris paribus* clauses. On this version of Empiricism, we cannot make a principled contrast between the "strict" laws of physics and the *ceteris paribus* laws of psychology, because physics also involves *ceteris paribus* laws.

But there are also difficulties for this variant of the Empiricist view of laws more generally. We have already seen, in our discussion of Cartwright's critique, that the scope of such laws would be quite narrow, and the instances about which they would say anything at all would be woefully few. Such laws would be far narrower in scope than the gravitation law and similar laws are generally understood to be. The gravitation law is not irrelevant to cases in which other forces are also at work, and hence a logical reformulation of that law ought not to exclude such cases by way of *ceteris paribus* or boundary conditions. Moreover, the truth of such limited-scope laws would shed no light on the legitimate explanatory and predictive power that real laws afford in the many cases that lie outside the *ceteris paribus* conditions. The gravitation law does not tell us exactly how bodies will fall in a fluid medium or when a magnetic field is present, but it does tell us something that is crucial to understanding their kinematics in such situations.

If laws are interpreted individually as materially true universal kinematic claims, they are either false or unrecognizable. If they are not hedged by *ceteris paribus* clauses, they are false; indeed, it is doubtful whether they have many, or any, true substitution instances. But if they are hedged by the necessary set of *ceteris paribus* laws, they are no longer the familiar physical laws, which tell us things about situations falling outside the *ceteris paribus* conditions.

Moreover, Newton's formulation of the gravitation law,

$$F = G \frac{m_1 \times m_2}{r^2},$$

says nothing directly about motion. What it looks like, and what Newton understood it to be in the first instance, is a force equation, claiming that the gravitational force between two bodies is proportional to the product of their masses and inversely proportional to the square of the distance between them. The law does yield kinematic descriptions and predictions with appropriate computational additions, as Newton showed. One mass accelerates toward the other according to the formula

$$\left| \frac{d^2 \vec{r}}{dt^2} \right| = a_1 + a_2 = G \frac{m_1 + m_2}{r^2}.$$

For the most important of Newton's derivations of motion—the proof that the inverse-square law allows derivation of Kepler's laws—little more is required, as the velocity of planets in stable orbits is a function of their distance. However, in cases such as rogue comets or projectile motion the gravitation law alone does not suffice; it must be combined with the contributions of the inertial state of at least one of the bodies. Thus, the piecemeal quantified interpretation is either a bad interpretation of classical mechanics (because it interprets a dynamic claim—a claim about forces—as a kinematic claim) or an interpretation that applies only to special cases in which inertial and other non-gravitational forces can be discounted.

5.4 Piecemeal Dynamic Claims, Global Kinematics

The foregoing suggests an alternative interpretation. Individual laws are materially true, universally quantified claims. But they are claims about dynamics rather than about kinematics. That is, they are claims about forces acting on objects rather than about the objects' behavior. Such an interpretation—suggested by the uses of the term 'force' in physics—has several advantages over the kinematic view.

First, at least in cases such as the law of gravitation, the dynamic interpretation does not require that we screen off with *ceteris paribus* clauses all cases in which other forces are at work. As a result, the laws can have broad scope without thereby becoming materially false. The dynamic interpretation also makes it unnecessary to formulate separate laws (or disjunctive laws) for systems with different numbers of bodies. Forces occur between any two bodies with mass. Moreover, the dynamic approach accords in an important way with scientific practice. Since Newton, we have viewed the kinematics of a mechanical system as resulting from, and described and predicted by, a summation of forces, calculated using vector algebra. This interpretation would view laws as individually stating materially true universal claims about forces ranging over n-tuples of objects. Its kinematic implications, however, would be framed in terms of a summation-of-forces equation ranging over the entire system.

It is harder to say just what we should make of the similarities and differences between physical and psychological laws on such a dynamic interpretation. It seems somewhat strained to speak of the psychological variables that are at work in psychological laws as "forces." But this need not be a serious problem. The notion of "force" also seems strained in biology, and we already have, from Cartwright and others, a suggestion of more general expressions, such as "causal powers" or "causal capacities." I have general misgivings about such terms, but they are no stronger in the case of beliefs or emotions than in the case of, say, explanations of genetic drift. To the extent that we are content to individuate beliefs or emotions as occurrent events of psychological kinds, and to speak of mental causation at all (and I am aware that not everyone is content to do so), it seems clear enough that we need to speak of them as having the capacity to make causal contributions. Their ability to do so is, of course, contingent on other states of the organism. But this is compatible with a dynamic account whose kinematic implications are determined globally. It is, for example, the sort of idea that has been explored in accounts that view the mind as a Turing machine whose causal dispositions are expressed globally in the form of a Turing table (a view of the mind I do not wish to endorse, but only to mention).

What the dynamic approach notably lacks is something corresponding to the principled distinction between strict laws and *ceteris paribus* laws. In all cases, dynamic laws must be supplemented by something more—a rule for interactions and composition of forces—in order to yield kinematic results. The exact nature of this rule might be different in psychology than in physics, but it probably also would be different in chemistry than in biology, and perhaps even between different areas of physics. In short, it is not clear that one can make the original distinction between strict laws and *ceteris paribus* laws on the dynamic account.

The piecemeal dynamic interpretation, however, has problems of its own. Some (e.g., Cartwright) see the idea of "component forces" as unsuitable for a realist interpretation. I do not see any reason not to speak of component forces in the case of the gravitation law applied to a system with more than two bodies, though it may become more problematic with laws of the special sciences such as population genetics. More problematic, to my mind, are the issues of how to interpret the summation of forces and the relation between laws and prediction in a fashion consonant with the Empiricist quantified interpretation of laws.

Despite its naïveté, the piecemeal quantified kinematic approach had the advantage of providing a straightforward account of the relationship between laws and prediction. (Summation of forces was not a part of its story in the first place.) All we needed were the laws themselves, taken one by one. But if the laws directly make claims only about instantaneous forces, we need something in addition to the laws to account for change. We need some additional claim, such as "The kinematics of the system is determined by a comprehensive summation of forces." And, in contrast with specific laws, we cannot spell out such a claim in detail without an understanding of what all the forces are. We can state the gravitation law in ignorance of what other forces there may be. But to state a summation claim without knowing what is to be summed is to say something that is not very perspicuous. Such a claim at least starts out as an open-ended one, and as one that either is ill-defined or achieves definition only by quantifying over an open-ended set of forces, known and unknown.

There is also an additional difficulty here. We can make a summation-of-forces claim concrete through simple vector algebra only to the extent that the forces operate in the same way in isolation as when combined. This works well enough for gravitation and electromagnetism; but laws in the special sciences, and many in physics, do not deal with causal factors that are truly independent of one another. Take Cartwright's example of laws governing how a compound C interacts with an acid and with a base. Now suppose that we wish to know what will happen if compound C is mixed with an acid and a base at the same time. If we simply take the individual laws and combine their results, we will get an incorrect answer, because the acid and the base interact preferentially with one another. In such cases, which are probably the norm in the special sciences, a summation of forces requires more than vector algebra over the results of individual laws. And what it requires differs from case to case. The task of specifying a general summation-of-forces equation is thus both daunting and disturbingly piecemeal and open-ended. This is troublesome both for the project of giving a logical reconstruction of the notion of summation of forces and for turning laws into predictions.

Moreover, it is not even clear how we should interpret the supposedly universal character of such nomic claims as those in Cartwright's example. In contrast with the gravitation law, it is not clear that it makes sense to view laws of chemical combination as expressing forces. Forces such as those found in mechanics may be a paradigmatic example of dynamic invariants; however, if we are to treat all laws in a similar fashion, we must treat them all as expressing forces. And even if we do so, we face problems with the quantifier. Forces tend to combine. The causal dispositions expressed by chemical laws, by contrast, seem to be conditional in character. If we say that the dispositions are absent in some cases, we are back in the position of treating them as *ceteris paribus* laws. If we say that they are present, we need some further notation to capture the conditions in which they are and are not expressed, whether within our reconstruction of the laws as dynamic laws or in the summation-of-forces equation. (Any formula that could capture all of the ways forces do or do not combine in different cases would not be an elegant piece of vector algebra but a motley disjunction of special cases, requiring the use of logical machinery in addition to vector algebra.)

The relationship between laws and prediction is also problematic in additional ways. First, if the notion of summation of forces can be spelled out, the resulting account will underwrite predictions only when we know what forces to sum, and how to sum them. It underwrites nothing about cases in which we have only partial information. And we are normally in such a case, even under carefully controlled laboratory conditions. But even in such cases, the individual laws often afford us strong predictive power, even though they do not yield exact predictions. We should want an account of laws to explain why they have the pragmatic virtue of often yielding good-enough approximate predictions in such cases. Second, even when we know what forces to sum, the resulting equation may not be computationally tractable.

5.5   Truths about Kinematics in Ideal Worlds

We started out with an interpretation of laws as universal claims that are materially true of actual objects and their kinematics. This foundered on problems related to the many cases in which the kinematic behavior does not conform to the laws. We then explored the alternative view that laws express materially true universal claims, not about actual kinematics, but about dynamics. This approach avoided the kinematic view's inability to find a way of making the laws simultaneously true and useful for prediction in the broad range of cases in which they are actually employed, though it was met with compelling objections as well.

There is, however, an alternative kinematic interpretation. It begins with the Empiricist suggestion that laws individually make true universal claims about objects and their kinematics. Of course, we have seen that law claims would turn out false if interpreted in this way and applied to the actual world. But we might preserve the idea that the laws are at least materially true by assuming that their domain is not events in the real world, but in some ideal world. (Suppe 1989; Horgan and Tienson 1996; Giere 1999). For example, the gravitation law does make true claims about a world that is "ideal" in the sense that we use in speaking of ideal experimental conditions—i.e., those that isolate the variables we are interested in. So the gravitation law, interpreted as a kinematic law, would be at least materially true, for example, of a world in which gravity was the only force at work, all bodies possessed mass, and so on.

This interpretation would indeed make the laws turn out to be true. Indeed, the risk is that it makes them true by definition, and also makes it too easy to come up with "laws" that are "true." After all, any non-self-contradictory universal claim C is materially true of some world W, if we define W as a world in which C is true! It also risks saying nothing about how laws actually function in science. The scientist may in some sense be interested in "ideal worlds," but she is also interested in the real world, and laws are of scientific (as opposed to philosophical) interest only insofar as they say something about the real world. The mere fact that a law statement is true of some ideal world does not ensure this. After all, there are also ideal worlds in which entirely different laws hold.

Moreover, even in ideal worlds described by laws we actually use, it is not clear that the domain of the laws could be the same. The real objects to which the laws are applied do have other physical properties (for example, mass and charge). So whatever objects exist in the ideal world are not the same in kind as anything in the real world. And the types of real macroscopic objects the sciences actually make claims about could not even exist in a world without strong or weak force. Securing material truth by appeal to ideal worlds would seem at best to risk making laws irrelevant to real science, and at worst to risk making them applicable only to objects that could not exist in the actual world.

But there is a strategy that might address at least some of these worries. Laws, thus conceived, might afford understanding of the actual world without being materially true of its kinematics. They might, for example, be "approximately true" of the actual world. But it is hard to know just what "approximate truth" might amount to. If "approximate truth" is supposed to be a logical or a semantic notion, it is a rather odd one, as it requires us to formulate a logic and a semantics without the law of excluded middle. Alternatively, we might view such a notion in pragmatic terms: the laws, though not materially true of the actual world, nonetheless give us the ability to make predictions that are often within an acceptable margin of error. Indeed, if one can define a suitable similarity relationship between worlds, the truth of laws in ideal worlds might even explain our ability to use them for approximate predictions in the actual world.

I am doubtful about this strategy in general. But it seems most conspicuously problematic when we look for an account of summation of forces in real-world science. An ideal gravitational world and an ideal electromagnetic world are entirely separate things. They have completely disjoint sets of laws, and I suspect that no objects that could exist in one could exist in the other. Even if each such world, taken individually, could explain predictive success in the application of a single law, the ideal-worlds model tells us nothing about how to understand cases in which we would normally say that multiple laws are at work. It is not clear to me how understanding a world W_1 as governed by law L_1 and a very different world W_2 as governed by L_2 should explain the kinematics of the actual world, especially if the latter is composed of objects found neither in W_1 nor in W_2.

And, most fundamentally, the ideal-worlds view would seem to require us to modify our normal assumption that law statements "say something true" about the actual world. Unless forced to do otherwise, we should favor a view that either (a) ends up with the laws saying something true about the actual world, or else (b) if 'truth', understood as entailing material truth, is not a suitable predicate for laws, we at least need to articulate an alternative success term for law statements that captures what we take to be the epistemic virtues of law statements.

And this, I think, forces us to abandon the assumption that laws are in the business of making (or implying) materially true universal claims about kinematics. And although this suggestion may initially sound shocking to philosophers, it ought not to be a cause of shock or scandal. After all, no scientist since Newton has thought that laws individually imply anything exact about real-world kinematics. Composition of forces, at least, has been a general feature of physics for some time now. The fact that some of the Logical Empiricists ignored it in their discussions of the nature of laws simply shows that they were less concerned with attending to the science than with forcing scientific discourse into a particular logical mold. Perhaps we can do better if we approach science in a different way.

5.6   Moving Forward

This chapter pursued two agenda. The first was to clarify and assess variations on the Empiricist account of laws. The second was to assess its implications for the claim that there is a principled difference between the "strict" laws of physics and other natural sciences and the *ceteris paribus* laws of the sciences of the mind.

One overarching theme here has been that there are several relevant variations of the Empiricist account and that they must be assessed separately. What they share in common is a view of laws that (a) interprets laws as claims employing a quantified logic and (b) holds that laws either are materially adequate truths about kinematics or else are used to generate such truths. They differ with respect to such questions as whether only some such laws employ *ceteris paribus* clauses, whether the quantified statements directly express kinematic or dynamic claims, and whether the kinematic implications are about the real world or about some ideal world.

The simple piecemeal Empiricist approach treats physical laws as "strict" kinematic laws (laws that express exact generalities about their real-world behavior) at the cost of making them turn out false. Adding *ceteris paribus* clauses to the physical laws deprives us of a way of distinguishing them from psychological laws by their logical form. Treating the quantified parts of laws as expressing dynamic rather than kinematic claims likewise deprives us of such a principled distinction. And treating the laws as strict kinematic laws whose domain is something other than the real world obscures how the laws say something correct about the real world, and how they are useful in explanation and prediction. In short, no variant of the Empiricist account (or at least none that we have explored here) seems adequate as an account of laws, and only the first variant (which makes all the laws false) supplies us with a principled distinction between physical and psychological laws.

We are thus in need of a better account of laws generally. Only when we have a better account in hand can we return to the question of how to assess the similarities and differences between laws in the physical and psychological sciences. I shall offer such an account in the next chapter, drawing on several themes I have already explored. From Cartwright and the dynamic interpretation I shall take the theme that laws express causal capacities. From Giere I shall take the ideas that laws involve a form of modeling and are in some sense idealized. However, I shall embed these assumptions in a cognitivist account of the nature of laws.

6 Laws and Idealization

My intention in this chapter is to lay out a view of laws that will capture what was right about Cartwright's analysis, but also to move beyond it in the ways I described at the end of chapter 4. In its basic orientation, the view is cognitivist, pragmatist, and pluralist. It is cognitivist in that is looks at laws as they are encountered within the cognitive task of modeling features of the world. It is pragmatist in that modeling is viewed as a kind of action performed by a thinking organism in ways that seek to optimize particular interests (even if those are largely theoretical and explanatory interests, as is often the case in science). And it is pluralist in that it ends up taking the view that our scientific understanding consists in an ability to understand the world through multiple models and to find practical connections between them, rather than an ability to understand the world by unifying multiple models into a single axiomatic system. This view of laws is part of a larger view that I have elsewhere dubbed Cognitive Pluralism (Horst 2007).

One of the mistakes of the Empiricist approach, in my view, was the attempt to characterize laws simply in terms of their logical form. Never mind that, even so, the Empiricists got the logical form wrong. My suggestion, by contrast, is to start with the pragmatics. Laws should be understood in terms of the roles they play in enterprises that involve modeling features of the world. Modeling the world is something we do in many contexts other than science as well, but scientific modeling is related to modeling in general as species to genus. (Whether it is a single species or a group of species I shall not attempt to adjudicate here.) But as such, it bears distinctive features of both the genus (modeling) and the species (specifically scientific modeling). In particular, modeling involves abstraction and idealization: it involves bracketing some features of the world in order to attend to others, and it sometimes involves further idealization of some of the features that are modeled.

Mental modeling is a very basic aspect of human cognition, and probably also in the cognition of many animals. Scientific modeling is a highly regimented form of this general cognitive skill, characterized in part by its standards of rigor. It has at least two pragmatic goals. One goal is to afford theoretical understanding by representing real and deep invariants in nature. Another is to provide tools for prediction and description of the real-world behavior of objects.[1] Laws are a particular kind of representation found in scientific modeling. They are used both to represent such invariants and to describe and predict real-world behavior. One of the interesting discoveries of recent philosophy of science is that these two goals sometimes pull against one another, and that what makes a law good for one of them often compromises its ability to do well with the other. In particular, three features of scientific modeling—*qua* modeling—contribute to this tension: (1) the specific (and sometimes incompatible) idealizing moves that go into the formation of each particular model, (2) the formal features of the representational systems employed in each, and (3) the sometimes divergent pragmatic goals to which the models are held accountable.

6.1 Modeling

We encounter laws in the context of scientific modeling, and modeling is something we do. This does not mean that the laws are purely an artifact of our own projects or our own cognitive architecture. Indeed, one characteristic that distinguishes scientific laws, theories, and models is precisely the exceptional extent to which they are optimized to track features that are independent of idiosyncratic facts about the theorist. Nevertheless, it is fruitful to approach laws from the standpoint of a study of modeling. And modeling is an activity that is much more widespread than the special case of scientific models. Scientific modeling is an especially exact and regimented variant of things that we do all the time.

Consider what goes on in understanding something. We live in a complex world. In any situation we encounter, there is more going on than we can say or imagine at one time. Understanding requires us to bring order to what we encounter by unifying it under concepts and principles. This involves, first, treating the particular and concrete in terms of the general and abstract. The primitive projectile-wielding hunter does not think about the rock in his hand in all its peculiar particularity, but simply as a rock of a certain size, or perhaps as a projectile. And viewing it as such, he can apply all his acquired (or perhaps natively endowed) ballistic know-how to flinging it at his prey. The prey also is not regarded in all its particularity, but in some simpler fashion: as a member of a kind about whose movements the hunter has acquired some understanding, or perhaps simply as a target moving at a given speed and in a particular direction. The simplified "projectile schema" and "gazelle schema" allow the hunter to grasp the kinds of invariants in the particular situation that are relevant to his task of bringing home meat for his family.

In reducing the particular to the general, the hunter is also doing something else: regarding the situation from a particular cognitive perspective. A single particular situation can be understood from a variety of cognitive perspectives. But we can employ only one perspective, or only a few, at a time; we can't employ them all at once. (Of course, there are also many perspectives available in principle that may not be in the repertoire of any particular individual.)

In some sense, the hunter has mental models of such things as throwing a projectile and the behavior of a gazelle. It is possible that a hunter might have a single integrated model of throwing things at a gazelle; however, that is probably not the norm, as people who can throw a projectile accurately at one target can usually throw one accurately at a very different sort of target too. (Stone Age hunters already have some of the qualifications to be NFL quarterbacks.) More likely, the hunter's brain is, in some way, integrating its projectile-throwing schema and its model of gazelle behavior (and thus the person who is best at hitting a stationary target may not also be the best at landing a gazelle on the run, because he may not anticipate when the gazelle is going to zig or zag). The hunter probably knows a lot of other things about gazelles and rocks, too—things that are largely irrelevant to his present task and potentially distracting—and so it is good if he has models of the situation that abstract away from all that other information. He isn't there to daydream or to think deep thoughts. There will be plenty of time for adopting other cognitive perspectives later, by the fire, with a belly full of gazelle.

Mental models can be better or worse for particular tasks. A model that treats a moving gazelle as a stationary object is not as good (for hunting with projectiles) as one that treats it as moving at a steady speed on a fixed course, which is in turn not as good as one that also incorporates some of the characteristic features of gazelles' style of running; a model of projectile motion that does not treat it as parabolic is not as good as one that does; and so on.

6.2 Theoretical Models

In the particular cases just discussed, the models are probably not explicit: they are not something the hunter could articulate in words or draw a diagram of. Rather, they are probably encoded as a kind of know-how and perhaps a mental simulation of gazelles on the run. Theoretical models, on the other hand, are made explicit. Whereas intuitive and explicit models aim at tracking the relevant invariants of a particular kind of situation or state of affairs, explicit models employ explicit representations of the relevant features. (Of course, some cognitive psychologists take the view that even implicit models involve similar symbolic representation, but that such representation occurs at an infraconscious level that does not admit of conscious inspection and correction. Whether one takes this view isn't relevant to the present story.)

In many respects, the scientist's use of scientific models and theories is like the hunter's. In approaching a problem, such as projectile motion, a theorist begins with a messy and complicated world and tries to find ways to simplify it so that the factors that do not matter for his (explanatory rather than hunting) purposes are bracketed off as irrelevant and the factors that do matter are represented explicitly and accurately. Given an interest in understanding a particular phenomenon, apt choices of what to bracket and what to make explicit are constrained by how the world is. The Aristotelian strategy of looking at "motion" in terms of the specific nature of the thing that is moving is apt for some tasks, such as predicting what a gazelle will do rather than what a lion will do. It is poorly suited to other tasks, such as modeling the motion of a projectile. For that, one does better with the Galilean strategy of bracketing specific nature and treating a projectile simply as a "body" with a particular mass. (Of course, sometimes one needs more. For example, a ten-gram piece of paper moves differently if you crumple it into a ball than it does if you fold it into a paper airplane, and only one of them is going to be well described by Galilean ballistics. And healthy birds do not fall like cannonballs when released from a tower. All this means is that one should choose a model that suits the problem at hand.)

Notice that the physicist, like the hunter, is choosing a particular cognitive perspective (the ballistic features of the situation) and performing abstractions (treating features other than mass, location, and a rough approximation of the aerodynamic properties of the projectile in question as irrelevant). But what really counts as irrelevant depends on the problem. For some tasks, such as launching a cannonball at a pirate galleon, it is good enough to employ Galilean ballistics and not worry about aerodynamics or wind resistance. For other tasks, such as getting an airplane to fly or plotting a trajectory of a small metallic object through a strong magnetic field, other things (including aerodynamics and electrodynamics, respectively) clearly matter. If you are asking about how things fall when dropped from the Tower of Pisa, it turns out that Aristotelian specific nature is irrelevant (at least so long as you are not dealing with things that fly under their own power): you don't need separate dynamics for cannonballs and kings; they both accelerate in the same way and hit the ground more or less together. The political consequences, of course, are quite different, and so the idealizations that are innocent in ballistics may not be so innocuous in politics (and vice versa). I shall use the term 'idealization' to mean "abstractions where what is bracketed really makes a difference to what happens *in vivo*."

6.3   Laws, Models, and Scientific Theories

Scientific theories tend to be models that apply quite generally. These often involve the discovery of robust invariants in the world that can be expressed in a systematic, and often mathematically exact, way. Some, in particular, are expressed in the form of algebraic equations. Such expressions are paradigmatic cases of laws. Laws, thus understood, are typified both by their form, and by the role they play in a particular type of modeling. According to this characterization, whether something counts as a law does not depend on whether it gets the invariants right. In my usage, Descartes' law of conservation of motion counts as a law, even though it is momentum, not motion, that is really conserved in mechanics. It is a law, in my sense, just not a very good or apt one. One could, of course, reserve the word 'law' for the ones that get it right and use another expression (perhaps "putative law") for the larger class. But anything that can be said in one usage can be said in the other. They are what the mathematicians call "notational variants," and there is only rhetorical reason, not substantive reason, to argue over the usage.

Laws thus present themselves within the context of enterprises of modeling. And modeling ultimately serves two functions that can sometimes pull in different directions. One function is that of accurately describing and predicting how particular situations will unfold *in vivo*. The other is that of finding genuine and robust invariants in nature that apply across many particular instances and account for what happens in those instances. And a model can thus be evaluated along two different axes: for how elegantly and accurately it captures robust invariants, and for how useful it is for description and prediction. Of course, models that do a good job of the former will do an increasingly good job of the latter to the extent that one is dealing with situations in which only the features modeled are in play, and their performance will degrade as the influence of other factors is increased. Thus, to test a model we must set up experimental situations in which other features are excluded to the greatest extent possible. However, for purposes of prediction, and likewise for the explanation of actual events, the messy complexities that are smoothed over in the formulation of individual laws, and are screened off in experimental set-ups, often matter a great deal.

6.4 Idealization and the Pragmatic "Aptness" of Models

As a result of the fact that laws serve a variety of theoretical and practical purposes, what features are counted as virtues in a model may depend on whether one is interested in theory or in application and testing. For the theorist, it might count as a good thing to leave a constant (say, the gravitational constant, or the speed of light) represented by a constant letter rather than using a particular representation of its value. For testing and prediction, however, it is necessary to use some finite approximation of such a value. Whether a particular approximation is "good" is really a question of its aptness for a particular application. Truncating at five decimal places may be more accuracy than one needs for sending a projectile into a pirate ship, but less than one needs for sending a rocket to Jupiter. The practical failure of an application of a model using a finite approximation need not impugn the model in its theoretical form. In the limiting case of chaotic systems, there may be no finite approximation that is good enough to turn the model into a prediction that meets the standards of accuracy that are in play. (Hence, in such cases there is a principled difficulty in testing whether a failure of prediction should be attributed solely to computational intractability, or to the presence of yet-unknown causal factors, or to a more basic flaw in the model.)

Likewise, it is a virtue of a model of gravitation that it isolates a single force by bracketing everything else that might be at work in a real-world situation (what I shall call a *bracketing idealization*). The theoretical insight afforded by the model is a direct result of its isolation of a unique invariant. But this insight is bought at a price: precisely because it is idealized in this way, the model becomes increasingly unsuited to the task of prediction as non-gravitational factors become more influential in the situation to be predicted.

On the other hand, often a model introduces assumptions (explicit or implicit) that distort or limit its fidelity. I shall call these *distorting idealizations*. For example, in classical particle mechanics it is customary to treat bodies as point masses and collisions as perfectly elastic. Such assumptions are sometimes needed to make the model more elegant or computationally tractable, but they introduce assumptions that are known to be false of the things modeled. I shall treat this kind of "massaging" of the representation as another kind of idealization. As is true of other idealizations, it is likely to make a difference in some predictions and descriptions of real-world behavior and not in others. Note, however, that the assessment of what "makes a difference" is ultimately a pragmatic assessment, and that it depends on the demands of the task at hand.

While the physicist knows that perfect elasticity and point masses are distorting idealizations, he may not always know when other idealizations distort their subject matter. Until fairly recently, for example, no one had considered the possibility that the human mind assumes that it is dealing with "classical objects"—an assumption that is almost always good enough for the problems human beings historically encountered, but not good enough for certain types of very basic physics. Or a cosmologist of an earlier century might not have realized that the Euclidean metric he was employing quite generally is not apt when dealing with objects moving near the speed of light, or in the vicinity of a black hole, or even that there were consistent non-Euclidean geometries to be had.[2]

What are we to say about the model in such a case? Are we to say that the old model (for example, classical mechanics) has been proved false? I do not think this is the best way to put it. Most fundamentally, two levels of felicity terms seem to be needed here, one for saying that a model is well suited to a given situation or problem and one for saying, once we are working within a particular model, whether a given claim (e.g., that a constant has some particular value, or that an object described by the model would behave in this way rather than that way) is accurate. I prefer to use 'true' and 'false' for the latter distinction, and 'apt' and 'inapt' for the former. On this usage, a model defines a space of possible assertions, and the world "decides" which are true or false. Rigorous questions of truth and falsity are well posed only once the model in play has been fixed. Whether a model is a good one, or whether one model is better than another, is a question of aptness.

6.5   Integration of Models and Cognitive Triangulation

Sometimes distinct models of the same phenomenon are to be viewed as competitors, but sometimes (perhaps more often) they are not. In the simplest case, gravitational and electromagnetic models are not competitors; they are models of different invariants that may be relevant to a given situation. In a more complicated case, evolutionary and mechanical or biochemical models of a historical process need not be competitors. Even if the natural history of a species is in some sense a result of mechanical and biological processes, the invariants of biological variation and selection are not a construction out of the mechanical features that contributed to a particular natural history. The same is true of functional kinds: the invariants characteristic of circuits such as AND-gates may be resultant from physical properties in every individual case, but the functional kinds and regularities are not a construction out of physical kinds and laws, and these regularities cannot be stated except in the functional terms. More problematic still, the relativistic model of gravitation and the quantum-mechanical understanding of strong, weak, and electromagnetic forces are inconsistent with one another, yet both are considered apt models.

Given the *de facto* plurality of models employed in the sciences, one is inexorably drawn to the question of how they fit together. (As Kant pointed out, the human mind has a strong drive to unify what it knows.) Much of modern philosophy has been drawn to a particular model of integration, which may be the limiting case. Rationalists, including Descartes (and Hobbes was, at least in this respect, a Rationalist), supposed the following.

Rat1: *Fundamentalism.*   There is a single set of *fundamental* principles from which all the rest can, in principle, be *derived*, in much the fashion that one derives the geometric theorems from a conservative set of definitions and axioms.

Rat2: *Rationalism.*   These principles are completely *intelligible* to human minds.

Rat3: *Realism.*   They reflect the real, fundamental and mind-independent natures of things.

Rat4: *Apriorism.*   They can be known *a priori*.

Apriorism (Rat4) has, of course, been largely abandoned since the early eighteenth century; but Rat1–Rat3 have proved hardier, and indeed form part of the core of the Positivist/Logical Empiricist orthodoxy. That orthodoxy, however, is not the only possible alternative; it was roundly rejected by some of the British Empiricists (e.g., Locke and Hume) and by Kant, all of whom denied Rat2 and Rat3 (and, at least in Kant's case, Rat1). The Empiricist orthodoxy has also been the target of much work in post-Positivist philosophy of science; it has been argued (and is now more or less the consensus view in philosophy of science) that the relationship between theories is not well conceived on the model of an axiomatic system, and that the "patchwork of laws" we see in present-day science is not simply a consequence of the current state of science but rather a sign of deeper disunities either in the world itself (Dupré 1993) or in how we model it (Horst 2007). This question (of whether we should accept R1–R3) should not be regarded as closed, but it is important to regard it as a question and not simply assume that R1–R3 are true. (Indeed, the majority view in philosophy of science today probably is that at least some of them are false.)

In order to test R1–R3, it is necessary to do three things. The first of these is, of course, to continue doing science, including attempts at integration of different scientific models. That project lies outside the scope of a philosophical investigation such as the present one. The second is to continue to pursue research projects in philosophy of science that look at the various forms that inter-theoretic relations really take.[3] The third is to present philosophical accounts of how an abiding plurality of scientific models might come about.

The cognitive-pragmatic approach I have been pursuing in this chapter goes a considerable distance in the third project. Scientific models, thus understood, answer not only to the world, but also to cognitive and pragmatic constraints. To zero in on real invariants, and to apply the models to particular situations, it is necessary to look at the world from one cognitive perspective at a time, and to represent the world as being a certain way (i.e., to employ a particular representational system to represent some aspect or feature of the world). Doing this may introduce artifacts of our own cognitive architecture into the model, as well as reflecting the particular ways we possess of interrogating and intervening in the world by way of experiments. The idealizations needed to get a good model of one feature may make it impossible to integrate it smoothly with a good model of another feature. And we may have only a limited stock of representational strategies, no one of which may be good for all problems, and there may be aspects of the world for which we lack adequate representational strategies altogether. (Of course, if we are utterly lacking in ways to represent a phenomenon, we may not even know it, as it does not "appear on our cognitive radar.") If we start from the reasonable assumption that we are finite, perspectival, pragmatically embedded cognizers, the fact that we have proved capable of developing a cognitive toolkit that allows us to successfully model various features of the world no longer gives us reason to assume that we should also be able to integrate them into a single super-model. Not all forms of representation submit to this form of integration.

But if models are not like axiomatic systems, what are they like? Consider, as an alternative, two other paradigmatic forms of representation: pictures and maps. A picture is always a picture from a particular perspective, taken through a particular lens, in particular lighting conditions, and so on. We can assemble many photos and drawings of the same object from different angles, at different resolutions, in different lighting, on different scales, and on different types of film. And the accumulation of such photos adds to the information we have about the object. But we cannot paste them together into a single picture of everything (visible) about the object, from all angles at once, under all lighting conditions. Pictures don't work that way. Even though we can use many pictures to form a more adequate understanding of the object pictured, we do so, not by forming an (impossible) God's-eye picture, but by a kind of cognitive triangulation. Moreover, there are non-visual features that do not show up in pictures at all. If we were to assume that the real is that which can be pictured, we would make ourselves unnecessarily oblivious to what cannot be pictured. (See figure 6.1.)

Maps tend not to have the same sort of variation in physical or directional perspective as pictures. (They are, for the most part, represented as views from above.) But they do exhibit a kind of cognitive perspective. One map uses lines to represent elevation; another abstracts away from elevation and uses lines of different colors to represent roads and municipal borders; a third abstracts away even from actual geometric form and represents subway stops topologically as points on a straight line, even though the real train tracks wind this way and that and even up over bridges and down into tunnels. Each map employs idealizations that allow the user to do certain tasks well while eliminating the information needed for other tasks: it is optimized for how well the reader can extract a particular type of information from it and employ it in particular tasks. A topological map is better than a topographic map for getting from one subway stop to another, but worse for an overland trek on foot. One cannot simply lay transparencies of various maps of, say, Boston (figure 6.2) on top of one another and have "the" map of the city. Rather, one has to know how to move from one map to another, and how to coordinate the knowledge afforded by each map with the knowledge afforded by the others.

Scientific models are not exactly like either pictures or maps. But they are not exactly like axiomatic systems either. (And, of course, even with axiomatic systems, it is not a given that two such systems can be integrated into one. There is no consistent integration of Euclidean and non-Euclidean geometry, for example, as they involve contradictory axioms.) If scientific models are perspectival, idealized, and optimized to pragmatic constraints, they share important features with photographs and maps. And whether they can be integrated into a "unified science" along Carnapian lines—i.e., a single axiomatic system—turns out to be a substantive question not only about the world but also about human psychology. (It is worth noting that not even all of the Positivists shared Carnap's understanding of "unified science." Otto Neurath conceived of the "unity" of "unified science" on the model of the unity of an encyclopedia, which contains a wealth of distinct entries on different topics (Cat, Cartwright, and Chang 1996). Encyclopedia entries may be liberally cross-referenced, and the reader can use them to mutually inform one another, but they do not stand to one another in the relation of axioms to theorems.)

How, then, may we sum up this view of laws and models? First, models are cognitive entities—elements in an enterprise of modeling. Second, each model is idealized and cast in some particular representational system optimized for particular practical or theoretical interests. Third, models aim at capturing real invariants. Consequently, fourth, they pick out potential partial causal contributors to the kinematics of real-world events. The law of gravity, for example, picks out gravitational force, which is one contributor (but seldom if ever the only one) to real-world kinematics.

6.6 Limits to Integration: A Partial Inventory

There are a number of situations that we may find ourselves in when we wish to integrate scientific models. The familiar cases from classical mechanics stand near one end of a spectrum; cases in psychology and neuroscience stand near the opposite end. I shall differentiate several such situations here in an attempt to show why it should be no surprise that the gap between models and *in vivo* behavior should be far greater in psychology and neuroscience than in physics. Here I am mainly concerned, not with theoretical integration (reducing one theory to another, or finding any of a number of connective relationships weaker than integration), but with practical integration (using what we know from a variety of laws,

Figure 6.1
Three photos of the Tower of Belém, in Lisbon: one taken from a distance, one taken looking down from the top of the tower into the inner courtyard, and one taken within one of the tower's floors. Each of these pictures conveys information about the tower not conveyed by the others, but it is not possible to integrate this information simply by combining them into a single picture of how the tower looks from the outside, from the top, and from within all at once.

theories and models to describe or predict real-world behavior). Understanding the complications of the former is a worthy project (see Horst 2007), but we started with the observation that generalizations in psychology and psychophysics appear to be much messier and more prone to "exceptions" (i.e., inability to translate theory into prediction) than generalizations in physics.

6.6.1 Independent and Factorable
The best-case scenario for practical integration is when the factors bearing on the behavior of a system are exhaustively covered by the laws and models, factorable into mutually independent contributions, summable,

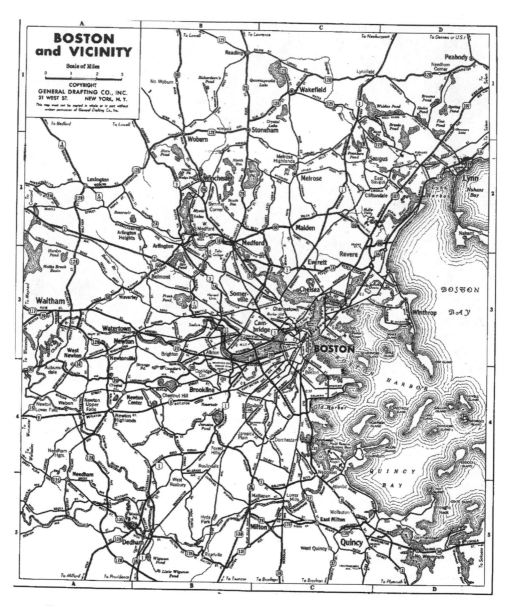

Figure 6.2

Figure 6.2
(continued)

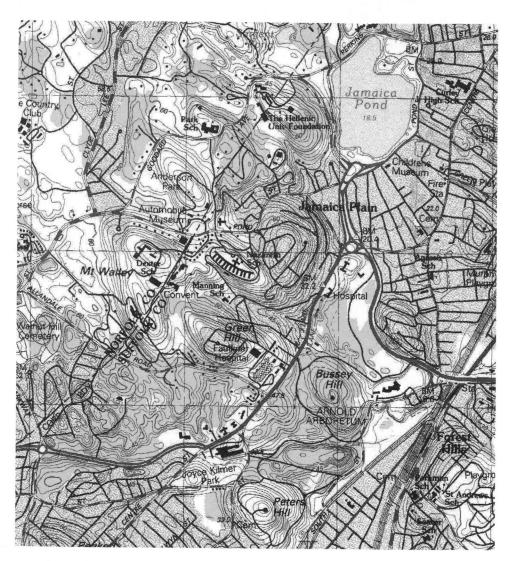

Figure 6.2
(continued)

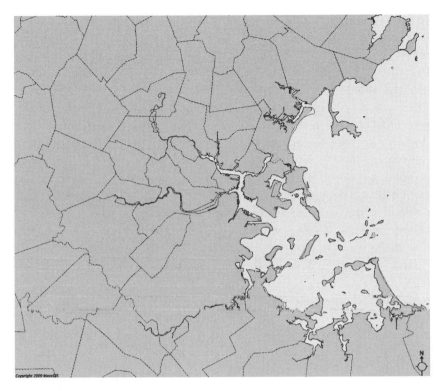

Figure 6.2

Four maps of Boston. In the road map (reproduced from *Official Arrow Atlas: Metro Boston/Eastern Massachusetts*), geographic relationships are drawn to scale and roads are indicated by lines. The Massachusetts Bay Transit Authority's map (copyright 2009 MBTA; downloaded from www.mbta.com) makes some attempts to approximate the geometry of the points mapped but is not geometrically faithful. However, its most important information—the connections between subway stops—is not geometric but topological. (The MBTA used to have maps on its trains that were completely topological, but I have not been able to find one of those for reproduction.) In the USGS 7.5 minute topographic map of Boston South (N4215-W7100/7.5), geographic relationships are drawn to scale, and thin topo lines (brown in the color original) represent elevations. Streets are represented by double lines and locations of points of interest are indicated with textual labels. The fourth map (copyright 2009 MassGIS; generated from the MassGIS OLIVER program; downloaded from http://maps.massgis.state.ma.us/) shows township boundaries without other features.

computationally tractable, and entirely deterministic. If the assumption of determinism fails in any one case, there will be a gap between model and prediction even if only one force is in play, and so we shall not consider that variable here. Computational intractability crops up fairly quickly even in classical mechanics, indeed even if one is considering only one force. The classical two-body gravitational problem is tractable. The three-body problem, famously, is not, though one can make good enough approximations for a viable celestial mechanics. Computational intractability does not impugn the theoretical virtues of a model, but much of even classical mechanics is not in the best-case scenario for prediction and description. Even Laplace's demon could not compute the world's kinematics if it had to employ the kinds of mathematical techniques humans can use: in chaotic systems, the gap between computational techniques and *in vivo* kinematics is not one of performance but one of competence, as there is no level of exactness at which the problem caused by chaos sorts itself out.

6.6.2 Distorting Idealizations

I have already mentioned that many idealizations misdescribe their phenomena in known ways. For example, particle collisions are treated as perfectly elastic, bodies are treated as point masses, and people are treated as ideally rational and omniscient decision theorists. These distorting idealizations clearly describe their subject matter in ways that are false and are known to be false. Such idealizations often buy computational tractability, which is, in practice, something worth paying a lot for. And sometimes they cost relatively little. For example, sometimes idealizations that radically falsify the picture at a microscopic level cancel each other out in large numbers, so that treating objects (say, gas particles) in a simplified-but-false manner (say, as point masses that collide with perfect elasticity) allows us to do statistical calculations that explain important features of macroscopic properties (e.g. pressure and temperature) quite nicely. Or, the economist insists, applying a decision-theoretic model of the person can generate good-enough predictions of an entire economy, even if it radically misdescribes individuals.

One important use of distorting idealizations is in situations in which they represent limiting cases. Real-world collisions involve varying degrees of elasticity and asymptotically approach simplified models that assume perfect elasticity as the actual elasticity approaches the ideal. The Euclidean space is a limiting case of the curved spaces needed for General Relativity. Limiting cases bear some resemblance to reductions in that they are special cases of more general theories, much as a reduced theory is a special case of the reducing theory. But there is also an important difference. With genuine reductions, the truth of the reducing theory entails the truth of the reduced theory; but the truth of a more general theory does not entail the truth of the limiting case. Indeed, when the limiting case cannot be fully reached, but only approached asymptotically, the general theory entails that the limiting case cannot be an exact description of reality.

6.6.3 Conflicting Idealization Classes

Things become more complicated in a principled way when there are mismatches in the idealization conditions of two laws. Take Cartwright's example of a substance that reacts in known ways both to acids and to bases. We can write each reaction as an equation, but in so doing we are in each case implicitly idealizing away from all the factors that might prevent or interfere with such a reaction (such as the interaction of an acid with a base if both are present). As a result, it is possible for there to be an interference between idealization classes for two laws cast at approximately the same level. Ideally, in such cases, we wish to appeal to a more fundamental theory that will explain both the individual reactions and the more complex case. Sometimes we have such a theory, sometimes not. When we do not, we may still be able to determine experimentally what happens in the complex case, and then add this knowledge to the patchwork of laws.

Similarly, when we make use of two or more models whose objects are of different levels of complexity, the different ways the models are idealized may interfere with one another. Consider, for example, what happens if we wish to know how known effects in cognitive and social psychology can affect economic behavior. For example, when people are in a highly aroused state, they make decisions differently from when they are in a "cooler" state, giving greater weight to current stimuli and doing a worse job of forecasting their own future attitudes. Likewise, people act differently in groups than when making decisions alone. Our economic account may treat people as idealized decision theorists; our cognitive and social psychologies examine, among other things, how people approach or depart from this ideal in different conditions. If we ask how economic forecasts would differ if the population should be more stressed, or aroused, or isolated, we are asking a question that cannot be cast in terms of a purely decision-theoretic economics without massaging the psychological laws to reinterpret them in decision-theoretic terms. Ideally, one might look for a broader foundation for economics that has the decision-theoretic form as a limiting case; but such a model may not be available, or may not be as good for computation, and we may have to supplement our "pure" economic theory with a set of heuristics (or, better, with what computer programmers call "kludges") to get realistic results.

6.6.4   Non-Independence and Feedback

Yet more problematic are cases in which the variables represented in different models are not independent. Here one cannot do the straightforward sort of factoring and summation of forces that one can do in the simplest case. A paradigmatic case of such a situation would be separate models of two or more processes that form part of a feedback network in which the behavior of one process influences the normal behavior of another. Even if each "unit" of the system can be given a functional description of its own, that only specifies its dynamics at an instant. Because the causal evolution is not linear (i.e., is not one-way from unit A to unit B, but goes both from unit A to unit B and from unit B to unit A), the dynamics of the system can be computed only globally and over time. This, however, may not be fully comprehensible in the form of a global model. And the desiderata for having a model of unit A that is good for some particular theoretical purpose may well have involved treating the behavior of other units as "normal" or even as nonexistent. If you isolate an object from all non-gravitational influences, it will behave just as your model of gravity predicts. But if you take some unit in a feedback system— say, some unit of the brain (perhaps the lateral geniculate nucleus) and really isolate it from other causal influences, it doesn't behave like an "ideal" lateral geniculate nucleus; it behaves like a piece of raw meat.

Psychophysics, belief-desire psychology, and neuroscience all tend to produce models of the last sort. Any generalization about what people will do given assumptions about beliefs and desires is, in fact, sensitive to a great many other psychological and neural factors not been mentioned in the model. It is probably not possible to have a model of all mutual influences of beliefs and desires, and so partial models are the best one can hope for. But partial models inevitably idealize away from things that are not really independent variables, such as other beliefs and desires, and the relations between these and non-cognitive factors, such as arousal level and hormones. Hence, the relationship between model and description or prediction of behavior in psychology is very complex, far more so than it is in basic physics. Similar observations can be made with respect to neuroscience—nearly every part of the brain has feedback inputs from many other parts of the brain that modulate its normal behavior. It is probably not possible to have a comprehensive model of all the causal influences, so partial models probably are the best models one can have. But because partial models will leave out things that may matter to actual neural dynamics, there is a large and complicated gap between models and description or prediction.

The upshot of this is that psychology and neuroscience are, in a principled way, more complicated than basic physics. In physics, we are blessed with a small number of fundamental forces, and they are mutually independent. In psychology and neuroscience, we are faced with a great number of interconnected factors, which are mutually interdependent for their normal functioning. As a result, there is bound to be a much greater gap between models in their theoretical role of providing understanding and uncovering real invariants and models in their practical role of description and prediction.

6.6.5 The Prospects of Scientific Unity

What does all of this imply about the prospects for unifying scientific models? The first and most basic point I wish to make here is that whether scientific models can be unified in a single "super-model" that is at once comprehensive and consistent is not a question that can be settled on *a priori* grounds. Moreover, its answer depends not only on facts about the objects of the sciences but also on facts about how the mind forms models of these objects and the relationships between them.

In this section I have outlined several characteristics of different types of models that can, in principle, result in barriers to their integration. This, of course, falls short of a demonstration that theory unification is impossible. It may turn out that the models we actually apply in the sciences do not suffer from these problems. And even if they do, we may prove to be capable of radically re-conceptualizing scientific domains in ways that avoid these problems. However, the general failure of attempts at inter-theoretic reductions ought to give us pause whenever we are inclined to suppose that inter-theoretic integrations must be possible. (See Horst 2007.) And even if inter-theoretic integrations prove to be possible in the long run, this would likely involve not only new ways of integrating models but also substantial alterations to the scientific models we now employ. And the models we *do* employ surely *do* involve barriers to integration that stem from ways the models are idealized. If these problems can be avoided, they will be avoided because there are particular models (thus far undiscovered) that are immune to them, not because modeling *per se* is not plagued by them.

Embracing a pluralistic account of scientific models does not bar us from pursuing various types of unification as regulative ideals. There have been important unifications in the history of science, some partial and some complete. For example, mechanistic explanations provide partial inter-level explanations, and Newtonian mechanics provided a unified account of various types of motion. We certainly should pursue such inter-domain explanations; they represent scientific progress when they can be had, and we can tell when they can be had only by looking for them. What seems problematic to me is turning this regulative ideal into a metaphysical claim about how the world is or must be, and then using this as a kind of *a priori* norm for judging the merits of particular models in the special sciences. We should not embrace "white-flag epistemology" (as I was once accused of doing at a talk), but we should not rush to "declare-victory-and-go-home epistemology" either. Questions about scientific unification are ultimately to be decided by actual scientific progress, not from an armchair. My Cognitive Pluralist account is meant to be a defeasible hypothesis about why we find examples of scientific disunity, not a replacement of an aprioristic unity claim with an equally aprioristic disunity claim.

6.7   The Davidsonian Problematic Revisited

We are now in a position to return to the Davidsonian Problematic. We were looking for a solution that preserved Cartwright's insight that laws in psychology and physics are not so different as the stark contrast between "strict and exceptionless" laws and *ceteris paribus* laws, but avoided her problematic retention of the notion of *ceteris paribus* laws and her appeal to "capacities"; that provided a satisfying account of how psychological and physical laws are alike; and that explained why there would nonetheless be a greater gap between model and prediction in the case of psychology and its related disciplines. The account outlined in this chapter, I believe, satisfies these three goals.

On the one hand, physical laws, like psychological laws, occur within the context of models that serve both the theoretical aim of identifying real invariants in a comprehensible way and the practical aim of generating descriptions and predictions of real-world behavior. Both physical laws and psychological laws involve abstraction and idealization, and as a result there are gaps between model and prediction (especially if models are taken singly). One way in which the two kinds of laws differ is that models in basic physics isolate forces that are independent of one another, and hence one can build a more complex dynamic model licensing good predictions through factoring and composition of forces, calculated through the application of vector algebra. In psychology (and indeed in psychophysics and neuroscience), by contrast, one is normally faced with a large number of models of things that are not really independent of one another—indeed, are mutually interdependent—and hence one cannot simply calculate the contribution of each force separately and then combine the contributions through vector algebra. This being the case, we should expect psychological models, even when they capture real invariants, to provide only rough predictions and descriptions of real-world behavior.

This account resolves—or, better, dissolves—the Davidsonian Problematic at a theoretical level. The difference between translations from model to prediction in physics and in the sciences of the mind is not that physics has laws and the sciences of the mind do not have laws, or that physics has strict laws and the sciences of the mind have *ceteris paribus* laws. At a generic level, both are very similar modeling activities. In both cases, there are potentially serious gaps between model and real-world behavior. It is the details of the models, and the implications for how they can be combined, or used for prediction individually, that account for the difference between physics and both psychology and neuroscience. The difference is not a deep ontological or philosophical one, but a difference in technical details.

6.7.1 The Vindication Problem Revisited

The Vindication Problem was based on an intuition that a lack of strict laws compromised the methodological integrity of the sciences of mind. In chapter 2, I cast this in the form of an argument:

V1: Strict laws are a necessary feature of legitimate (pure, mature, first-rate) sciences.

V2: Psychology (necessarily) lacks strict laws.

Therefore,

V3: Psychology is (and cannot be) a legitimate (pure, mature, first-rate) science.

V1, however, has shown to be false by Cartwright's critique, and my independent critique in chapter 5. If V1 is interpreted according to Empiricist lights—i.e., as a claim that sciences must make true universally quantified claims about real-world kinematics—then it would imply that even physics is methodologically suspect, as we have seen a variety of reasons why the sciences do not trade in such claims. On the other hand, if "strict laws" simply means laws that express potential and partial causal contributors, we must reconsider what "strictness" really amounts to. If it means that the causal contributors (e.g., forces) in question apply to all objects (i.e., have universal scope), then indeed psychophysical, neural, and psychophysical generalizations are not "strict" in this sense, as they apply only to certain types of organisms, and not at all to inorganic matter. But by the same token, most of the generalizations of the special sciences are about objects within their proprietary domains, and are not unrestricted in scope. And even basic physical laws are limited in scope: gravitation applies only to particles with mass, electromagnetic laws only to charged particles, and so on. This interpretation of "strict laws" is strong enough to imperil the sciences of the mind on methodological grounds, but only at the cost of imperiling the sciences generally, and thus it is too strong an interpretation.

Suppose, however, that "strict laws" is interpreted still less strongly, as indicating generalizations that pick out invariant causal contributors that are always at work in their appropriate domains. It is not clear that this interpretation threatens the status of the generalizations made in the sciences of the mind. Take the example of conflicting belief-desire motivations from chapter 3: A mother sees her children trapped in a burning building and is both inclined to stay away from the flames because she fears them and inclined to rush to her children's aid because she loves them and wants what is best for them. At most one of these motivations will find expression in action, but that does not mean that they are not both at work as dynamic forces as the mother is deciding what to do. If generalizations such as "people tend to avoid things they fear" express psychological invariants that are only partial and potential causes of behavior, rather than universal claims about actual behavior, two generalizations that lead to divergent predictions can still both be apt.

However, we saw in chapter 3, and will see further in the case studies in part III, that many generalizations in psychology, in neuroscience, and even in psychophysics can break down under various conditions. For example, there are well-known conditions under which psychophysical laws (e.g. the Weber-Fechner laws) do not hold good, such as when the visual apparatus is not operating "normally" (e.g., when one has been staring at a light before exposure to a stimulus, or when transmitter levels are abnormal); people who are self-sabotaging may not desire what they believe to be best for them; and so on. In this respect, such generalizations are narrower in scope than laws of gravitation and electromagnetism. But this is because they are generalizations about how a complex system operates when it is operating normally, and the conditions of "normalcy" can be undercut by breakdowns in the system's component parts or by its relations to a larger system of which it is a part. And this is a feature shared by complex systems generally. Generalizations about the tensile strength of a metal break down when it approaches its melting point, for example, and many biochemical and neural generalizations no longer hold good when toxins are introduced to an organism. The dividing line here is not between the natural sciences and the sciences of the mind, but between generalizations that are scale-independent (and apply even to the smallest particles) and generalizations that apply only to particular types of complex systems. Even this more lenient notion of strictness would result in compromising the methodological integrity of most scientific laws.

And more fundamentally, it is a mistake to try to cash out the scope of scientific generalizations in terms of the universal quantifier in the first place. Scientific generalizations are idealized claims, and the often-complicated issue of their scope is bound up in their idealization conditions. Finding a situation in which a generalization fails is often seen, not as falsifying the generalization, but as uncovering a hitherto unforeseen boundary condition on its scope. Since idealizations are essentially open-ended, this does not result in falsifying or modifying a law, but in making explicit things that had been inexplicit and unarticulated.

In short, there seems to be no way of saving the distinction between "strict" and "*ceteris paribus*" laws in a fashion that compromises the integrity of the sciences of the mind without, in the process, compromising the integrity of a much broader class of scientific generalizations too. We would do well to reject this distinction as one that is not doing productive work in philosophy of science, and with it the vindication problem it spawns.

None of this, of course, is meant to imply that explanations in the sciences of the mind are *in all respects* like those in physics or chemistry, or that the cognitive sciences may not suffer in the comparison. Indeed, it provides reason to *expect* that fundamental physics is in some ways a limiting case of exact understanding. Fundamental physics deals with independent forces singly. As a consequence, it allows for experiments that control for exogenous variables in a fashion that is not possible in more complicated causal systems. This allows for comparisons of the different explanatory virtues found in models of different scientific domains. What it precludes is a very particular sort of charge leveled against psychology and the cognitive sciences: that they are scientifically illegitimate because they do not trade in strict laws.

6.7.2 The Ontological Problems

The ontological problems arose from identifying "real" or "natural" kinds, and hence ontological legitimacy, with kinds to which strict laws apply. However, if we reject the dichotomy between "strict" laws and "*ceteris paribus*" laws, it is no longer possible to get such arguments off the ground. If "strict laws" are interpreted according to Empiricist lights, there are few if any strict laws; hence, if real or natural kinds are those to which strict laws apply, there are few if any such kinds. If "strict laws" are those with universal scope, similar considerations follow. And if they are those with universal scope within the intended domain of objects, only fundamental kinds are real or natural kinds. Although some philosophers are prepared to allow only fundamental particles into their privileged ontology, this would rule out many of the kinds (e.g., biological species) that philosophers use as paradigmatic examples of "natural" kinds; moreover, it would mean that what counts as a "natural" kind is not determined by the sciences themselves, but by an armchair philosophical criterion. It is thus possible to motivate the ontological problems (at least, those that are based on considerations of the differences between laws in different sciences) only at the cost of an extreme ontological purism that seems out of touch with the natural sciences.

6.8 Conclusion

In this chapter, both the vindication problems and the ontological problems for philosophy of psychology have been undercut. Those problems rested on a misguided logical reconstruction of the nature of scientific laws. A more adequate account of laws—as elements in regimented mental models of aspects of the world, models that are idealized and cast in particular representational systems—reveals both the continuities between physical and psychological generalizations and an important way in which they differ. This also represents a step beyond Cartwright's account, which undercut the Empiricist interpretation of laws but did not provide a way of seeing the nature of the continuities and differences between laws in the physical sciences and laws in the sciences of the mind.

II   Laws and Freedom

7 Laws and Freedom

We now turn to a second question concerning laws and the mind: whether our actions are all causally determined by natural laws and prior events, or whether at least some of our actions involve free will.

This chapter will discuss the relevant notions of freedom and determinism, and then explain why belief in laws of nature is sometimes thought to entail determinism and hence to threaten freedom. Chapter 8 will assess whether a commitment to laws really implies a commitment to determinism. I shall argue that it does so on the Empiricist account, but not on causal accounts, of laws. Chapter 9 will briefly discuss several types of attempts to argue for determinism on somewhat broader grounds related to the sciences.

The basic "plot arc" of these chapters is a case to the effect that our commitment to scientific laws does not entail a commitment to determinism, and hence that acknowledging that there are such laws does not give us reason to doubt the existence of free will. That is, free will is compatible with the existence of natural laws, properly understood. I shall not, however, offer any new arguments for free will. Nor shall I argue that determinism is, or must be, false. Indeed, I am highly skeptical about whether claims for either freedom or determinism are capable of being proved. These chapters are thus intended, as much as anything else, for those who already think there is *prima facie* reason to believe in free will but suspect that it is incompatible with the existence of natural laws. My conclusion is that they are *not* incompatible, and that the sciences provide no reason to give up any existing commitment to the thesis that we are capable of acting freely.

7.1 Are Our Actions Free, Determined, or Both?

Immanuel Kant put forward the somewhat paradoxical view that our actions are both free and determined. Viewed through the lens of theoretical reason, we are phenomenal objects existing in space and time, and hence it is a synthetic *a priori* truth that what we do is causally determined, as are the behaviors of all phenomenal objects. Viewed through the lens of practical reason, however, we are agents who are at least capable of acting in accordance with reason by adopting a maxim consistent with the Categorical Imperative. We are thus, as Kant put it, phenomenally determined but noumenally free. In the *Critique of Pure Reason*, Kant states part of the resolution of the problem as follows:

[W]e could say that if reason can have causality in regard to appearances, then it is a faculty through which the sensible condition of an empirical series of effects first begins. For the condition that lies in reason is not sensible and does not itself begin. Accordingly, there takes place here what we did not find in any empirical series: that the condition of a successive series of occurrences could itself be empirically unconditioned. For here the condition is outside the series of appearances (in the intelligible) and hence not subject to any sensible condition or to any determination of time through any passing cause.

Nevertheless, this very same cause in another relation also belongs to the series of appearances. The human being himself is an appearance. His power of choice has an empirical character, which is the (empirical) cause of all his actions. There is not one of these conditions determining human beings according to this character which is not contained in the series of natural effects and does not obey the laws of nature according to which no empirically unconditioned causality is present among the things that happen in time. Hence no given action (since it can be perceived only as appearance) can begin absolutely from itself. But of reason one cannot say that before the state in which it determines the power of choice, another state precedes in which this state itself is determined. For since reason itself is not an appearance and is not subject at all to any conditions of sensibility, no temporal sequence takes place in it even as to its causality, and thus the dynamical law of nature, which determines the temporal sequence according to rules, cannot be applied to it. (Kant 1998, p. A552)

Kant's solution requires that we identify free actions with those that are "empirically unconditioned"—that is, not determined by prior empirical events and the "laws of nature," which Kant understood to mean Newtonian mechanics. Each human action "belongs to the series of appearances" (i.e., is a phenomenon). But actions performed on the basis of reason can also be understood in another way, for reason is not in the "series of appearances." As a result, reason "does not begin," and thus does not require a further cause. (Indeed, as time and causation are themselves confined to phenomena, reason could neither begin nor have a cause.)

I begin with Kant partly because, perhaps more than anyone else, he succeeded in highlighting the fact that our minds seem to be deeply drawn both to determinism and to the thesis that we can (at least sometimes) act freely. But I also begin with Kant to highlight the fact that by the late eighteenth century the realization that there are laws of nature was already being connected to a belief in determinism. This connection has endured to this day, both in academia and in the popular imagination. More recent discussions, however, have taken some important turns away from Kant's understanding of how laws and freedom come into conflict, and it is with these more recent discussions that I am ultimately concerned.

The most obvious difference, of course, lies in the fact that few contemporary philosophers embrace Kant's distinction between phenomena and noumena. But there are also other important differences. For Kant, the most compelling argument for (phenomenal) determinism stemmed, not from the success of Newtonian mechanics (though he thought quite highly of it), but from a distinctly Kantian argument that, because the relation of cause and effect is one of the categories that structures all sensible experience, any possible object of sensible experience (that is, any event in the world) must be understood to be the effect of some cause. Many other philosophers, however, have embraced determinism for a different reason: they regard features of the sciences themselves (particularly their nomic character) as entailing determinism. Finally, Kant identified the locus of freedom in actions in accordance with specifically rational principles. Most contemporary proponents of free will, by contrast, think of it as an ability to choose between two prospective actions that are both possible, and indeed to count as "free" choices that are arbitrary as well as choices that are rational. Voluntary spontaneity has, in effect, replaced rational spontaneity as the touchstone of freedom.

In remainder of this chapter, I shall discuss the relations between free will, determinism, and laws of nature along these non-Kantian lines. But in order to do so, I shall first engage in some preparatory discussion of the key notions involved—freedom and determinism—and of the relations between them.

7.2 Notions of Freedom

The topic of freedom of the will, as one might expect, has accumulated a huge philosophical literature. And within this literature there are discussions of many different notions of freedom. It is beyond the scope of this book to do even rough justice to the literature, and mastery of it is not needed for the reader to follow this chapter. However, it will be necessary to talk briefly about several different notions of freedom that may occur to the non-specialist—most important, notions that a non-specialist might, if not properly forewarned, wrongly assume to be operative in the discussion that follows. Indeed, even specialists sometimes equivocate between different notions of freedom—at least, they often accuse one another of having done so.

The notion of freedom that I am concerned with here is what philosophers sometimes call "libertarian free will." In the libertarian sense of 'freedom', a free action is one in which the agent was able to do otherwise. Libertarian freedom is, in large measure, a metaphysical notion. When one says "Paul acted freely" in this sense, one is making the claim that, at the moment just before Paul acted, there was real indeterminacy in what Paul would do, and that that indeterminacy was settled through a choice Paul made that was itself not fully determined by prior events. To be committed to this type of freedom is thus to be committed to a fairly robust metaphysical claim.

There are also weaker notions of freedom in this general vicinity that don't involve any heavy metaphysical lifting. In a courtroom, "free" actions are contrasted with actions that are coerced and with behavior that is compulsive. If Peter had put a gun to Paul's head and had threatened to shoot unless Paul punched Andrew, a court would probably say that Paul had not punched Andrew freely but under coercion, with the consequence that Paul either had not perpetrated a crime or else was guilty of a lesser crime than he would have been guilty of had he decided to punch Andrew of his own accord. Similar considerations would apply if Peter had hypnotized Andrew and planted a post-hypnotic suggestion that he punch Andrew. If Paul had punched Andrew accidentally, in the midst of an epileptic seizure, Paul would likewise be said not to have punched Andrew freely. This time, the exonerating circumstance is not external coercion, but internal compulsion: Paul was not in control of his body, and hence what he did was not a voluntary action. There are also psychological compulsions: Paul may be unable to control his temper, for example, in which case he might still be judged culpable of a crime of passion rather than a premeditated act; the action might even be treated as a result of a type of insanity. A coerced act can also be free in the libertarian sense. A person who possesses libertarian free will might be capable of refusing to act under coercion, but might choose not to do so because of the consequences. Internal compulsions are, by contrast, cases in which a person lacks the ability to control his actions.

There is also a philosophical tradition, running from the Stoics through Augustine, Spinoza, and Kant, that has articulated another notion of freedom: that a free action is one that is in accordance with reason. I view this as a special variation on the notion of freedom that is opposed to internal compulsion. The basic idea here is that most of human life is spent acting under the tyranny of the passions, and that the only alternative to this servile mode of existence is to understand one's motivations and actions so fully that one can be guided by reason rather than passion. This notion of freedom strikes me as compatible both with libertarian freedom and with its denial. One might truly *choose* to act in accordance with reason, being capable of doing otherwise. But a rational automaton would also be free in this sense.

There are also political and legal notions of freedom that are less easily confused with libertarian freedom. These are concerned with what actions a person is legally permitted to perform. In this sense, I am free to quit my job and move to another state—a type of liberty that was not legally permitted to, say, a Russian serf. A lack of a political liberty is, of course, quite compatible with a person's being capable of acting in a fashion that is against the law. A serf might have been fully capable of trying to desert a *boyar*'s estate, just as I am fully capable of driving through a red light.

7.3 Why Do People Believe in Libertarian Freedom?

Not everyone believes in libertarian freedom—which I shall henceforth call simply "freedom" or "free will." But it is surely a widespread notion, and one that many people find intuitively plausible. Why do we believe in it?

One reason stems from experience. There are certainly times when we find ourselves just acting out of habit, and even out of miserable compulsions that we cannot conquer. But there are also moments when we experience ourselves as at a crossroads—when alternative courses of action seem truly to be available to us. Sometimes the context is mundane, as when, in a restaurant, I feel equal inclinations to order flounder and to order shrimp, and no reason to prefer one over the other. In the end, I just have to make a choice, and the power to choose between alternatives at least *seems* to be within my power. But sometimes a choice is morally significant. For example, I might have to decide whether to blow the whistle on criminal activities my employer is engaging in, and I might be aware that the entire future course of my life (and perhaps my state in whatever afterlife there might be) hangs in the balance. At least at times, I experience myself as being truly capable of doing either one thing or another.

The assumption of freedom is also wrapped up in our practices of moral assessment. When we blame people for their actions, we generally assume that they acted freely and could have done otherwise. And when given reason to believe that someone truly could not have done otherwise, we tend not to assign blame—at least, not the same sort of blame. If Paul freely struck Andrew, he is blameworthy; but if he did so accidentally, as a result of an epileptic fit, he becomes an object of pity instead of blame. If Paul is truly unable to rein in his violent impulses, we may still be angry, and react with contempt and loathing, but we no longer blame him for his particular actions (although we may blame him for any past choices that contributed to his present state).

We likewise connect the assumption of freedom with assessments of moral desert. We feel that someone who caused harm of his own free will deserves punishment. (And this may include cases where the person acted out of habit or passion but was capable of foreseeing the consequences and of acting differently.) However, when a person does harm that is not a result of his own choices, our attitudes are more complicated—perhaps even so different that we may even hold him blameless. (Depending on the circumstances, we may alternatively regard someone as being, at least in some corners of his life, less than a true human agent, and thus to be avoided, locked up, or dealt with through reward and punishment as a non-human animal would be.)

Thus, to give up the assumption of free will is to imperil a whole constellation of ways we assess our own actions and those of others in moral terms. Kant took a strong view of this position, holding that it is nonsensical to ascribe to someone a duty to do something he is incapable of doing. As Kant put it, "ought implies can." However, one need not go that far in order to believe there is a strong and essential relationship between freedom and moral evaluation. For example, Saint Paul, in his epistle to the Romans, expresses a view that would seem to be contrary to Kant's:

I do not understand my own actions. For I do not do what I want, but I do the very thing I hate. Now if I do what I do not want, I agree that the law is good. But in fact it is no longer I that do it, but sin that dwells within me. For I know that nothing good dwells within me, that is, in my flesh. I can will what is right, but I cannot do it. For I do not do the good I want, but the evil I do not want is what I do. Now if I do what I do not want, it is no longer I that do it, but sin that dwells within me. So I find it to be a law that when I want to do what is good, evil lies close at hand. For I delight in the law of God in my inmost self, but I see in my members another law at war with the law of my mind, making me captive to the law of sin that dwells in my members. Wretched man that I am! Who will rescue me from this body of death? (Romans 8:15–24)

Here Paul's view seems to be that, at least sometimes, when we experience weakness of will, we feel the moral duty to act in one way while simultaneously findings ourselves unable to do what we believe duty requires. Alcoholics Anonymous and similar programs are based on a similar experience of lack of power over an addiction. In both cases, the resolution to the problem is said to lie in divine grace, which confers on a person the ability to do something he or she previously desired but wasn't able to do. Such a position might be seen as escaping Kant's charge of nonsensicality in that being in such as a state as to be capable of doing what one acknowledges to be right is itself a contingent condition. There is nothing about being a human being *per se* that keeps one from acting in accordance with duty, only the besetting sins or addictions that a particular person is subject to. Duty is assigned in accordance with an ideal standard of human action, and not with respect to the capacities of an individual at a particular time. The condition of (original) sin, like that of addiction, is viewed as a kind of sickness that results in wrong actions and from which one must be delivered or healed.

More generally, freedom is often viewed as tied to our sense of ourselves as agents. When we act under compulsion or coercion, we do not view ourselves as the agents of what we do. Indeed, without a sense of agency, we might view what we do as mere behavior, and not real action. And if we come to believe that all of our actions are determined by our genes or our environment, we similarly feel our sense of genuine agency to be threatened.

Freedom is thus closely tied to a number of assumptions that are central to our self-image as human beings. We are moral beings—that is, beings capable of acting morally, and subject to moral evaluation—and moral evaluation seems tied to the assumption of actions that are performed freely. To treat the actions of other people as inevitable consequences of impersonal or sub-personal forces is to treat other people as less than fully human. Likewise, to believe oneself to be other than free results in a feeling that one's own status as a human agent is in peril.

7.4 Why Do People Doubt Free Will?

There would be no "free will problem" if everyone thought that the assumption of freedom was without difficulties. Just as there are several reasons people have believed in free will, there are at least as many ways that it has been brought into question. For some, including Saint Augustine, close examination of their own lives has led to the conclusion that their actions were not free, or at least that moments of true freedom are considerably less numerous than common sense might suppose. Others have denied that humans are free because of their religious or theological beliefs—for example, that God predestined some individuals to be saved and others damned. Most recent philosophical critics of free will, however, have doubted it because they have believed that there is good reason to believe in determinism, and that determinism and free will are incompatible. They thus reason as follows:

1. Determinism is true.

2. Free will is incompatible with determinism.

Therefore

3. We do not possess free will.

Much of the philosophical literature on free will is concerned with whether the relevant notion of freedom is compatible with determinism. The thesis that the two are compatible is called *compatiblism*. The contrary thesis is called *incompatiblism*. The libertarian notion of freedom I am concerned with here is generally assumed to be incompatible with determinism. Compatiblists are generally concerned to argue that some other notion of freedom is both able to underwrite all that we want (or ought to want) out of a notion of freedom and compatible with determinism. (For example, one might plausibly argue that the legal distinction between acting freely and acting under duress is compatible with *both* sorts of actions' being causally determined, the difference being that free actions are not conditioned by a threat of harm from another person.) Thus, at least some of the argument between compatiblists and incompatiblists turns on an ambiguity in proposition 2 above: whether or not "free will" is meant in the libertarian sense. Since I have stipulated that I'm talking about a notion of freedom that is generally regarded as incompatible with determinism, I shall take that incompatibility as given.

But on what grounds do people believe that determinism is true? There are several distinct breeds of determinism, and they require different sorts of arguments to support them. My main concern will be with what I take to be a fairly widespread assumption that serves as the ground for many people's determinist affinities. The broad form of this assumption is that *something* about what the sciences tell us about the world entails that the world is deterministic. Now, there might be multiple features of scientific claims that might serve as grounds for determinism. But this book is concerned primarily with laws. And so the narrow form of the assumption, to which I wish to devote the bulk of this chapter and all of the next, consists in the views (a) that the sciences commit us to the thesis that the natural world is governed by natural laws and (b) that a commitment to a law-governed world entails a commitment to a deterministic world. I believe that (a), properly understood, is correct, but that (b) is false.

7.5 Nomological Determinism

Not all forms of determinism make crucial use of the nature of natural or psychological laws. Kadri Vihvelin's article on "Arguments for Incompatiblism" in the online Stanford Encyclopedia of Philosophy distinguishes three varieties of determinism: theological, logical, and nomological (Vihvelin 2007). Theological versions of determinism that are concerned with the relationship between God's will and events in Creation are not our concern here. Logical determinism is concerned with necessary or constitutive relations between cause and effect. Hume, for example, might be construed as making a claim of this kind when he says that no one has ever denied that the sum total of causes ensures the effect without specifying what kinds of causal factors he has in mind. One way of reading Hume here is as saying that it is part and parcel of our use of the words 'cause' and 'effect' that the total cause ensures the effect. If one accepts this as an analytic truth, one can nonetheless believe in agent causation that is not determined by prior physical states and natural laws, as the notion of a "total cause" is unrestricted with respect to what sorts of causes there can be. But this would lead to a dilemma: the act of will that leads to the behavioral effect must either be causally undetermined or else require a regress of causes. However, this type of logical determinism seems to trade on a subtlety. It may be plausible that our notions of cause and effect are such as to entail that everything that is correctly describable as an effect has a total cause that ensures it. But it is less clear that it is a logical truth that every event, or every state of affairs, has a cause. (Kant, at least, seems to have realized this between the A and B versions of the *Critique of Pure Reason.*) Those who champion spontaneity of the will could hold that free decisions of the will are uncaused events, thereby denying that they are effects.

Vihvelin goes on to characterize nomological determinism as follows:

At a first approximation, nomological determinism (henceforth "determinism"), is a contingent and empirical claim about the laws of nature: that they are deterministic rather than probabilistic, and that they are all-encompassing rather than limited in scope. At a second approximation, laws are deterministic if they entail exception-less regularities; e.g., that all F's are G's, that all ABCD's are E's, and so on. At a third approximation, the fundamental laws of nature are probabilistic if they say that F's have an objective chance N (less than 1) of being G's. (Note that so-called "statistical laws" need not be probabilistic laws; see Armstrong 1983, Loewer 1996a.) The laws of nature are all-encompassing if deterministic or probabilistic laws apply to every-thing in the universe, without any exceptions. If, on the other hand, some individu-als or some parts of some individuals (e.g., the nonphysical minds of human beings) or some of the behaviors of some of the individuals (e.g., the free actions of human beings) do not fall under *either* deterministic or probabilistic laws, then the laws are not all-encompassing.

Given these rough definitions of the difference between deterministic laws, proba-bilistic laws, and limited laws, we can understand determinism as the thesis that a complete description of the state of the world at any time *t* and a complete state-ment of the laws of nature together entail every truth about the world at every time later than *t*. Alternatively, and using the language of possible worlds: Determinism is true at a possible world *w* iff the following is true at that world: Any world which has the same laws of nature as *w* and which is exactly like w at any time *t* is exactly like *w* at all times which are future relative to *t*. . . .

This characterization of nomological determinism is cast in the form of an account of its constitutive claims, not an argument for its truth. However, we can see how nomological determinism would seem to be an inevitable consequence of any view of laws that took them to be both deterministic and all-encompassing. More exactly, even if there are also some things in the sciences called "laws" that are probabilistic and/or limited in scope, so long as there is *some set* of laws that is both deterministic and all-encompassing, nomological determinism, as characterized by Vihvelin, is entailed by definition.

This connection between laws and determinism is widely found in the philosophical literature on freedom. A. J. Ayer (1954, p. 271) locates the problem of free will squarely within the context of the assumption that our actions are governed by natural laws:

When I am said to have done something of my own free will it is implied that I could have acted otherwise; and it is only when it is believed that I could have acted otherwise that I am held to be morally responsible for what I have done. For a man is not thought to be morally responsible for an action that it was not in his power to avoid. But if human behaviour is entirely governed by causal laws, it is not clear how any action that is done could ever have been avoided. It may be said of the agent that he would have acted otherwise if the causes of his action had been different, but they being what they were, it seems to follow that he was bound to act as he did. Now it is commonly assumed both that men are capable of acting freely, in the sense that is required to make them morally responsible, and that human behaviour is entirely governed by causal laws: and it is the apparent conflict between these two assumptions that gives rise to the philosophical problem of the freedom of the will.

According to this formulation, human actions are determined because they fall under the scope of natural laws. And if they are determined, they are not free.

Timothy O'Connor (2000, p. 3) likewise characterizes determinism in terms of natural laws, as "the thesis that there are comprehensive natural laws that entail that there is but *one* possible path for the world's evolution through time consistent with its total state (characterized by an appropriate set of variables) at any arbitrary time."

Peter van Inwagen (1983, p. 65) offers a characterization of determinism that is similarly framed in terms of natural laws. He defines determinism as the thesis that

For every instant of time, there is a proposition that expresses the state of the world at that instant;

If p and q are any propositions that express the state of the world at some instants [and q describes a state later than that described by p/SH], then the conjunction of p with the laws of nature entails q.

A few pages later (p. 70), van Inwagen puts forward an argument for incompatiblism. Consider the question of whether some person J could have raised his hand at time T. Let L be the set of laws, let P be a complete actual state of affairs at T that includes J's *not* raising his hand at T, and let P_0 be a complete actual state of affairs at some earlier time. Van Inwagen then argues as follows:

(1) If determinism is true, then the conjunction of P_0 and L entails P.

(2) It is not possible that J have raised his hand at T and P be true.

(3) If (2) is true, then if J could have raised his hand at T, J could have rendered P false.

(4) If J could have rendered P false, and if the conjunction of P_0 and L entails P, then J could have rendered the conjunction P_0 and L false.

(5) If J could have rendered the conjunction of P_0 and L false, then J could have rendered L false.

(6) J could not have rendered L false.

So (7) If determinism is true, J could not have raised his hand at T.

Van Inwagen frames the argument in such a way as to highlight the ideas that, according to the determinist, (A) laws and complete state descriptions together imply unique future-state descriptions for each subsequent time, and that acting in a fashion incompatible with that future-state description would (*per impossibile*) "render [the laws] false," and (B) we are incapable of rendering laws false. The view of laws suggested here is one on which exceptions to the laws are equivalent to falsifications of them. And this, in turn, suggests that the philosophical account of laws that van Inwagen has in mind is one in which laws are interpreted as universally quantified claims ranging over objects and events—that is, something like the Empiricist account of laws I discussed in chapter 2.

To look at the matter in the opposite way, the Empiricist account of laws would seem to entail the kind of incompatiblist determinism that van Inwagen describes here—at least if we assume that the laws are, in Vihvelen's words, "all-encompassing." If laws imply true material conditionals relating past and future states, and the laws cover every event, then there are no events that are not the consequents of some true material conditional with a true state description of a previous moment in time, cast in terms that fall under natural laws, as the antecedent. Laws, construed in this way, imply determinism and incompatiblism. (I shall explore the connection between determinism and the Empiricist account of laws further in the next chapter.)

I do not wish to give the impression that an analysis of the consequences of a commitment to natural laws is the only reason philosophers have been drawn to determinism. (Indeed, there were determinists among the ancient philosophical schools, long before our modern notion of natural laws came onto the scene.) My concern here, however, is not with the relationship between *determinism generally* and freedom of the will, but with the relationship between *laws* and freedom. The foregoing is thus meant to substantiate the claim that *one threat* to freedom stems from an analysis of the implications of the assumption that the world is governed by natural laws.

7.6 Psychological Laws and Freedom

Although the bulk of discussion of the relationship of laws to freedom and determinism has been concerned with physical laws, psychological laws pose an equal, and indeed a more direct, problem. One of the few writers I am aware of who singles this fact out, Alisdair Macintyre, writes:

[I]t is paradoxical that refutations of theoretical determinism—of Laplace's dream, for example—which satisfy most contemporary philosophers have been propounded and accepted in a period in which for the first time there has been accomplished what the opponents of classical determinism most feared. The threat of classical determinism did not arise so much from its total programme as from that part of its programme which concerned human action in general and moral action in particular. Consequently it is not the physical sciences which should arouse the apprehension of the anti-determinist, but psychology and the social sciences. Sufficient has been already achieved in these sciences to make it clear that we can expect from them ever increasing success in explaining and predicting human behaviour. (Macintyre 1957, p. 28)

On the next page, Macintyre writes:

[T]here appears a dilemma. either horn of which seems intolerable. The discovery of causal explanations for our actions, preferences and decisions shows that we could not have done other than we have done, that responsibility is an illusion and the moral life as traditionally conceived a charade. It makes praise and blame irrelevant, except in so far as we discover these to be causally effective, and while the moral judgements of agents might therefore retain some point, those of spectators and critics would be pointless. But even the moral judgements of agents would be affected by such discoveries, since in considering what I ought to do my whole assessment of alternatives presupposes that there are alternatives. The gradual establishment of determinism suggests a Spinozistic elimination of distinctively moral terms. Yet we find it difficult to believe that moral praise and blame are appropriate only because and in so far as we are ignorant; or rather, that they are not, but only seem appropriate. But to react against this is to discover that the other horn of the dilemma is equally menacing. For the only possible alternative seems to be a pious hope that psychological and sociological explanation should in fact prove impossible. To believe that human behaviour is inexplicable is to offend against all that we have learned from the successive victories of the sciences. (ibid., p. 29)

In other chapters of the present book, I attempt to defend the status of such explanations in psychology and other sciences of the mind. If the existence of such laws indeed implies determinism, then I have, in effect, provided the basis for a much more direct attack on freedom and on any moral norms that require it. Instead of a sketchy and circuitous route to determinism from the laws governing physical particles, we will have taken a short and direct step from the thesis that the mind is governed by laws to the conclusion that its operations are completely determined.

Of course, once again, the move from a commitment to laws to a commitment to determinism is in need of some scrutiny. Psychophysical laws (e.g., Fechner's Law), and, more important, psychological discoveries about action (e.g., various effects that bias choice) do not logically preclude that some actions are free. It is only when we view laws through a particular interpretive lens that they lead to this conclusion. Specifically, it is only when we hold that such laws are true universal claims about our thoughts and actions, and that *all* our thoughts and actions fall under the sway of at least some such laws, that a bridge can be built between a commitment to laws and a commitment to determinism. Thus, we must apply our previous general analysis of laws to the question of whether a commitment to the actual laws of the physical sciences or the psychological sciences entails a further commitment to determinism and the denial of freedom.

7.7 A Blind Alley: "Quantum Indeterminacy"

It is necessary to make a brief digression here in order to discuss an objection that is likely to occur to the reader. The reader might well think that exploring the consequences of deterministic laws is pointless, on the ground that our best scientific understanding of the most basic physical events—that supplied by quantum mechanics—should have disabused us of classical mechanics' assumption of deterministic laws. We often hear talk, after all, of "quantum indeterminacy," and of Einstein's famous characterization of quantum mechanics as amounting to a view on which God "plays dice with the universe."

Such a characterization, however, is not strictly correct. It is true that quantum mechanics supplies well-verified descriptions of the behavior of sub-atomic particles and an account of strong, weak, and electromagnetic forces. And it is true that it employs probabilistic functions and the Heisenberg Uncertainty Principle. But quantum mechanics has been given a number of distinct interpretations, not all of which involve indeterminacy. One influential family of interpretations—most famously, the Copenhagen interpretation enunciated by Bohr—indeed ascribes objective indeterminacy to nature. But there are other interpretations available. The hidden-variable interpretation (most famously held by Einstein) holds that the machinery of quantum mechanics, though useful and empirically probative, is descriptively incomplete, and that the appearance of indeterminacy is a result of unknown variables which, if discovered, would yield a deterministic account. Another view, the many-worlds interpretation (DeWitt 1970), holds that *all* of the quantum possibilities become actualities, and reality itself splits into multiple alternative universes at each such juncture. Since quantum mechanics has consistent interpretations that do not imply indeterminism, it does not supply the basis for an outright empirical refutation of determinism.

Moreover, it is not clear that even the interpretations that posit true indeterminacy are of help in defending free will. True, they would defeat objections to free will based on the assertion of determinism. But although determinism and libertarian freedom are incompatible, they are not the only alternatives. If my actions are results of probabilistic laws, with only brute chance determining everything that happens at indeterministic junctures, this is every bit as inconsistent with voluntary spontaneity as is determinism. Acting randomly is not the same thing as acting freely. It may be possible to freely make a random choice. But randomness grounded in brute physical chance does not amount to free will. Indeed, if my actions are ultimately governed by chance phenomena involving the quarks and leptons that make up my body, my actions are not free.

There may be interpretations of quantum mechanics that are more congenial to free will. Some interpretations, for example, take the talk of "observation" in Heisenbergian uncertainty quite literally as requiring conscious states, and treat consciousness as a fundamental variable in determining the actual sequence of events in nature (Wigner 1970). But even this interpretation does not *ensure* freedom of the will. There is nothing about our understanding of consciousness that entails freedom. That is, consciousness could be a fundamental force in nature, yet also be itself deterministic or random.

I thus regard quantum mechanics as itself neutral on the question of whether the will can be free. On some interpretations, free will is prohibited. On others, it is at best possible but not ensured. The availability of an interpretation of quantum mechanics consistent with libertarian freedom may be all the advocate of free will really needs in order to maintain her position. However, some authors have claimed that freedom is literally incoherent in the context of an indeterministic interpretation of quantum physics (Pereboom 2001). Pursuing the question of whether quantum mechanics provides any kind of defense of free will would require a great deal of discussion of some very difficult matters in philosophy of physics, and I shall not pursue it further here. Instead, I shall turn to an independent line of thought, drawing on the discussions of laws in previous chapters. First, I shall argue that the problems raised for the Empiricist conception of laws, raised independent of the question of free will or indeed of mental causation generally, bear directly on the status of the inference from that conception of laws to a deterministic conclusion. Then, I shall pose the question of whether laws, when interpreted as expressions of potential partial causal contributors to real-world events, would likewise lead to a deterministic conclusion, or whether they leave room for free will.

7.8   Why Might One Think a Law-Governed World Must Be Deterministic?

First, let us try to understand why someone would think that accepting that there are laws of nature would also require an acceptance of determinism. This was by no means always the prevailing assumption. Descartes, who has as good a claim as anyone to being the originator of the modern, scientific use of the expression 'natural law', intended the legislative overtones of the expression quite seriously. He viewed laws as decrees laid down by God. But he also believed that human beings have absolute freedom, not only with respect to how they shall act, but also with respect to what they shall believe. And he likewise regarded God, the legislator, as above the laws He laid down, and free to work miracles or even to change the laws. Newton, whose mechanical laws made up the core of modern science for two centuries, likewise believed in free will and miracles. There were, of course, determinists even in the seventeenth century, including Spinoza (and, more controversially, Hobbes and Leibniz). But determinism was not fashionable until the late eighteenth century. Laplace, the great physicist who tidied up Newton's mechanics, shocked and titillated Napoleon's court with a mechanics that was wholly deterministic, leaving no room for either human freedom or divine miracles.

Laplace famously described his deterministic view of the universe in the image of an exceedingly powerful being, which others dubbed "Laplace's Demon." Laplace claimed that such a being—one with a mind vast enough to know the laws of nature and the exact state of the whole universe at any time—could, on the basis of this knowledge, predict, with perfect precision, the exact state of the entire universe at any subsequent time. Asked by Napoleon what place God had in this system, Laplace is said to have replied "I have no need of that hypothesis." Napoleon did not ask about free will—or if he did, history has not preserved the incident—but we may reasonably assume that Laplace would have answered that it required no place in his system either.

The image of Laplace's Demon introduces two distinct issues. It is framed as a claim about prediction. Laplace claims that a knowledge that encompasses the combination of the complete set of laws and the complete description of the world at any time can, in principle, be used to predict, with perfect accuracy, the state of the world at any subsequent time. Of course, Laplace did not suppose that any human mind could actually work out such a prediction. Human minds are too limited in knowledge and in calculating power for that. Thus, Laplace conjured up the image of an imaginary being that could, like us, know laws and facts about the world, but was freed (by stipulation) from our limitations. The Demon is, in effect, a way of thinking about an ideal limiting case of the kind of knowledge we are capable of possessing but which we possess only in limited degree. But in order for Laplace's claim to be true—in order for knowledge of laws and of the state of the universe to afford such predictive power—one must also assume a second sort of claim to be true. This is a metaphysical claim rather than an epistemological one: that the combination of laws and the state of the universe at a particular time determines the state of the universe at all subsequent times.

Let us refer to this first thesis as *Laplacean predictability*. The second thesis corresponds to a claim of *nomic determinism*. Laplacean predictability is a stronger claim than nomic determinism. Nomic determinism could be true but not underwrite predictions if there are objective laws that, when combined with physical states, determine future events, but there is no expression of those laws that affords exact computations of the sort needed for prediction. Determinism is a claim about the world. Laplacean predictability involves further claims about representations of invariants in the world, and about their computational tractability.

One might quite reasonably ask: *Given* that we have reason to believe that there are natural laws, why do determinists think we should we also embrace nomic determinism? We might distinguish four broad types of answers:

1. A particular understanding of laws in fact already entails determinism, with no need for further theses.
2. Nomic determinism is not entailed by the laws themselves, but is entailed by other commitments of the sciences.
3. Nomic determinism is not entailed by anything in the sciences, but receives evidential support (e.g., inductive support) from them.
4. Nomic determinism requires commitments from outside the sciences for its justification—e.g., philosophical or theological commitments.

In the next two chapters, I shall explore these answers, and I shall argue for the following claims:

• An Empiricist interpretation of the nature of laws can entail nomic determinism. This may explain why the move from a commitment to laws to a commitment to determinism seems so natural for many. But it should carry little weight, as that account of laws has been shown to be problematic on independent grounds.

• On the principal rival view, the causal capacity interpretation, a commitment to laws clearly does *not* imply a commitment to nomic determinism.

• There is a limited methodological principle to the effect that, in certain contexts, one should treat the universe as a system causally closed under natural laws, but this should not be taken to be either an empirical claim or an *a priori* claim about how the world is or must be.

• Any arguments that we could currently marshal to the effect that the sciences provide inductive support for determinism are question-begging.

• Commitment to nomic determinism is a brute philosophical commitment that should be regarded as no more than an expression of philosophical taste.

8 Freedom, Determinism, and Two Accounts of Laws

The preceding chapter suggested that one important reason that the assumption of human freedom has been called into question over recent centuries is that people have believed that the discovery of natural laws has proved freedom to be impossible. A law-governed world, it is claimed, is a deterministic world. And determinism is incompatible with (libertarian) free will. Since we have good reason to believe that there are indeed natural laws, we thus have good reason to suspect that our actions cannot truly be free.

But in previous chapters, we examined two alternative accounts (or families of accounts) of the nature of scientific laws: the Empiricist and causal accounts. In order to assess the claim that a commitment to laws entails a commitment to determinism, we must bring to bear the insights gleaned from those earlier chapters. In this chapter, I shall argue that the Empiricist account indeed provides a direct link between laws and determinism, but that the causal account does not do so. The popularity of the Empiricist account of laws in the twentieth century may explain the prevalence of the assumption that a law-governed world must also be deterministic. But the argument from Empiricist laws to determinism is no better than its premises, and we have already seen that there are compelling objections to the Empiricist account of laws. These, it turns out, also undercut any support that account might give to determinism. To the extent that we ought to favor a causal account of laws, whether those posed by Cartwright and Hacking or the one developed in my Cognitive Pluralist formulation, a commitment to such laws is perfectly compatible with a commitment to free will.

8.1 From Empiricist Laws to Determinism

What is the connection between laws and determinism? We make the connection quite naturally, supposing the discovery of natural laws to imply that the world is something like a grand machine. But a bit of reflection shows that it is not quite so simple. If the discovery of laws means simply that *some* natural phenomena are governed by laws, this leaves open the possibility that others are not. It is only if *all* natural phenomena are governed by laws that determinism lurks in the wings. Moreover, many of the laws we find in the sciences are merely probabilistic, not deterministic. If there are events that fall only under probabilistic laws, determinism is false. And if we consider the original context of the metaphor of laws of nature—that is, the idea that God set down laws for matter to obey—this suggests that the laws themselves are not truly fundamental, as they depend on God's will and could be set aside or suspended if God so chose.

However, if we adopt the philosophical analysis of laws favored by the Logical Empiricists, the connection is much more direct. The Empiricists understood laws to be true, universally quantified claims about real-world objects and events. Some of those laws are laws about how things change—kinematic laws. And a universally quantified claim about kinematics, if it is true, says something about how particular types of change unfold in nature. Whereas the initial formulations of the Empiricist account were framed merely in terms of material implication, more careful formulations are modally strengthened to cover counterfactuals. Such laws, if true, say something, not only about how certain processes of natural change *do* always unfold, but also about how they *would* unfold in the relevant counterfactual circumstances.

This is still not quite enough for determinism, as some events might not fall under any such law. But we can get from modally strengthened Empiricist laws to determinism by adding just one more assumption: that every event in nature is a product of change that is governed by at least one such law. This is not a trivial assumption, especially in the wake of quantum mechanics; however, my goal here is not to argue for determinism, but to make intelligible how people might reasonably have been led to believe that a commitment to natural laws, suitably understood, leads to a commitment to determinism.

Given such a picture of the natural world, what is one constrained to say about human thoughts and actions? There are only two possibilities. The first is that they are themselves natural events, bound up in the web of deterministic laws. The second is that they may involve components that are non-natural and/or non-nomic, but that these can have no effects on the natural world that are not already determined by natural laws and the state of nature. If dualism is true, and the physical realm is deterministic, there may still be free *thoughts*, but they cannot result in free bodily *actions*, because such actions involve the body, which is wholly material and which consequently can engage only in actions that are determined nomically by past physical states. Both determinism and the denial of free action are thus straightforward consequences of the Empiricist view of natural laws, supplemented only by the assumption that every physical event falls under at least one deterministic law.

8.2   Revisiting Some Problems

We saw in previous chapters, however, that there are compelling objections to this Empiricist account of natural laws. First, most or all of the laws, taken singly, would turn out to be materially false. Where multiple laws are in play, the real-world kinematics does not correspond exactly to what any one of the laws legislates. Indeed, since it is the norm that multiple forces act on any kinematic situation, it is doubtful that even "fundamental" laws, such as that of gravitation, have any true substitution instances. If nomic determinism entails that such universally quantified kinematic claims are at least materially true, then nomic determinism is false. This, however, is not so much a proof of indeterminism as another way of stating the conclusion that was argued in chapters 4 and 5: that there is something wrong with the Empiricist account of laws. Indeed, the very feature of this account that seem to provide a short road to determinism—universal quantification over actual objects and events—is precisely the feature that renders the account unacceptable. If, say, the gravitation law makes a true universal claim about the real-world kinematics of bodies with mass, this is probably enough to rule out free actions, as human physiology is made up of bodies that have mass. But by the same token, it is also enough to rule out bodies with mass being subject to any other forces, such as mechanical force or electromagnetism, that might also influence their behavior. The quantified kinematic interpretation of laws makes them very powerful claims, and its modally strengthened cousins are stronger still. Unfortunately, they are so strong as to be empirically false (and badly so) and to generate contradictions when multiple laws are in play.

On the other hand, if we do not get materially true universal claims out of the laws, a commitment to the truth of the laws does not imply determinism. Indeed, if we had no other account of laws to work with, we might well conclude that the world was pretty radically indeterministic, since the world either never behaves as any single law predicts or at best does so only in very carefully controlled circumstances shielded from other forces (what Cartwright calls "nomological machines"). Indeed, the piecemeal kinematic interpretation of laws makes the world seem a great deal less deterministic than we have reason to believe it to be (an indictment against it that we might add to the list). For if all that matters about laws is exact kinematic accuracy, and laws are in fact seldom or never accurate in this way, it is hard to understand why they yield the kind of predictive power and theoretical understanding that they in fact yield.

Here we return to a second, and more fundamental, criticism of the Empiricist account. The Empiricist attempt to reconstruct scientific laws in logical terms was misguided to the extent that it viewed the expression of exact kinematic truths (whether material or modally strengthened) as the sole or even the principal explanatory virtue of such laws. A law can, for example, be good enough for useful predictions even if it is not, and does not imply, a materially true exact claim about kinematics. Likewise, even if materially false with regard to real-world kinematics, a law can afford theoretical understanding—say, of one force that is a partial causal contributor to real-world kinematics—and can sometimes be good enough for practical approximations.

Both of the foregoing observations were noted by philosophers who remained close to the Empiricist formulation by suggesting that we substitute "approximate truth" for "truth" or that we substitute "truth about ideal worlds" for "material truth." These adjustments will not preserve the initial version's ability to entail determinism. If the laws do not determine exactly how things behave, then anything falling within the margin of uncertainty or error is compatible with the laws. This might be enough to exclude some types of miracles (say, the parting of the Red Sea as depicted by Cecil B. DeMille, with the water standing up in sheer walls ten stories high), but it is by no means clear that it would exclude free will. We have no idea how small a neural or sub-neural change would be involved in a spontaneous contribution by an anomic will. But it would almost certainly be smaller than the error that would result from, say, calculating the ballistics of a paper airplane by assuming it was not acted on by aerodynamic factors. Similarly, if the laws are true of "ideal worlds" but not of the real world, it follows that determinism is true of those "ideal worlds," but nothing at all is implied about the real world. Free will might be exactly the sort of thing that makes the actual world depart from this theoretical ideal.

Another way of trying to save the Empiricist account involved a multiplication of boundary conditions and *ceteris paribus* clauses. This had its own shortcomings, ranging from theoretical inelegance to an inability to explain composition of forces. If one handles departures from the behavior predicted by the laws by appealing to boundary conditions and *ceteris paribus* clauses, one has taken a step that can be extended to include indeterminacy. The boundary conditions or the *ceteris paribus* clauses might, for example, be ones that exclude cases where free will is at work. Whereas a view of science based in strict and universal kinematic laws led to determinism and militated against invoking additional special conditions, the situation is quite different if the laws are, quite generally, framed in a hodgepodge of *ceteris paribus* clauses. Of course, the prevalence of boundary conditions and *ceteris paribus* clauses by no means ensures that free will exists. But if our understanding of the relationship between law statements and real-world kinematics is vulnerable, in an open-ended way, to exclusions and special cases, our understanding of laws does not itself give us reason to rule spontaneous anomic causation out of court.

Now let us turn to what seemed (in chapter 5) to be the two most promising variations on the Empiricist analysis: the global kinematic and dynamic accounts. The global kinematic account says that law statements do not individually make claims about how the world actually behaves. Instead, it makes a claim to the effect that each law expresses only a contribution to real-world kinematics, with the real kinematics to be obtained only through a global summation of forces. Such an account might seem to be appropriate for describing some scientific achievements, such as Galileo's proving that the motion of a projectile is parabolic by decomposing the motions into vertical and horizontal components. In most cases, however, there are not real component motions, but only component *forces*. The Moon is attracted by both the Sun and the Earth, and its motion is (partially) caused by these two gravitational interactions, but it does not reach its resultant position by moving first as the two-body equation involving the Earth would dictate and then as the two-body equation involving the Sun would dictate. There is only one resulting motion. To be a realist about a globally determined kinematics, one must interpret the component interactions dynamically rather than kinematically.

On the dynamic interpretation, laws express something on the order of *forces*, though once one moves from physics to chemistry and biology it becomes less plausible to use the term "force" and more plausible to use "causal powers" or "capacities". A dynamic interpretation of laws is compatible with determinism, as it is possible that all forces are nomic and that there is a well-defined equation for their summation. It is *possible*, I say. Whether it is *true* is another question. We are misled if we concentrate on the Newtonian model of vector summation of component forces, because some laws—e.g., chemical and biological laws—simply do not work this way. As Cartwright points out, we cannot simply combine equations for what happens when you mix a compound C with an acid and what happens when you mix it with a base to see what will happen when you mix it with an acid and a base together. And indeed, in many cases we do not know how to combine laws. And in many cases their conditions for applicability are very severely constrained, in such a fashion that the conditions for two laws cannot be jointly satisfied. We sometimes have mathematical techniques that do well enough, but those are heuristics that resist any realistic interpretation. It was this situation that prompted our reconceptualization of laws in pragmatic and cognitivist terms as idealized models. We shall reconsider the relation of laws to freedom in light of that account shortly.

For present purposes, we would do well to note that a dynamic account introduces something that was absent from the original Empiricist formulation. If laws are universal kinematic claims, they imply at least some measure of determinism: the behavior of entities that fall under a law would be determined by that law. But dynamic claims do not directly say anything about how an object will behave. Individually, they express only partial causal contributors to real-world behavior. One gets from dynamics to real-world kinematics only when all the causal contributors are in hand and there is a well-defined function for their summation. But nothing about the laws themselves tells us what the complete list of causal contributors might be. The law of gravitation tells us nothing about magnetism. Indeed, even when we list all the laws we know about, this does not tell us whether there might be other laws. And, more important, it does not tell us whether there might also be causal factors that are anomic. For this, we need some other type of principle—one that is not implied by the laws, and is very different from them. Consider the different strengths of the following three claims:

(C1) Laws $L_1, \ldots, L_n$ are true.

(C2) $L_1, \ldots, L_n$ are all the laws there are.

(C3) Events are causally closed under $L_1, \ldots, L_n$.

If evidence for the truth of scientific laws commits us to any of these claims, it is C1. Of course, any commitment to C1 is hedged by the fact that we also believe that at least some of the laws we endorse today will be superseded in the long run. But more than that, the laws themselves are essentially open-ended. Each picks out some one set of causal factors while bracketing others. But to bracket other causal contributions is not the same thing as to deny that there are other causal contributions. To endorse a gravitation law is not to say that it is the only law, or that the universe is causally closed under gravitation.

Even if we have reason to believe (C2) that we have found the complete list of natural laws, moreover, this does not license the further claim (C3) that events are causally closed under those laws. That a certain set of laws is the complete set of laws does not imply that there cannot also be causal factors that are anomic. Nothing in our commitment to a set of laws as true and complete (i.e., as being the complete set of true laws) excludes the possibility that there could be additional, anomic causes (that is, causes for which there is no corresponding natural law). And if anomic causes are not ruled out, there is nothing in our commitment to laws (be they psychological or physical) that is directly in conflict with the possibility of libertarian freedom. There may be other reasons to reject libertarian freedom, but determinism is not entailed by the truth of laws.

C3 goes beyond C1 (which is directly evidenced by the sciences) and even C2 to claim that once we have listed all the nomic contributions to the world we have determined the whole causal story. But where does this principle come from, and whence comes its authority? It is not implied by the laws themselves, at least on the dynamic interpretation. It seems to have sprung up from nowhere to add "That's all folks!" like Porky Pig at the end of a Warner Brothers cartoon. However, C3 has gained a following under the name of the "principle of causal closure," and so I shall return to it later (in chapter 9). For now, the moral is this: Even if one is drawn to such a principle, this does not amount to inferring determinism *from scientific laws*. The original Empiricist account *did* imply at least some measure of determinism, because it was directly a claim about events, but was untenable for reasons having nothing to do with questions of free will. Most of its variants achieved (partial) freedom from its failings in ways that deprived them of this implication. Approximate truth, ideal worlds, *ceteris paribus* clauses, and the quantified dynamic interpretation all separate laws from real-world kinematics in ways that would allow for free will to be compatible with the truth of the laws themselves. To rule out free will, one would have to appeal to some additional principle that says, once the nomic contributions are in place, that is the entire causal story. Such a principle might be true, or it might not. But it is not implied by our commitment to the laws themselves. It is an independent philosophical commitment.

8.3 Freedom and Causal Accounts of Laws

Let us now turn to the major alternative to the Empiricist account: the family of views often called "causal accounts." What these accounts share is the view that what laws express are properties related to causal capacities. These properties are sometimes called "causal powers." I prefer to say the laws express "potential partial causal contributors" to real-world processes. But I shall call such accounts "causal accounts" for short, and I shall treat my Cognitive Pluralist analysis as falling within this family.

The quantified dynamic interpretation of laws might itself be classified as a causal account. But causal accounts, such as Cartwright's, Hacking's, and mine, are not usually framed in terms of quantified statements. Like Giere, I emphasize the role of laws within idealized mental models. And like Cartwright and Hacking, I view them pragmatically, as tools for understanding, prediction, and control. Laws—and, more generally, scientific models—allow us to cut through the mind-boggling complexity of nature by bringing into focus natural invariants, one or a few at a time. When one actually hits upon real causal invariants, this affords theoretical insight. Often it also affords predictive ability and control. But theoretical insight and predictive power are bought at a price: the very idealizing moves by which we isolate one invariant (bracketing idealizations) also screen out everything else. As a consequence, the world as seen through the lens of the model departs from the real-world kinematics. Often, we also idealize in ways that distort the phenomena we are trying to understand—say, by treating collisions as ideally elastic. Comprehensibility and suitability for use in computation are also bought at a price.

On this view of laws, we start out acknowledging their piecemeal character. Each law aims at modeling some systematic feature of nature in isolation from others that may be present in real world situations, but the set of models itself is not systematic, or at least does not start out that way. Individual laws can be brought into theoretical contact with one another—occasionally wholesale, by way of inter-theoretic reduction, but more often only partially, through heuristic knowledge of how to take insights from one model and apply it within another. And unlike the piecemeal Empiricist approach, we acknowledge from the outset that our laws and models are idealized and hence are unsuitable for providing true universal claims about real-world kinematics that are materially true. From this perspective, it is obviously a substantive question whether the "patchwork of laws" can be tailored into anything like the kind of systematic account that could underwrite something like Laplacean predictability. Indeed, sometimes when we inspect the idealization conditions of different models we can plainly see that they involve incompatible assumptions about their domains or are cast in incommensurable mathematical formulations.

What consequences does this have for determinism? It would seem to block the easy road that takes us to determinism through Laplacean predictability. In order to have Laplacean predictability, the laws would need to be such that

1. some set of them covers all events,

2. they are consistent with one another,

3. there is a well-defined function F for summation of forces,

4. F is deterministic,

and

5. F is computable.

There are reasons to be skeptical that conditions 2, 3, and 5 can be met, and without them it is question-begging to assert condition 1 or condition 4.

The most obvious problem for Laplacean predictability is computational tractability, and it is a serious problem for actual prediction, though not for determinism. A century before Laplace, Newton had already shown the dynamics of problems as simple as three bodies under gravitation to be computationally intractable, and things only get worse as the system becomes more complex. This is a real problem for actual computation, of course, and I am not sure it is resolved by Laplace's artifice of a computing demon who is freed from our computational limitations. If the demon uses the same sorts of computational methods we use, only faster and to a greater degree of accuracy, it can at best asymptotically approach exactitude in predicting real-world events. But it may not even be able to do that much. For chaotic systems, there is no finite degree of computational approximation that suffices. One might suppose, alternatively, that the demon understands the same laws we can understand, but works out their kinematic consequences in some other way. But we can never know how this might work, as by supposition the demon's way of working out the consequences is unavailable to human minds. But without such specificity, it is unclear what this proposal would amount to.

However, computational intractability is not inconsistent with *determinism*, as opposed to *prediction*. A deterministic function can be computationally intractable, and so computational intractability is not incompatible with determinism. One can, in short, have determinism by satisfying conditions 1–4 without 5. Indeed, my Cognitive Pluralist version of the causal account seems to lend comfort to those who would wish to assert determinism without predictability, as it locates the difficulties we face combining different models in facts about human cognition rather than in facts about the world. At very least, from a Cognitive Pluralist perspective, abiding barriers to prediction are compatible with the universe itself being deterministic. However, so long as the sciences we have do not give us a comprehensive set of laws that yields Laplacean predictability, they give us no direct reason to suppose that the universe is deterministic. To hold on to determinism, one must either place one's hope in a future science very different from the science we have today or else hypothesize that the "real" principles by which the universe operates are not fully intelligible to us.

Cartwright has pointed out that we often do not know how to integrate the insights gained from different laws or models into a prediction of kinematic consequences. My Cognitive Pluralist account provides several sorts of reasons that this might be so, stemming from incommensurabilities between the representational systems employed in different models and conflicts between their idealization classes. But this account must be separated into two claims. One is the comparatively modest claim that the ways certain pairs of scientific models are idealized and the ways they represent their domains render it impossible to integrate their results. This may be a significant fact about particular scientific models; but even if that is so, it may point only to an inadequacy of *those* models—an inadequacy of the sort that spurs researchers to posit new models. The laws with which we are familiar cannot all be combined in a fashion that entails a deterministic understanding of the world, and thus our commitment to those laws does not entail a commitment to determinism. But neither does it entail a commitment to indeterminism. Lacking a comprehensive way of combining the laws to imply kinematic consequences, we simply do not know whether the universe is deterministic or not.

The more ambitious claim that the Cognitive Pluralist might make is that the human mind is *incapable* of devising a set of models of the world that is at least equal in explanatory power to the set of models we now possess while also being comprehensive and consistent and yielding a well-defined function for kinematic outcomes. I sketched, in broad outlines, some ways in which a cognitive architecture *could* be plagued by such a limitation, but in doing so I did not mean to imply that it *must* be so with respect to us. It does strike me as unlikely that minds built through natural selection to avoid predators, to procreate, and to use simple tools would thereby be endowed with something infinitely grander: an ability to come to a kind of God's-eye understanding of nature. (Neither does it not strike me as particularly likely that finite creatures of a benevolent Creator who took special care in their design would necessarily have such abilities.) But that is really just an expression of my own leanings, and I am happy to admit that it is epistemically possible that the present state of our sciences is only a passing phase, and that the final completed state of the sciences would meet all the conditions needed to imply determinism. My concern here, after all, is not to argue that determinism must be false, or that free will is real, but only to argue that our commitment to laws does not entail a commitment to determinism. And our present understanding of laws clearly does not do so. And this is all that is needed to show that a commitment to laws is consistent with a commitment to free will. (I shall raise concerns about speculations on the characteristics that some future "ideally completed science" might possess in the next chapter.)

But the difficulty of getting from laws to determinism is not confined to our not knowing how to combine some of our laws to yield kinematic predictions. Some of our laws are inconsistent with one another. Worse, our two best-confirmed and most fundamental theories—general relativity and quantum mechanics—produce inconsistent or incoherent results. This is not some minor difficulty in knowing how to juggle two theories in order to solve an engineering problem. It is a glaring inconsistency between the best theories the scientific mind has ever proposed. Such a formal inconsistency need not pose a challenge to the aptness of either theory, within the Cognitive Pluralist interpretation, because each theory's aptness is assessed with respect to particular pragmatic goals involving explanation and prediction, and the inconsistencies may be artifacts of the idealizations and representational systems needed to confer such aptness. But the fact that we find such inconsistencies between the best theories we have suggests at least the possibility that we might not be able to attain an understanding of the world that is at once consistent and comprehensive. The source of the problem would not be that the *world* is inconsistent. Indeed, the world is not the sort of thing that can be consistent or inconsistent. Only representations can be consistent or inconsistent with one another. In this respect, cognitivism takes some of the sting out of pluralism, rendering it only mysterious rather than magical.

Again, I should emphasize that this type of abiding pluralism resulting from features of our cognitive architecture is a *possibility*, rather than something that I have shown *must* be the case. And indeed it is this very inconsistency that drives the search for a unified field theory in physics. But on the other hand, the notion of a unified field theory is likewise only an epistemic possibility, and not something that we know *must* be attainable. The illusion that it *must* be attainable on *a priori* grounds stems from a Rationalistic assumption that everything about the world must be intelligible to us in the form of a single theoretical framework. However, Rationalism involves not only an assumption about how the world is but also an assumption about our minds. And the question of what our minds are suited to understanding is surely an empirical one. Moreover, once we frame the question explicitly, it seems quite hubristic to simply assume we can understand everything.

What implications does this have for determinism and free will? Most directly, two theories that are apt but inconsistent cannot be combined to produce deterministic results. Indeed, in some cases they produce contradictory results. And thus our present scientific theories do not combine to imply a deterministic world. This does not imply that the world is indeterministic, either (except on interpretations of quantum mechanics that hold that it is itself committed to indeterminism). But it does show that, whatever the source of our inclination to assume that determinism is true, it is not to be found in the laws, the models, or the theories that we possess.

Less directly, we might look at the moral to be drawn from the inconsistencies we find between theories. On the Cognitive Pluralist interpretation, these inconsistencies do not point to facts about the world itself, but to consequences of the ways we represent the world within the capacities offered by our own cognitive architecture. We are free to assume that each model singles out real causal invariants. But we must recall that our representations of these invariants are framed in particular representational systems and idealized in particular ways. As a result, a model yields a good approximation of how things really behave in nature in some circumstances but not in others. And the degree of approximation is proportional to the extent to which the invariants singled out by the model exhaust the causal factors at work in a given situation. Conversely, to the extent that a situation involves causal factors that are *not* modeled, the model will stray from the real-world behavior.

But what sorts of causal factors might be left out? The models themselves cannot tell us this. The idealized character of a model does not consist in an explicit set of boundary conditions or *ceteris paribus* clauses. If it did, models, laws, and theories would be falsified every time we found other causal forces that we had not anticipated. Idealization is aimed at explicitly singling something out, not at explicitly excluding all other things by name. The class of things bracketed by a model is thus essentially open-ended. The gravitation law says nothing about what other causal factors there may be in nature. It does not exclude the possibility of other nomic causal influences. Nor does it exclude anomic influences.

Here we have hit upon a more general implication of the causal account of laws for freedom and determinism. If laws express potential partial causal contributors, then a commitment to a law or to a set of laws leaves us absolutely agnostic with respect to what other causal contributors—lawful or spontaneous—there might be. In this respect, the causal account of laws provides space for free will. Laws make no claims beyond their own limited domains. And because free will of the relevant sort—libertarian free will—is by definition anomic, the laws, understood as expressing causal capacities, can say nothing about it. This is not, of course, a proof that the will is free. But it is a proof that free will is not inconsistent with a commitment to scientific laws, properly understood.

Where does this leave us? The answer depends on just what assumptions one starts out with. Some people believe there is good *prima facie* reason to believe in free will. For them, the discovery that there are natural laws might have seemed to pose a challenge to this belief, perhaps even to represent the basis for an argument that their assumptions in favor of libertarian freedom must be false. For such people, the arguments I have presented here are intended to lift the cloud of doubt and worry, as I hope to have shown that a commitment to laws is fully compatible with a commitment to freedom. Other people, however, may start out with deterministic convictions that are at least as strong as their commitment to free will, or may even lack any such commitment. Nothing I have said here is intended to give those who do not already believe in free will new reason to do so. The arguments will, I hope, persuade those whose belief in determinism is grounded solely in a mistaken assumption that it is implied by the existence of natural laws that they should reconsider their commitment to determinism. But the existence of natural laws is not the only reason that might lead a person to believe in determinism. There are also other reasons, both scientific and philosophical, that have led people to embrace determinism as a thesis independent of a particular understanding of the nature of laws. I shall address some of these concerns in the next chapter.

9 Three Appeals and a Kantian Conclusion

The preceding chapter was an extended argument for a fairly modest point: that being committed to scientific laws does not entail a commitment to determinism and hence is compatible with free will. This does not mean that an analysis of scientific laws commits us to the existence of free will, either. But if the reader has independent reason to believe in free will, scientific laws pose no direct threat to that belief.

One might be satisfied to stop there and leave it at that. Indeed, I suspect that some readers who came to this book looking for a way to preserve their belief in free will may already have gotten what they were looking for. However, there are several replies that I regularly encounter in response to the previous line of argument, and these should be addressed.

First, there are appeals to other scientific principles. These concede that acknowledging the aptness of some law (such as that of gravitation), or even some set of laws, does not entail determinism. However, they hold that something else the sciences tell us *does* entail determinism. The two main variants of such appeals are appeals to specific laws (e.g., conservation of energy) that are supposed to entail determinism or prohibit free will and more general appeals to the causal closure of physics (i.e., the view that the universe is causally closed under physical laws).

Second, there are appeals to the future. These acknowledge that the sciences as we currently understand them do not entail determinism or prohibit free will. But they go on to argue that this is (or at least might be) merely a symptom of the present unfinished state of the sciences, and that an "ideally completed science" would (or at least might) produce laws that imply determinism or prohibit human freedom.

Third, there are appeals to mystery. These admit that our present scientific understanding of the world does not commit us to determinism or prohibit free will, and even that we might not be able to produce an "ideally completed science" that would do so, perhaps on Cognitive

Pluralist grounds. But they go on to object that this does not mean that the real causal forces that govern the world are not deterministic, even if it must be in a fashion that is unintelligible to us, and perhaps even that we are rationally constrained to suppose a real (if unintelligible) causal determinism.

9.1 Appeals to Other Scientific Principles

Let us begin with appeals to other (putative) scientific principles. I have argued that a commitment to the truth or aptness of laws does not entail a further commitment to determinism. Another way of saying this is to say that the laws themselves do not imply that the universe is causally closed under those laws. But neither do they imply that it is *not* causally closed. And some philosophers have argued that we *should* be committed to a principle of causal closure, either as a special consequence of the content of particular laws (though not of the nomic character of laws generally) or as an additional commitment required by the sciences.

9.1.1 Conservation Laws and Causal Closure

One argument for causal closure takes its starting point, not from a general understanding of laws, but from the content of a particular set of laws: those of conservation of mass/energy and entropy, which assert that there is conservation of mass/energy in physical reactions but that the total entropy of the system is always increasing. If one additionally assumes that a free action would require an exogenous cause, and that such a cause would add mass/energy to the system, the conservation law would be violated. And since the conservation laws are among the best-confirmed laws in physics, there is an enormous assumption against such exogenous causation, and hence against free will.

There are several things to be said about this argument. I shall only note in passing that it is a substantive assumption that free action would require an addition of energy to the system (Polkinghorne 1989). But my concern is with other assumptions. First, it looks as though the conservation law is being taken as an unrestricted universal claim about objects and events. It is only if we understand it thus that we generate a problem for free will. This construal of the conservation laws might be compatible with a rejection of the Positivist and Empiricist analysis of laws *per se*, since the conservation laws might be viewed as implying a universal quantifier not found in other laws. But a great deal depends on what we understand the conservation laws to be claiming (or perhaps what claims are really licensed by the empirical base). Do they really claim, for example, (a) that the total mass/energy of the universe is constant? Or do they claim only (b) that mass/energy is conserved in physical interactions of particular types? Claim (b) implies claim (a) only if we make the additional assumption that there are no exogenous causes imparting energy to the system, or no other types of physical interactions in which conservation does not hold. And clearly the experimental base supports (b) only directly and licenses (a) only insofar as it is implied by (b). But in the current context, in which we are asking about whether the conservation laws prohibit exogenous causation, it is illicit and question-begging to simply assume that the total mass/energy of the universe is constant.

There is also another way of understanding the assumption that there is no exogenous causation: that the exclusion of exogenous causes is part of the implicit idealization class of the law. That is, in doing thermodynamics, one has bracketed off the possibility of exogenous causes such as free will and miracles as possible contributions that will not be modeled. But if exogenous causes are excluded simply by idealizing away from them, one reasons from the law to the impossibility of exogenous causes at the cost of the fallacy of idealization—that is, of treating an idealized model of a phenomenon P as though it were an analysis supplying necessary *and sufficient* conditions for being a P. In so doing, one mistakes the partial and idealized claims within the model for the whole truth, and mistakes things that do not appear in the model only because they have been idealized away for things that are incompatible with the truth or aptness of the model.

Let us consider the problem from another angle. The conservation laws seem to be well supported in a wide variety of cases. But what if we wanted to test the hypothesis that in certain kinds of human action there are exogenous causes that might contribute energy to the system? Do the experiments actually performed in physics and chemistry labs conclusively confirm or refute this hypothesis? Only on the assumption that there are no causal influences in the case of human action that are not present in the laboratory cases already tested. But *that* assumption would be question-begging here, since that assumption is itself part of what we wish to put to the test. And how could we put it to the test? How much energy would we expect a free decision to add to the world? How would we measure it? Presumably it would involve something on the order of putting a human being in a very sensitive calorimeter. But this is well outside of the tolerances of such experiments (not to mention those of human-subjects committees). The energy imparted probably would be extremely small, probably much smaller than the margin of error involved in calculating the total mass/energy of a human being in a calorimeter. And that person would also be undergoing all kinds of metabolic reactions that were themselves making exchanges of energy, probably on a level that would drown out any blip caused by libertarian decisions.

But suppose we could do such an experiment, and suppose we were to find evidence of energy imparted by some exogenous cause. What would we then say? Would we conclude that the conservation laws had been proved false? I suspect there would be claims of this sort in the popularized accounts of science, but I doubt that this is how the scientific community itself would view the matter in the long run. Rather, I think it would conclude that the conservation laws were true, and that they had very wide scope, but that the scope was not universal. That is, in most classes of interaction, mass/energy is conserved. The knowledge of which cases are which becomes part of the practical knowledge of the scientist, as is the knowledge that the equation of heat with kinetic energy is to be applied when one is talking about gases and liquids but not when one is talking about solids or plasma.

An alternative way of responding to the challenge posed by the Second Law of Thermodynamics is as follows: Sometimes the Second Law is expressed as a claim about the total sum of matter and energy in the universe—as "Matter/energy can be neither created nor destroyed," or "The sum of matter/energy in the universe is constant." But such formulations are contentious. Looked at more carefully, what the Second Law claims is that, matter/energy is conserved *in a closed system*. The former versions of the law follow from this only if one assumes that the universe is a closed system. By this, however, one might mean either of two things:

(CS1)   The universe – i.e., the complete system of physical objects and their physical interactions – constitutes a closed system.

(CS2)   The universe – i.e., the complete system of all entities and processes – constitutes a closed system.

CS2 interprets the word 'universe' as broadly as is possible. In this sense, "the universe is a closed system" would seem to be a tautology, as there is nothing else to interact with elements of the system. However, it potentially includes any non-physical entities or processes (God, Cartesian souls) there might be, and hence its closure does not imply the closure of the physical universe. Moreover, it is not clear that the Second Law could be interpreted in a fashion applicable to the "universe" in this broad sense, unless it is somehow possible to attribute scalar measures of mass or energy to any non-physical components. Since CS2 does not itself make use of such notions, it is not rendered incoherent by this problem. What seems to be barred, however, is the claim that the Second Law can be applied coherently to "the universe" as understood in CS2.

CS1 invites objections as well. First, neither the proofs of the Second Law nor the experimental evidence supporting it entail that the physical universe is a closed system. Thus, to make use of a version of the Second Law that assumes that the physical universe is a closed system is to go beyond what is well-established science. Second, in this particular context such an assumption is perilously question-begging, as the openness of physical processes to free agency is precisely what is under discussion. (We shall return to the topic of causal closure in subsection 9.1.4.)

9.1.2 Double Causation and Epiphenomenalism

Another objection to attempts to drive a wedge between laws and determinism appeals, not to any features of laws themselves, but to some additional principle of a philosophical rather than a scientific nature. One popular topic in recent philosophy of mind has been that of *mental causation*—particularly, whether mental states can cause physical events without themselves *being* nothing but complex physical events. This is a broader topic than free will, as it concerns *any* mental event, whether free or causally determined. But concerns about the possibility of mental causation *generally* also have implications for *free* mental events. And recently there have been influential arguments to the effect that mental events cannot have physical effects.

This issue, discussed most thoroughly by Kim (1993), may be put as follows: The theses A–D listed below constitute an unstable tetrad—that is, they cannot all be true at once.

(A) *Independence of the Mental*   Mental events are not physical events.

(B) *Causal Closure of the Physical*   All physical events have sufficient physical causes.

(C) *Mental Causation*   At least some mental events cause physical events.

(D) *No Double Causation*   An event cannot have two independent causes.

If we assume that the physical universe is causally closed in the sense that every event has a complete physical cause, then it seems impossible to provide an account of human action that does contradict one or more of the other three theses. Mental events could still produce physical effects if they are also physical events, but this would violate (A). Independent mental events could exist but be epiphenomenal (have no physical effects), but this would violate (C). An event could have both a complete physical explanation and also be the result of a mental state, but this would violate (D).

This tetralemma is commonly posed as a problem for mental causation generally. But it applies to any free actions we may suppose there to be, as well as to any we may suppose are not performed freely. And there are some additional issues that arise when we confine our investigation to *free* actions. If mental events are also physical events, and the universe is causally closed under physics, then there are no free actions. But if mental events are *not* physical events, and this implies that they have no physical consequences, we are equally deprived of any meaningful notion of freedom. There might be free *thoughts*, but *we* are not free to *act on* them.

Those who have explored this puzzle have tended to assume Causal Closure and No Double Causation, and to argue either for physicalism or epiphenomenalism (or to argue simply that there is a forced choice between the two). I wish, however, to focus on the claims that are more generally assumed. I shall discuss the denial of Double Causation first, and then turn to Causal Closure.

9.1.3 Double Causation

What is supposed to be the problem with double causation? And where does the principle on which we deny it come from? The problem seems to lie in an intuition that, if we have a sufficient causal explanation for an event, it must also be a "complete" explanation. And if it is a "complete" explanation, it must leave nothing out. But this seems to me to trade on an equivocation. If 'complete' just *means* "causally sufficient," then having a complete explanation (a set of circumstances sufficient to ensure the consequence) does not entail that it is a comprehensive explanation in the sense of including all causal factors. But if 'complete' means that no causal factors are left out, then sufficiency does not entail completeness.

Consider the following type of example, often used to explore issues of double causation: Two assassins are sent to kill the king. Luthor the Loathsome stabs the king in the heart, thereby ensuring his death. But at exactly the same moment, Hektor the Horrible shoots the king in the head, equally ensuring his death. Who killed the king? It seems to me that, if the events are appropriately timed (the sort of thing one can do by fiat in thought experiments of this sort), there is no unique answer. Both

Luthor and Hektor did things that were individually causally sufficient to kill the king, and because of the serendipity of timing neither sequence of events that was set in motion brought about a state ensuring his death before the other. Had Luthor lingered, the king would still have died, and likewise had not Hektor hastened. The king's death was causally overdetermined.

Nor, I think, need we appeal to such contrived thought experiments to make the point. In the cognitive sciences, and indeed in biology, causal redundancy is a familiar idea. Biological systems, especially neural systems, often employ multiple parallel pathways that lead to the same result. For example, the human visual system extracts information about depth from a number of different cues, processed along different neural channels (including shadows, motion, and occlusion). This is a good design feature, as sometimes only a subset of such cues are actually available, and sometimes an organism is presented with stimuli that are ambiguous or potentially illusory and require multiple cues to resolve them. But in ordinary circumstances it is often the case that we would be able to infer the same information about depth from any of the individual cues without the others. Having any of a number of subsets of the cues, and a normal visual system, would be enough to ensure correct depth computation in many situations. And in such situations, I think, it would be as wrong to insist on a *unique* answer to the question of how the brain computed depth as it would to insist on a unique answer to the question of who killed the king.

The intuition that there cannot be Double Causation seems to me to be a philosopher's intuition, but one of the sort that we can be disabused of if we are sufficiently aware of the role that causal redundancy plays in biological systems. When we assert that there must be some set of events that was *the* cause, it seems to me, we are insisting on an armchair notion of causation. We would do better to attend to the practice of the sciences, which seems to allow multiple causes.

Some philosophers will no doubt be willing to bite the bullet here and insist that dispensing with causal redundancy is not too high a price to pay to retain a particular metaphysical notion of causation. Others might seek to analyze examples where scientists speak of causal redundancy in a fashion that shows the phenomena described to not really be examples of Double Causation. I find these strategies unpromising, but I shall not try to anticipate replies here. For the denial of Double Causation really provides the basis for a challenge to free will and mental causation only when combined with Causal Closure, a thesis that has arguably been far more influential in recent philosophical debates.

9.1.4 Papineau's Argument

Let us then turn to the other disputed principle, Causal Closure. Discussions of mental causation, freedom, and physicalism often explicitly assume that the universe is causally closed under laws. David Papineau puts the principle this way: "All physical effects are fully determined by law by prior physical occurrences." (2001, p. 8). In his 2002 book *Thinking about Consciousness*, Papineau indicates that he had originally thought that the closure of physics was

not a problematic issue. . . . The one assumption that I did not expect to be controversial was the completeness of physics. To my surprise, I discovered that a number of my philosophical colleagues did not agree. They didn't see why some physical occurrences, in our brains perhaps, shouldn't have irreducibly conscious causes. My first reaction to this suggestion was that it betrayed an insufficient understanding of modern physics. Surely, I felt, the completeness premise is simply part of standard physical theory. However, when my objectors pressed me, not unreasonably, to show them where the completeness of physics is written down in the physics textbooks, I found myself in some embarrassment. Once I was forced to defend it, I realized that the completeness of physics is by no means self-evident. Indeed, further research has led me to realize that, far from being self-evident, it is an issue on which the post-Galilean scientific tradition has changed its mind several times. (Papineau 2002, p. 45)

In *Thinking about Consciousness*, Papineau devotes an appendix to the task of describing the history of the thesis of causal closure. He quite rightly notes that Descartes'[1] and Leibniz's assumptions of causal closure were closely tied to their assumption that there is only one causal mechanism at work in nature—contact mechanical interaction—and that this assumption was overthrown by Newton's conception of forces, which was taken up by the vitalist tradition in physiology in the eighteenth and nineteenth centuries. Likewise, Papineau notes that "early Newtonians themselves certainly saw no barrier to the postulation of *sui generis* mental forces" (ibid., p. 239).

Papineau characterizes the principle of causal closure as an empirical claim that became well supported only in the twentieth century, and he traces the rise of physicalism in the latter part of the twentieth century to this growing evidence for causal closure. The beginnings of the case for causal closure are found in the addition of the conservation laws to Newtonian mechanics, from the early work of d'Alembert (1717–1783), Lagrange (1736–1813), Laplace (1749–1827), and Hamilton (1805–1865) through Joule's (1819–1889) discovery of the equivalence of heat and mechanical energy, and culminating in Helmholtz's (1821–1894) work "showing that there are fixed equivalences between [electric and magnetic forces], heat, and mechanical energy" (ibid., p. 248). In spite of this, however, the vitalist tradition continued in physiology. Helmholtz was also a pioneer in physiology, and a reductionist rather than a vitalist, but his reductionism was largely programmatic—the result of a kind of orthodoxy learned from his teacher Johannes Müller. As Papineau notes, "there is no outright inconsistency between the conservation of energy and vital forces, and many of the nineteenth-century figures were quite explicit, not to say enthusiastic, about accepting both" (ibid., p. 248). Papineau sees no contradiction between the conservation of physical forces and existence of additional nomic vital (or mental) forces. But he does think there is a problem for anomic vital (or mental) forces: "The content of the principle of the conservation of energy is that losses of kinetic energy are compensated by buildups of potential energy, and vice versa. But we couldn't really speak of a 'buildup' or 'loss' in the potential energy associated with a force, if there were no force law governing the deployment of that force. So the very idea of potential energy commits us to a law which governs how the relevant force will cause accelerations in the future." (ibid., p. 249) Here, however, Papineau seems tacitly to be making the assumption that the conservation laws should be viewed as unrestricted in scope—as making universal claims about the real-world behavior of systems of objects. As we have seen, this assumption seems to be unwarranted, especially if one has embraced the causal view of laws.

The remainder of Papineau's appendix deals with the death of vitalism and emergentism in physiology and biology at the hands of accumulating evidence from biochemistry and neurophysiology in the twentieth century. Oddly, Papineau does not directly discuss the case of anomic or even independent *mental* causes at all. The argument seems to be as follows:

1. The threats to causal closure perceived in the nineteenth century came from reasons to think there are independent vital and mental causes.

2. The reasons for thinking there are independent vital causes are undercut by empirical work in biochemistry and neurophysiology.

3. Therefore, the threats to causal closure have all been undercut.

Clearly, however, this argument is not valid. The threats from independent mental causes, including free will, have simply been left unaddressed. And yet these threats are crucial to Papineau's overarching agenda in the book, which is to make a case for physicalism. As he says in the concluding section, "Without the completeness of physics, there is no compelling reason to identify the mind with the brain." (ibid., p. 255) Given this recognition of the crucial importance of the mental cases, it is baffling that does not address them directly. Moreover, Papineau himself finds the argument for causal closure inconclusive:

Of course, as with all empirical matters, there is nothing certain here. There is no knock-down argument for the completeness of physics. You could in principle accept the rest of modern physical theory, and yet continue to insist on special mental forces, which operate in as yet undetected ways in the interstices of intelligent brains. And indeed, there do exist bitter-enders of just this kind, who continue to hold out for special mental causes, even after another half-century of ever more detailed molecular biology has been added to the inductive evidence which initially created a scientific consensus on completeness in the 1950's. Perhaps this is what Tyler Burge has in mind when he says that 'materialism is not established, or even deeply supported, by science', or Stephen Clark when he doubts whether anyone could 'rationally suppose' that empirical evidence 'disproves' mind-body dualism. If so, there is no more I can do to persuade them of the completeness of physics. However, I see no virtue in philosophers refusing to accept a premise which, by any normal inductive standards, has been fully established by over a century of empirical research. (ibid,, p. 256)

But just what premise has really been established here? At most, it would seem to be the claim that biological phenomena such as the processes of metabolism involve no new forces beyond those of basic physics. But that premise would generally be conceded by present-day advocates of mental causation and free will. Without a comparable examination of the problem case at hand—that of anomic mental causation—the argument that there are no additional forces in one domain (physiology) has little bearing on the question of whether there are additional forces in another domain (mental causation). Moreover, if the right method for establishing causal closure is what Papineau seems to say it is—a careful examination of the problem cases and a demonstration that they are, after all, completely accounted for by the normal suspects on the lists of natural forces—then one ought to apply *that* method in the case of agency too. But such an application is precisely what Papineau's chapter glaringly omits.

I applaud Papineau's intellectual honesty in exploring the case for causal closure. But the net effect of that exploration is to reveal that the arguments for causal closure are inconclusive. Nothing we know from the sciences is inconsistent with the possibility of free will, or with the denial of causal closure. Indeed, insisting that the universe must be causally closed under physics would seem to be an additional commitment—one more along the lines of an expression of philosophical taste than an inference from the sciences themselves. I have no objection to expressions of philosophical taste, but they place no rational constraint on those committed to contrary principles. A faith in causal closure is not irrational. But neither is it rationally compulsory.

9.2 Beyond Our Knowing: Appeals to the Future and to Mystery

I have argued that scientific laws as we understand them are compatible with indeterminism and freedom. But this does not render them incompatible with determinism. Scientific laws of the sort we possess today do not yield determinism, but their failure to do so may not reflect anything about the universe, but only something about the incomplete state of our present understanding of it (a possibility that is, if anything, brought to the fore by Cognitive Pluralism).

Here it is necessary to point out an ambiguity in the word 'law'. When we say "the laws of nature" or "scientific laws," we may mean the linguistic and conceptual entities we find in scientific *discourse*—our attempts to represent the regularities or causal powers found in nature. (For purposes of clarity, let us call these *law-representations*.) But we may mean the regularities or causal powers themselves—the things we are seeking to represent. (Let us call these *laws-in-nature*.) With this in mind, we can see that there are in fact two ways we might look beyond our current understanding to ground a belief in determinism. The first would be to suppose that our present-day law-representations fail to yield deterministic predictions because they are not yet adequately perspicuous representations of the laws-in-nature, but that we might someday reach a stage of scientific progress where they would do so, at which time the law-representations will yield deterministic predictions if the laws-in-nature are in fact deterministic. The second would be to acknowledge that the laws-in-nature may themselves be deterministic, even if we are not capable of producing a set of law-representations that adequately capture them and yield deterministic predictions. The first is an appeal to a possible type of understanding we might someday achieve, and hence is an appeal to the future. The second is more of an appeal to mystery. Both strategies require us to make a distinction between the "laws" the scientist trades in (law-representations) and "really real laws" (laws-in-nature) that govern change in nature.

We might view the two strategies as regarding our epistemic prospects with different degrees of optimism. The more optimistic scenario is one in which we can find law-representations that adequately reflect laws-in-nature. An attempt to preserve determinism in this way is, in essence, to appeal to a future possibility. The more pessimistic scenarios hold that we cannot develop a set of law-representations that adequately represent the laws-in-nature to an extent that would allow us to derive deterministic predictions, but that the laws-in-nature are nonetheless (collectively) deterministic. On this scenario, the ultimate nature of reality is to some extent mysterious to minds like ours, and thus seeking to preserve determinism in this way entails appealing to something mysterious.

9.2.1 Appeals to the Future

At the optimistic end of the spectrum would be the view that our current scientific understanding does not underwrite any unified understanding of nature—at very least because of inconsistencies between relativity and quantum mechanics—and that achieving this goal would require a revolutionary change on a par with that of the seventeenth century or that of the twentieth, but that such a unified understanding is something the human mind is capable of achieving, and with the result of a future theory that has recognizable continuities with present-day science. Of course, we do not know whether such a revolution is metaphysically possible for creatures with minds like ours, or whether it would make determinism seem more or less likely if it were to come about. Such a revolution would have to be assumed to result in some basic changes in our conceptions of the world and of scientific understanding, as was the case in the transitions to early modern science and to quantum mechanics. But as an optimistic scenario, it would have to involve either laws or other types of quantified models, and these would have to either directly license exact deterministic predictions or else be limited only by computational tractability.

I am willing to allow that this scenario is epistemically possible. That is, it may well be true that nothing we know about ourselves or the world is incompatible with it. Scientific revolutions, by their very nature, tend to usher in forms of understanding that seemed unavailable before, because they involve radical reconceptualization both of the world and of what it is to explain something. Cognitive Pluralism raises the possibility that there are principled limits to what minds like ours can achieve in this way; but so far this has been raised only as a possibility. To go beyond this, and claim that there *are* such limits, and that we can now *say* what they are, would be to go beyond what we know, and would be decidedly risky. Once, when I gave a talk on Cognitive Pluralism and scientific disunity,

I was accused of advocating "white-flag epistemology"—that is, of advocating that we simply give up on projects of uniting our scientific knowledge. This was a misunderstanding of what I was suggesting, conflating the suggestion of a possibility with an assertion of what is the case. But it points to a possible excess that the Cognitive Pluralist must take pains to avoid.

But there is also an opposite danger. Too often, the alternative to "white-flag epistemology" has been what we might call, in the same spirit, "declare-victory-and-go-home epistemology." This consists in the equally risky move of conflating an epistemic possibility about what we might someday understand with an assertion that we are in fact capable of such an understanding. To assume *now* that such an achievement is possible is essentially to take a stance of faith on philosophical grounds, as opposed to simply using our current understanding of nature to guide our view of the world, leaving what we do not know unsettled. And to assume that a major scientific change would result in a unified and *deterministic* understanding of the world would require another leap of faith. It is epistemically possible that we might come up with a unified deterministic theory of everything. But it is equally epistemically possible that we might come up with a unified indeterministic theory, or that we are not capable of coming up with an adequate unified theory at all.

Indeed, if we are trading in epistemic possibilities, it is epistemically possible that I might discover that everything I thought I knew about the world was the product of some ingenious deception—say, the type of virtual reality scenario depicted in the movie *The Matrix*. But it might be far more radical even than that: the real world might be fundamentally different from the simulated world, with different types of objects and laws. I do not, of course, worry about such epistemic possibilities. The point of the example is merely to show how risky it is to conflate possibilities with things we are entitled to assert, since the range of epistemic possibilities is so unconstrained.

Insistence on appeals to the future state of science often amount to statements of faith or philosophical taste. In some cases, they may amount to a bit more than this. We are probably justified in thinking, for example, that fifty years from now we will have a much more comprehensive understanding of biological and neural systems than we have now. We are justified in supposing this because there is strong inductive evidence that continuing to apply known methods of investigation will continue to yield additional insights, of familiar types, into these systems. But we do not have similar inductive evidence that the sciences will be unified, or that if they were to be unified the result would be deterministic. The present state of scientific understanding, with inconsistencies between our two best and most fundamental theories, involves what is perhaps the worst sort of disunity—inconsistency—to be found in the history of science. And inquiry into the nature of inter-domain relations in the sciences in recent decades has, if anything, given us more reason to be suspicious of scientific unity than has been the case since the end of Scholasticism (Horst 2007).

This is not to say that people are not entitled to their speculations, their faiths, and their tastes. I do not regard it as at all irrational for someone to suppose that progress in science might yield a unified and deterministic understanding of nature. But neither do I regard it as irrational to suppose that it cannot do so, whether because of concerns about the limitations of our finite minds or because of independent rational commitments to freedom of the will. What *is* irrational is to confuse embracing something on the basis of speculation, faith, or taste with showing it to be true or well grounded. This is the mistake made both by those who wave the white flag too early and by those who declare victory before the battle is done.

9.2.2 Appeals to Mystery

At the pessimistic end of the spectrum would lie the view that the human mind is constrained to think of the world only in ways that cannot be at once unified, comprehensive, and true. The sciences might make significant and even fundamental advances, but we would still be left with a patchwork of laws and models, with various types of explanatory gaps and mysteries. If such should prove the case, Cognitive Pluralism would at least provide a framework for explaining why this might be so. Now, so long as we are in a situation in which the law-representations we have do not combine to yield deterministic results, if we nonetheless wish to insist that laws-in-nature are deterministic, we are left in something analogous to the Kantian position of having to distinguish between phenomena (things as conceived by minds like ours) and noumena (things in themselves). In such a position, we cannot know or even conceive of the noumenal nature of things, and there are at least serious questions to be raised about whether notions such as causation and determinism are even applicable to them. If "the really real laws" means something like "noumenal laws," which are beyond our powers to conceive, it might be truly nonsensical to apply the concepts of 'causation' and 'determinism' to them. (Likewise, it is not clear that any positive notion of 'freedom' could be applied, though Kant distinguishes a purely negative idea—the denial of causal determination—that might be applicable.)

Noumenal determinism, if we may call it that, is not a scientific theory but a philosophical doctrine. And even as a philosophical doctrine, it treads a dangerous line as it attempts to make concrete claims about things that, even by its own lights, we cannot understand. We might do well to modify Wittgenstein's counsel here: What we cannot understand or conceptualize, we should pass over in silence.

A third possibility, suggested by Plato and Spinoza, is that there might be a form of understanding available to us—a form of understanding quite unlike what we employ in ordinary experience, in dialectic, or in the sciences—that would afford us a grasp of things that would be at once complete and consistent. Plato calls this *noesis*; Spinoza calls it intuitive understanding. Perhaps some people have even experienced this in mystical ecstasies. I happen to be very hopeful about the availability of such a form of consciousness, and about its prospects of conferring a deeper sort of understanding. But it is not clear how much light it would shed on questions about determinism. For one thing, such experiences probably cannot be translated into experiments and theories that could be tested in such a way as to provide evidence for either determinism or freedom. Such experiences might provide deep subjective conviction on the part of those who have them, and even broad inter-subjective agreement among them, but they would not be suitable for use in scientific demonstration or in philosophical argument.

Additionally, people who claim to have such experiences tend to have difficulty conveying their content at all, and crucial notions such as time, space, causation, and volition seem to be particularly unsuitable for expressing what is experienced. Such experiences seem not so much to present an answer to our questions about causal determination and freedom as to lead those who have them to call into doubt the very terms in which such problems are framed. And indeed, insofar as those who experience them are able to make any claims about the unity they intuit, they tend to describe it in terms very different from our sciences—for example, as "the Form of the Good" or "Divine Love." Such an understanding may be better than scientific understanding in many ways, but it seems to do little to answer questions about causation or freedom. I suspect that, were I dragged from Plato's cave to behold the Form of the Good directly, or to experience the Beatific Vision, I might share Thomas Aquinas' conclusion that my previous understanding looked like filthy rags by comparison. I probably would lose all interest in the philosophical and scientific questions that now engage me. But that would not be an answer to those questions. It would be a matter of moving on to something better, or at least to something different.

9.3   Speculations on the Sources of Our Urges Toward Unity and Determinism

It is instructive to ask why we have urges to speculate beyond what we know, and indeed why we confuse these speculations with things that we know to be so, or even with things we know must be so. Why are we drawn to the ideas of epistemic unity and determinism? Here, I think, Kant is once again a good guide. Kant might be regarded as one of the founding fathers of cognitivism, as his transcendental turn attempted to ground features of human understanding in principles of cognitive architecture. His approach emphasized synthetic *a priori* reasoning, whereas I would prefer to integrate insights gained from the empirical study of cognition, but I regard his project as an important ancestor of mine.

Kant used hypotheses about cognitive architecture at a number of different junctures. He postulated distinct but interrelated faculties of Sensibility (for receiving sensations and ordering them temporally and spatially) and Understanding (for applying concepts and forming judgments). He explained different forms of judgment as the products of twelve innate "categories," which seem to be both propositional forms and abstract concepts. And he postulated that the human mind has an innate drive to seek to unite its beliefs systematically. This last drive makes science and systematic thinking possible. But it can also result in certain "Dialectical Illusions of Pure Reason," which result when the mind forms propositions or conceives concepts that are beyond the realm of any possible experience. It is in this context that Kant discusses the dialectic between freedom and determinism and the Idea of "the world" as a comprehensive manifold of cause and effect.

Kant held that the situation we seem to be in—with deep commitments to contradictory claims of freedom and necessity—is based in a confusion. On the one hand, because causation is one of the categories of the Understanding, we are constrained to view every phenomenal event as having a cause. For the same reason, however, the category of causation can be rightly applied only to phenomena, and not to noumena. Hence we can be phenomenally determined but noumenally free. Moreover, though we are architecturally constrained to understand every phenomenal event as having a cause, we move beyond this when we project "the world" as a *comprehensive* nexus of cause and effect, because the world in its totality is outside the scope of possible sensible experience.

Here I wish to focus on what the Kantian account claims about human *psychology*. Kant is right, I think, to claim that we are driven to try to unify the things we understand in ever more comprehensive ways. (I am more skeptical about Kant's claim that there are exactly three of these, corresponding to three forms of syllogism. I suspect that this is actually a broader and more variegated phenomenon, but pursuing that line of thought would take us too far afield.) Our minds, having hit on a way of unifying beliefs, pursue the honest work of finding the connections between them. But we also do something more: we project what a comprehensive system of understanding *would* look like *if this method could be pursued to an ideal conclusion*. In doing so, we take a turn into speculative reasoning. This can be innocent so long as we bear in mind its speculative character. But we are prone at this point to make a grave philosophical error: to suppose that such an ideal completion could be reached, and that the world is such as to make it possible. We go from saying "If we could extend and unify our understanding of the world to the ideal limit, we would be able to understand it as a comprehensive and deterministic nexus of cause and effect" to saying "There must be a thing called 'the world' which is a comprehensive and deterministic nexus of cause and effect" and even "We can, in principle, understand the world as a comprehensive and deterministic nexus of cause and effect, and on this basis reason rightly about metaphysical truths."

Kant's argument that the Ideas produced by such a process of reasoning to an ideal limit are illusory was grounded in the distinction between the phenomenal and the noumenal and in the claim that categories are applicable only to phenomena. And his notion of "illusion" did not imply that the Ideas thus generated did not really correspond to anything. They were "illusory" in the sense of being claims to *knowledge* where no knowledge could be had through theoretical reasoning. I wish to take his insights in a slightly different direction—one that does not require us to buy into Kantian assumptions about phenomena and noumena.

The basic insight is as follows: We have drives that result in projecting how things would be if the world could be completely understood through an ideally completed extension of familiar unifying moves, such as causal and reductive explanation. And we are prone to assume that the picture that results from such speculative reasoning (glimpsed only abstractly) tells us something about how the world must be. But the fact that we are prone, or even constrained, to view the world in a certain way is no guarantee that it really is that way. This was where Rationalism went astray. It may be that God has endowed us with faculties and drives that are capable of leading us to understanding, in a comprehensive way, the real and fundamental natures of things (although this requires some weighty theological assumptions). It may even be that the luck of the evolutionary lottery might do so. But it may equally well be the case that some or all of our ways of understanding involve "forced errors"—ways we are architecturally constrained to *mis*represent the world.

Some such forced errors would be hard for us to detect, and we would have no way of correcting them. For example, if substance/attribute ontology is hard-wired into our brains, but is inapt for representing certain features of the world, we might never be able to know it, or even to formulate what it is that we are rendered unable to understand except negatively. (That is, we could only say "real ontology is not divided into substances and attributes"; we could not say what the alternatives might be.) But other forced errors might be more avoidable. In particular, things (such as Kant's Ideas of Pure Reason) that are not part and parcel of how we actually experience the world, but involve theoretical projections, can be avoided. (Or if we make the projections, we can distinguish them from things we know.) And indeed the very act of acknowledging that we have strong drives that result in such projective Ideas should alert us to the possibility that they may be artifacts of something about our own cognitive makeup, and to call into question our too-easy assumptions that they are deep metaphysical truths.

It seems quite likely to me that this story, or something like it, is the best explanation of why we feel so deeply drawn both to seeking theoretical unification of things we believe and to thinking that they provide deep metaphysical insight into necessary features of the world. And indeed such features *are*, in a certain conditional sense, necessary: *if the world is to be fully intelligible to us,* or to be intelligible according to a particular type of explanatory structure, it must be thus. But we are prone too easily to overlook the antecedent of the conditional. Likewise, there is a quite respectable sense in which the drive to unify counts as a "rational principle." It is a rational principle in the sense of a sound maxim to follow in investigating the world. If we are to find such order as there is in the world, we must investigate it as though it is orderly. If we are to find such connections as there are between our beliefs, we must proceed as if such connections are there to be found. But doing so is quite compatible with the possibility that there are limits to the extent to which such an enterprise can be carried out. The mistake comes in a subtle elision from a methodological maxim to a metaphysical manifesto.

Now, lest advocates of free will overestimate what has been shown here, I should also point out that our assumption that we are capable of acting freely is also a prime candidate for a belief that is constrained by—and perhaps an artifact of—our cognitive architecture. Indeed, there is recent evidence that, from a very early age (in infancy), we have several different schemata through which we understand the world. Some of these deal with perceptible objects and seem to involve at least primitive notions of causation; one of them is concerned with agency and lacks some of the constraints found in the object systems (Spelke and Kinzler 2007). If this research is correct, and if such innate "core systems" constrain our adult thought about objects and agency, our minds may actually have two different systems for understanding objects and agents, which represent their domains in incompatible ways. Our philosophical reflex may be to say "Then at least one of those two systems must be wrong." But perhaps, in view of the discussions of models in earlier chapters, it is better to say that each of the two systems captures something about the world that cannot be captured by the other, and that we seem to lack a single way of understanding the world that captures the insights of both systems while avoiding inconsistency.

9.4 Conclusion

The scientific laws we have are compatible with free will. If a "law-governed world" is simply one to which the sorts of laws we actually find in the sciences can aptly be applied, then a law-governed world need not be deterministic, and there is room for free will within such a world. The motivation for determinism must thus be found either in a misunderstanding of the laws we have received from the scientists or else in a commitment to some additional type of principle. The sciences supply no such principle at a metaphysical level, though they do employ methodological maxims that are easily mistaken for metaphysical principles. Appeals to someone's guesses as to what we would find in an "ideally completed science" are no guide to deep metaphysical truths. They are more like a Rorschach test for revealing a person's philosophical dispositions. And appeals to ways the world may be that are entirely unknowable to us or are knowable only through a form of consciousness radically discontinuous from science leave us in a position in which it is not clear we can say anything at all.

I conclude that if you feel that you have reason to believe in free will, you need not fear that this commitment has been shown to be mistaken by science. Scientific laws are compatible with human freedom. Anyone who says otherwise has misunderstood the scientific laws we possess or else is expressing a philosophical taste that is not itself vouchsafed by the sciences.

III Case Studies of Explanation in the Sciences of the Mind

10 Psychophysical Laws and Models of Early Vision

The chapters in part I of this book compared different theoretical resources for talking about the nature and status of laws in the physical and the cognitive sciences, and their implications for familiar problems in philosophy of mind. In writing those chapters, I opted to conduct the discussion at a purely philosophical level, without appeal to case studies. This was, in part, because the main burden of those chapters was to apply well-established ideas from philosophy of science to philosophy of psychology and philosophy of mind, and detailed case studies were not called for in the course of that argument. I am, however, the sort of philosopher of mind who thinks that philosophy of mind is best done in close dialogue with the sciences of the mind. Moreover, there are several issues that are left unresolved by part I of the book that would benefit from some case studies of a length that would have interrupted the flow of the main argument.

First, there is the question of whether various disciplines that study cognition really employ laws at all. In some cases, including psychophysics, laws (or at least putative laws), such as Fechner's Law or Stevens' Law, play a prominent role. Models in computational neuroscience also employ laws, and the models themselves are mathematically precise, though not always in the form of equations. It is less clear whether the mathematically imprecise generalizations of belief-desire psychology are well described as laws. Thus, even given that such laws as are found in various cognitive sciences may be continuous in character with physical laws, we might still do well to ask whether the types of generalizations found there are laws in the first place, and whether this matters.

Second, I have thus far largely spoken of "the sciences of cognition" as though they were a more or less homogenous group. (And indeed sometimes I have, for purposes of brevity, lumped a good many of them under the collective heading "psychology.") But one need not read very far into textbooks on neuroscience, neural modeling, psychophysics, cognitive psychology, developmental psychology, and ethology to see that their forms of explanation in fact look very different. This quite naturally leads to a project that can be approached only through case studies: the project of examining just what kinds of explanations are employed in each discipline, and whether this book's general account of explanation as mental modeling can handle them equally well.

To carry out these projects (especially the second) comprehensively would be well beyond the scope of this book. However, in the remaining chapters I shall attempt to walk through some examples from three distinct areas of the sciences of cognition in order to highlight their commonalities and their differences, and to render more explicit the kinds of generalizations they employ. This chapter will examine visual psychophysics and its connection to circuit-like models early in the visual system. Chapter 11 will examine neural dynamics of systems in the lateral geniculate nucleus (LGN) and visual cortex. Chapter 12 will examine several variations on belief-desire psychology.

10.1 Visual Psychophysics, Localization, and Modeling

It is fitting to begin with visual psychophysics, which was arguably the first of the sciences of cognition to which rigorous quantitative methods were fruitfully applied (Weber 1834; Fechner 1877). Fechner distinguished "outer" psychophysics (which was concerned with mathematical relationships between stimuli and percepts) from "inner" psychophysics (which involved relations to brain states). The word 'inner' here seems intended to pick out what is inside the head, rather than what is interior to experience, as Fechner's outer psychophysics involves subjective percepts. If what makes inner psychophysics "inner" is the fact that brain states are among its relata, Fechner's usage here is potentially ambiguous, as the expression "inner psychophysics" might be applied both to relations between stimuli and neural states and to relations between neural states and percepts. I shall distinguish these usages by calling them "early" and "late" psychophysics, respectively. We may thus distinguish the following:

outer psychophysics (relations between stimuli and percepts)
early psychophysics (relations between stimuli and neural states)
late psychophysics (relations between neural states and percepts).

(See figure 10.1.)

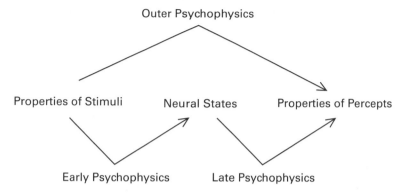

Figure 10.1

Diagram of the explanatory domains of outer, early, and late psychophysics. Outer psychophysics describes lawlike relationships between properties of stimuli (e.g., objective luminance) and properties of percepts (e.g., subjective brightness). Early psychophysics describes relationships between properties of percepts and neural states (e.g., firing rates of particular types of neurons in a specified anatomical region). Late psychophysics describes relationships between neural states and properties of percepts.

Outer psychophysics, as a discipline, has historically tended to proceed quite autonomously, measuring perceptual and discriminative abilities without reference to the mechanisms that underlie them. In Fechner's day this was unavoidable, as the technologies for examining neurons and neural connections did not yet exist. But it is also defensible on methodological grounds, as outer psychophysics supplies at least some of the data that must in turn be explained by neurally plausible models of underlying mechanisms. Psychophysics is thus, in the larger scheme of things, closely linked with two additional enterprises. The first of these is (mathematical) modeling of mechanisms that could perform the necessary informational transformations required to fit the psychophysical data. The second is finding neural localizations of these mechanisms in the form of bits of brain architecture whose causal structure corresponds to the psychophysical data, fits one or more of the models, and lies in an appropriate causal position in the perceptual cascade.

There is no strict rule about whether modeling or localization is undertaken first. Helmholtz (1867) put forward abstract models to explain psychophysical data without hypotheses about their underlying mechanisms; only later were his models confirmed as having plausible neural localizations. In such cases, nineteenth-century models (such as the three-color process model and the color-opponency model) provided concrete things to look for in the dynamics of cells involved in early vision. On the other hand, around the same time, Broca and other anatomists were discovering, through post-mortem studies of brains, that losses of particular psychological abilities are often correlated with damage to particular areas of the brain through strokes or traumas, thus providing at least candidates for gross anatomical localizations of the psychological functions in question. In some of these cases, we still do not have theoretical models for how the functions are performed. It is quite possible that in some cases modeling (e.g., of face recognition) will be guided primarily by a study of the actual relations between cells in the relevant areas. (See figure 10.2.)

All this is easily accommodated within the familiar framework of a black-box mechanism. Outer psychophysics provides a black-box description of various psychophysical data. Modeling provides abstract hypothetical mechanisms for realizing these functions, which can be further filled

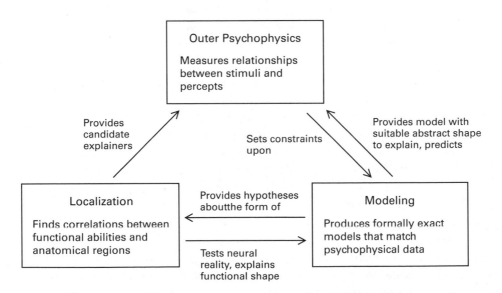

Figure 10.2
Diagram of the relations among outer psychophysics, localization, and formal modeling. Outer psychophysics provides data that set research agenda for localization and modeling. Models and localization hypotheses each provide partial potential explainers for these data, the models proposing the formal properties of the hypothesized mechanism and the localization hypotheses proposing the neural realization of the mechanism. The enterprises of localization and modeling can be mutually informative, and either can place constraints on the other.

in by understanding what goes on at the level of neurons and networks of neurons. One can either work *inward* from larger boxes to smaller boxes and eventually link these with neural behavior, or work *outward* from neural behavior to functional descriptions of brain areas that can then be linked with models at some level of abstraction.

Modeling of early psychophysical processes begins with an account of the transduction of environmental information by peripheral cells in the sensory organs and ends with a model that is neurally plausible and consonant with the outer psychophysical data. Late psychophysics, on the other hand, is entangled with familiar philosophical problems, such as the explanatory gap (Levine 1983), and arguably poses some problems that lie beyond the scope of empirical investigation. Outer psychophysics, as conceived by Fechner, relates stimuli to a phenomenological quality space. Early psychophysics is not complete until it discovers neural mechanisms that bear an appropriate relationship to the formal shape of phenomenological quality space, as charted by outer psychophysics. For example, early psychophysics of color vision comes to an end when it explains how the state space of some part of the visual cortex that seems causally implicated in color vision (say, V4) is isomorphic to the phenomenological color space obtained through outer psychophysics, and explains various psychophysical effects demonstrated in the laboratory. But neither outer nor early psychophysics explains why this V4 activity results in the particular types of color qualia it results in, or indeed why it results in any qualia at all. Outer and early psychophysics provide an explanation of why we can, say, distinguish red from yellow, but not of why a particular shade of red has the particular phenomenological character ("subjective feel") it has, or why it has any such phenomenological character at all. In doing the science, one simply assumes that there is some vaguely defined "realization" relation between phenomenological states and brain states. But there may be abiding explanatory gaps surrounding the question of why this realization relation obtains (Horst 2005).

10.2 The Weber-Fechner Laws

One paradigmatic example of outer perceptual psychophysics is to be found in the laws proposed by Fechner and Stevens as describing the relations between stimulus intensity and percept intensity. The data consist first and foremost of a set of data points representing how subjects can either identify stimulus-intensities (Stevens) or discriminate between them (Fechner). These are then interpreted in terms of a mathematical function whose curve fits the data points: either the logarithmic function $p = k \ln S/S_0$ (Fechner 1877) or the power law $S = kI^a$ (Stevens 1951).

Fechner's Law and Stevens' Law have all the hallmarks of scientific laws. They are expressed in mathematical relations between variables. They are empirically robust. They can be tested through experimental manipulation of the variables. They are useful for description, prediction, and diagnosis. And they help guide and constrain microexplanations involving neural substrates. To the question of whether there are laws of outer psychophysics, most scientists of perception would unhesitatingly answer in the affirmative. In subsection 10.2.3, I shall examine objections to this assumption raised by Wade Savage (1970) and Donald Laming (1997). First, however, I wish to pose questions about the nature and status of these laws, and about how they can be accommodated by my cognitivist account of laws. This I shall do by way of examining issues about the methodology and interpretation of these data that would be familiar to any psychophysicist.

10.2.1 Direct and JND Methods, Logarithms, and Power Functions

Fechner and Stevens employed different methods to obtain their data. Stevens had his subjects rate individual stimulus intensities directly, then normalized the subjective scales they employed. Most psychophysicists, however, have followed Fechner's experimental methodology of measuring subjects' abilities to discriminate between intensities using the method of just-noticeable differences (JND). Either experimental method yields a set of data points that is then subject to mathematical interpretation in terms of a curve answering to a particular mathematical description. Fechner proposed that percept intensity is a logarithmic function of stimulus intensity, with a different base for each perceptual modality. Stevens proposed that the data are better described by a power function.

Any such mathematical interpretation of data is subject to a number of issues of "curve fitting," such as that there are always multiple mathematical equations that fit the data with similar degrees of fidelity and that there are always data points that do not fall exactly on the curve defined by the mathematical function. Such problems are endemic to any mathematical interpretation of data; they are in no way specific to psychophysics, or to a particular psychophysical methodology. Real experimental data are always messy, with data points falling off the interpolated curve. (Indeed, if a lab report contains data that are too neat, that fit too exactly with the hypothesis, it is likely to be regarded with some suspicion.)

Some textbook expositions of the differences between Fechner's Law and Stevens' Law concentrate solely on whether the data points are best interpreted mathematically as logarithmic functions or as power functions. The mathematical curves described by these two types of function are in fact very similar. And indeed, for any set of data points, one could find functions (albeit perhaps less elegant ones) that were even more similar to it, even arbitrarily similar to it. What, if anything, is at stake in disputes over which function better fits the data? To some extent, it depends on practical considerations: are there cases where assuming the law to be logarithmic will produce results inconsistent with the data, but for which a power function will get it right (and vice versa)? To the extent that the differences between them don't matter, one might adopt either or both of them as bland and harmless idealizations. It is not clear that there is such a thing as *the* (unique, canonical) equation for any phenomenon in nature. Our selection of one equation over another will sometimes depend on inaccuracies that matter. But at other times it will depend on other things (e.g., mathematical simplicity or computational power).

But there are also other ways the choice of functions might matter. To take an extreme case, suppose we are looking at similar functions for the photosensitivity of a pixel of a digital camera, which takes luminance values as its input and some scalar representation as its output. Here, which equation we use to describe the camera's behavior may matter in a more fundamental way *if the camera employs a mathematical algorithm corresponding to one of the functions to compute the transformation.* If the transformation is mediated by a mere transducer, and no logarithmic or power-function algorithm is employed to generate the output, the equations may be equally good. But if it first measures luminance, then applies a power-function algorithm to it to obtain a result that parallels that of human vision, the power function has a kind of computational reality. Describing the behavior logarithmically might never matter for practical purposes in predicting the output within a given margin of error, but if taken as a description of *how* the camera does what it does, it would misrepresent it. Similarly, in the human visual system, transformations might be brought about by neural processes that are truly algorithmic in *employing* symbolic functions or might be brought about by neural processes that are *describable* tolerably well by one or more functions but are *accomplished* in a non-algorithmic fashion. As it turns out, the cells involved in early vision are almost certainly non-algorithmic in *how* they do what they do, and these do the burden of the work in explaining the psychophysical laws. But it is more contentious whether this is true of more sophisticated neural processes. Indeed, strong versions of the computational approach to psychology depend on the assumption that there are levels that are well described as *employing* algorithms. In short, the choice of equations may not always matter when one is doing *outer* psychophysics, but this does not imply that it never matters when one is doing *early* psychophysics—i.e., relating outer psychophysical transformations to the mechanisms that achieve them.

10.2.2   Complications in the Model

But there are issues in the wings that are more complicated. For example, the psychophysical laws are functions from physical luminance to subjective brightness, irrespective of the wavelength of the stimulus. But it turns out that human vision is differentially sensitive to light in different wavelengths. (And, of course, we cannot see infrared, ultraviolet, gamma, or cosmic radiation.) This is due to the fact that the photoreceptivity of the rod cells is realized through particular photopigments, such as rhodopsin, which are differentially responsive to light at different spectral wavelengths. (See figure 10.3.)

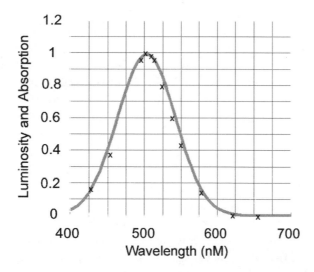

Figure 10.3
The chemical basis of vision. The curve represents the photosensitivity of the (dark-adapted) human eye. Gray x's represent amount of light absorbed at the same wavelengths by the pigment rhodopsin. (Source: Horst 2005. Based on a figure in Gregory 1978.)

The psychophysical laws are thus idealizations of a more perspicuous way of describing human photosensitivity in terms of a curve of responses to different wavelengths of light. Although the data are robust across subjects, they are a simplifying idealization of a more complex phenomenon. In some contexts, this idealization does not matter. But in other contexts (e.g., calibrating a computer screen so that it produces "true" colors) it does matter. And the more complicated curves that describe differential photosensitivity over different wavelengths are also "better" in another respect: they supply additional data for models and localizations of the mechanisms employed in photosensitivity to explain.

And things get still more complicated. The curves for sensitivities to different wavelengths of light are different depending on whether the subject was dark-adapted or light-adapted—that is, whether, in the period preceding the onset of the stimulus, the subject was in a dark room or in a normally illuminated room. This is due to the fact that in daylight vision the cone cells as well as the rod cells are active, and each of the cone cells has its own distinctive photoreceptivity curve. (See figure 10.4.)

Any single curve plotting the objective property of luminance (the intensity of the stimulus) at different wavelengths against brightness (the intensity of the percept) is thus cast against assumptions of particular background conditions. There is no single such curve for brightness perception; rather, there are at least two different curves—one for dark-adapted

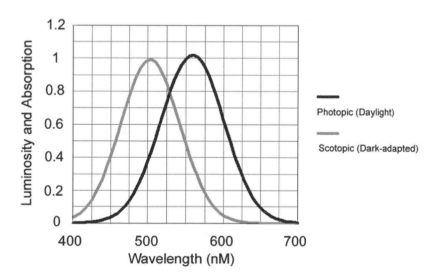

Figure 10.4
Photoreceptivity curves for daylight vision and dark-adapted vision.

and one for light-adapted vision. And since vision also takes place in states intermediate between those of full dark adaptation and full light adaptation, even the two curves represent data that are idealized away from the full range of variables present in real-life situations. A more adequate representation of brightness as a function of luminance could be obtained only by plotting it in four dimensions, corresponding to luminance, brightness, wavelength, and a measure of light adaptation. Such a representation, of course, could neither be produced in a three-dimensional space nor imagined in pictorial or graphic form. Breaking down the four-dimensional curve into separate graphs is thus a good strategy for understanding, given how the human imagination (not to mention the objects in the physical world employed to represent graphs) is in fact comported. The costs of the idealizations involved are more than offset by the fact that they allow information to be represented in a way that our minds can readily grasp. A four-dimensional model (say, in a computer database) is better for purposes of accommodating all the data at once, but worse for purposes of comprehension.

The data are also idealized in a second way, in that they represent data collected from multiple subjects, all of whom are deemed "normal." This averages away from individual variation among "normal" subjects; it also brackets subjects who are "abnormal"—e.g., subjects who lack one or more types of cone cell. To obtain a curve that exactly matched real-world behavior, one would have to map the four-dimensional curve for an individual subject under various background lighting conditions involving variations of previous exposure to different levels of light over different times. Such a curve would have several additional dimensions, and its accuracy would be bought at substantial cost. On the one hand, it would lose the generality needed for a science of (human) vision by representing the photosensitivity of only a particular individual; on the other hand, the extra dimensions might well obscure things that are brought out by the simpler curves, which turn out be connected with quite ecumenical neural phenomena: e.g., that light-adapted vision has a different sensitivity curve *because* it is a result of the additional contributions of cone cells, which are inactive in dark-adapted vision. The curves standardly displayed in textbooks lose a certain amount of descriptive accuracy in describing any particular subject in particular lighting conditions, but the idealizations that cost us this accuracy make understanding possible and are theoretically fertile in linking the simple mathematical model represented by a photosensitivity curve to properties of the underlying neural mechanisms.

On the other hand, it would be a mistake to view this as falsifying the Weber-Fechner laws. They are certainly not regarded as false by the vast majority of scientists. Indeed, it is not clear that "truth" and "falsity" are the right terms to apply here at all, at least if "truth" means "facticity"— i.e., description of the actual performance of a particular subject (Cartwright 1983). The laws should not be regarded as making exact descriptive or predictive claims about all human beings, or even about a single human being at a given time, as our hypothetical multi-dimensional curves would be. Rather, they are aimed at capturing robust species-typical generalizations about human vision that hold good against particular background assumptions and within an implicit acceptable margin of error. They bracket such cases as people with "abnormal" visual systems, people with normal visual systems in "abnormal" conditions, small individual variations among "normal" subjects, and ways a single subject might change over time. Indeed, exactly which cases are bracketed is essentially open-ended. Discovery of a new way in which particular subjects (or human subjects in general) might respond to light in a fashion that deviates from the Weber-Fechner curves need not falsify the laws; it may merely show that there are additional conditions in which those laws are not aptly applied. The scientist has an ever-growing and open-ended body of practical knowledge about the situations in which applying the laws is apt or inapt. As a condition comes to be known as rendering the law inapt, that condition also becomes regarded as "abnormal," and so the application of the labels 'normal' and 'abnormal' is likewise ever-changing and open-ended.

10.2.3   Are the "Laws" Really Artifacts?

A far more radical issue, raised by von Kries (1882) and James (1890), has been taken up by Savage (1970), Zuriff (1972), Tumarkin (1981), Boynton (1989), and Laming (1997). Their claim is that the data of various psychophysical experiments do not in fact reflect measurements of sensation or of the intensity of any inner variable. The most recent systematic discussion of this view is that of Donald Laming, and it is with his treatment of the issues that I shall principally concern myself here.

Laming first points out that the standard statements of psychophysical laws found in Fechner or Stevens really involve multiple claims that can be separated from one another. Most important:

1. The experiments performed by psychophysicists provide an adequate basis for assigning the type of metric to *whatever* it is that is correlated

with stimulus intensity that is needed to underwrite an algebraic law (i.e., a ratio metric).

2. This amounts to a measurement of relations between stimulus intensity and some feature of *sensations*.

Some of the writers Laming surveys (e.g., Stevens) seem to make different assertions at different times, sometimes asserting only a version of claim 1 that links stimulus intensity to some neural variable and at other times linking it to sensation. Laming thinks both of these claims are false.

The nub of the matter is that the type of "measurement" required to underwrite the kinds of algebraic laws put forward by Fechner and Stevens requires that data points be ordered on a particular type of scale, a *ratio scale*. There are also weaker types of scales. The most important of the weaker types are *ordinal* scales, which arrange values comparatively (e.g., as greater or less than one another) but do not license addition or division. Both Fechner's logarithmic law and Stevens' power law require a domain that can be ordered according to a ratio scale. One of Laming's central claims is that the psychophysical data support only an ordinal scale and not a ratio scale, and hence do not really license the kind of algebraic interpretations found in Fechner's or Stevens' laws.

One important type of evidence Laming marshals comes from comparing the data from different types of tests, such as those requiring difference detection versus those that require increment detection or cross-modal matching. Fechner was able to arrive at a logarithmic law because his tests involved only difference detection, and because he made additional assumptions, such as that all JNDs are subjectively equal. The need for such additional assumptions suggests that Fechner's algebraic interpretation of the data points may be an artifact of his methodology. And this suspicion seems to be supported by the fact that data collected by other means, such as increment detection, cannot be reconciled with data arrived at by Fechner's method through a single ratio scale. Similar considerations apply to Stevens' method. Laming summarizes the argument as follows:

1. If numerical magnitude estimates establish a valid scale of sensation, then that scale must be a ratio scale, because 'equal stimulus ratios tend to produce equal sensation ratios' (Stevens 1957b, p. 162), and the relation of sensation to the physical magnitude of the stimulus must be a power law.
2. If that ratio scale is extensive, not only are ratios of sensation meaningful, but *differences* as well, because an extensive ratio scale also has interval scale properties.

3. It then follows that magnitude estimates of differences in sensation should conform to the same power law as estimates of ratios. This is contrary to experimental observation.

Perhaps more surprising, Laming claims that the very same problems arise in trying to match stimulus intensities with intensities of neural activity through direct sampling, and hence they cannot be avoided by retreating from outer psychophysics to early psychophysics. The problem, if you will, is not so much that psychophysics does not measure *sensation* (as opposed to measuring something else, such as intensity of neural activity) as that it does not *measure* sensation (or anything else).

Laming's alternative interpretation of the data involves several separate theses. The first of these is that what Fechner and other experimentalists took to be reports of subjective intensities were in fact reports of perceived properties of the stimuli (in the sense of properties-of-stimuli-as-perceived). Previous writers, Laming opines, tended to fall into what Boring (1921) called "stimulus error." (See also Lockhead 1992.) In perception, we are in fact making judgments about the intensities of properties of objects. The stimulus error consists in mistaking these judged-intensities-of-properties-of-objects for intensities of sensations. (This is more or less the converse of the attribution error of projecting properties of one's psychological states onto external objects toward which they are directed.)

Laming's second claim is that the variances in psychophysical data obtained from different subjects and under different conditions suggest that subjects' discrimination abilities are consistent with no better than an ordinal scale. Actually, it is a somewhat complex ordinal scale, with five values(*much less, less, equal, greater,* and *much greater*) rather than *equal/unequal* or *less/equal/greater*. However, the crucial point is that it is not a scale that supports algebraic operations of addition or division.

Third, when subjects are required to give numerical estimates of differences or ratios between stimuli, they are in fact engaged in a process of judgment—a process that does not simply reproduce a scale already implicit in pre-existing neural or phenomenological states, but produces artifacts of its own. One possibility Laming explores for the origins of this imposed scale involves research on the subjective values of numbers: briefly glossed, human behavior in making numerical comparisons of stimuli actually yields results with a logarithmic bias, rather than conforming to canonical arithmetic. (One way of understanding this would be that humans have multiple internal modules for different types of mathematical operations, some of which conform to canonical arithmetic laws little better than ordinary reasoning conforms to Bayesian rationality.) Laming supports his thesis by showing that his five-value ordinal scale can help account for various data obtained by different experimental methods that proved recalcitrant so long as one assumed there must be a single ratio scale of internal intensities that is measured by psychophysical experiments.

Laming concludes that, when all the psychophysical data are considered together, they do not justify claims for psychophysical laws, such as those of Fechner or Stevens. The problem is not that those "laws" are not lawlike in form, but that the data as a whole do not fit the equations. Fechner's data *do* conform to Fechner's Law, but the larger set does not support a ratio metric when the data set is expanded to include data obtained through different methods. This is an important critique of widespread assumptions about psychophysics. However, it is not clear that it succeeds in undercutting the claim that there are psychophysical laws. What Laming has shown, at most, is that Fechner's Law and Stevens' Law must be viewed as idealized descriptions of the data. But, as we have already seen, the fact that a law is idealized need not compromise either its aptness or its probative power.

First, some ways in which a model can deviate from real-world behavior can be virtues. In a later section of this chapter, I shall examine one such case: a case in which Helmholtz's three-color process model failed to accommodate data about color vision. In one sense, this could be viewed as a flaw in the model, in that it was a good fit with only a carefully constrained subset of the available data. But in fact, as we shall see below, it turned out to be a useful guide to the mechanisms involved in one stage of processing of chromatic information (that of the cone cells). A more complicated model that was more empirically adequate—i.e., that covered a broader data set—would have masked something real that the model had hit upon, and would have lacked some of the probative power of Helmholtz's model. It could turn out that some of the processes involved in seeing brightness will likewise bear a closer relation to Fechner's or Stevens' Law.

Second, Laming's own mathematical analysis of the data, utilizing a five-value scale, can itself be viewed as a successor to Fechner's and Stevens' Laws. It is not a "law" in one important sense, in that it is not an algebraic equation. However, to the extent that it is a mathematically exact model, it fits well with my broader characterization of laws as mathematically exact models. Such a model would still allow us to speak of "psychophysical functions." They would just be much more complicated functions that cannot be expressed in simple equations, as Fechner's Law can.

Laming's critique does, however, raise questions about how psychophysics should now be pursued. In Fechner's day it was not possible to measure neural events involved in perception. As a consequence, outer psychophysics had to be pursued as an independent science. Today that is no longer the case. And insofar as Laming's more comprehensive investigation of psychophysical data as a whole suggests that the perceptual process involves something more complicated than a single informational transformation that can be described by a simple law, it seems to me that the proper moral to draw is that psychophysical experiments should now be pursued in tandem with investigation of the neural mechanisms involved in perception. This will necessarily draw us into the issues involved in modeling neural systems that have distinctive functions yet are interrelated in their performance of those functions. A model of one component system will have to idealize away from some of those interrelations, and the behavior of the model will therefore deviate from real-world behavior. And one should not expect a macromodel to be empirically exact in the absence of an understanding of how its components operate and interact. Such issues will be discussed in the next chapter.

10.3   Color Vision

Let us now turn to the exploration of other relations among psychophysics, localization, and modeling by way of another set of examples, taken from the study of color vision. This draws on physical optics, which reveals such things as that white light is a combination of various colored lights. The spectrum of colored light, in turn, is typified by various wavelengths of electromagnetic radiation. Phenomenological color perception also yields something like a spectrum, but there is not a one-to-one mapping between wavelength and phenomenological hue. Whereas a distribution of light along the electromagnetic spectrum is aptly represented by a two-dimensional scale of wavelengths and intensities, the set of phenomenological hues is best modeled by something like Munsell's three-dimensional color solid (figure 10.5).

The mapping from spectral stimuli to color perception of perceived hue is also complicated in other ways. A combination of pure wavelengths, for example, does not result in the perception of a visual "chord," as in the case of hearing two tones, but in the perception of a single hue. Indeed, for any hue there are a variety of combinations of light at different wavelengths that will result in perception of that same identical hue (figure 10.6). Such combinations that produce the same phenomenological hue are called *metamers*.

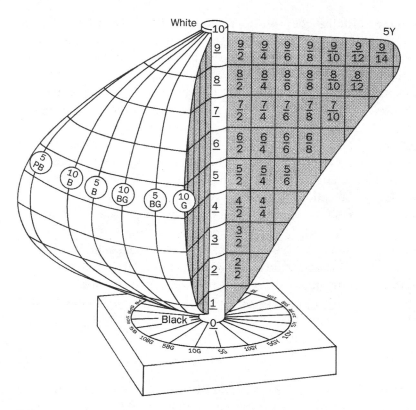

Figure 10.5
The Munsell color solid, a geometric representation of trichromatic human color space. A portion of the solid has been cut away to reveal the interior. (Source: Hurvich 1981, p. 274. Reproduced from Clark 1993.)

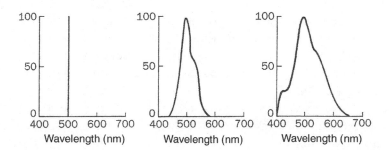

Figure 10.6
Light distributions and metameric matches. Each of these wavelength distributions will produce a sensation of a unique green—i.e., one that is not perceived as having any mixture of yellow or blue. (Source: Hurvich 1981, p. 78. Reproduced from Clark 1993, p. 43.)

The psychophysical data regarding color vision can be viewed as a function C from a set L of distributions of intensities over wavelengths in the visual spectrum to a set H of phenomenological hues. The data set is, of course, idealized in various ways. It is drawn only from "normal" subjects, for example, and not from colorblind people or dichromats (though of course their vision would be described by *different* functions). And it brackets any differences there may be in different parts of the visual fields of individuals (e.g., between foveal and peripheral vision) and any intersubjective differences over the population of "normal" subjects. These are idealizations of a sort familiar from any statistical model. They trade a loss in exact descriptive power in individual cases (one subject versus another, or a stimulus in this part of the visual field versus a stimulus in another part) for generality and explanatory power.

10.3.1   The Three-Color Process and Cone Cells

Helmholtz (1867) showed that all hues can be produced by combinations of three pure spectral frequencies. The so-called three-color process was posed as a model for candidate mechanisms that could explain the function C. This model, initially introduced at a purely theoretical level, turns out to have a neural basis in the three types of cone cells in the eye, demonstrating that Helmholtz's model is neurally plausible. Experimentally identified properties of the cone system generate properties of the three-color process model. In particular, algebraic combinations of absorption levels of different cone systems generate predictions of metameric matching.

The three-color process is a beautiful example of a model that is both richly generative and neurally plausible. It is neurally plausible because there are experimentally verified candidates for local neural architectures that indeed behave as the model, initially introduced to accommodate outer psychophysical data, supposes. It is generative in that the known properties of the cells predict the psychophysical data mathematically. The model thus underwrites a very strong form of explanation, as the data to be explained can in fact be generated out of known properties of retinal cells. Given that color vision in humans is partially mediated by retinal processing, we can demonstrate that it will have particular formal properties. Of course, this does not block off the possibility that other creatures might have the same phenomenological states in response to the same stimuli, but through different causal pathways. Nor does it explain why the process results in the particular phenomenology it does, or indeed in any phenomenology at all. (Presumably, a robotic simulation of the cone

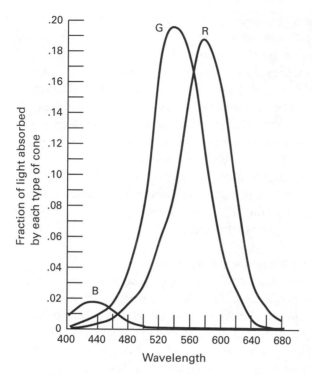

Figure 10.7
Response curves of the three cone systems in humans. Horizontal axis represents wavelength; vertical axis represents fraction of light absorbed by each type of cone. (Based on figure 8.9 on page 171 of Cornsweet 1970.)

Table 10.I
Sample data: absorption percentages, differences, and ratios of the M (medium-wavelength) and L (long-wavelength) cone systems. Note that the ratio M/L preserves information about wavelength regardless of intensity. Source: Clark 1993.

Wavelength (nm)	Quanta incident	Absorbed by M	Absorbed by L	Difference	Ratio
560	1000	192 (19.2%)	165 (16.5%)	27	1.16:1
520	1000	165 (16.5%)	62 (6.2%)	103	2.66:1
560	3814	732 (19.2%)	629 (16.5%)	103	1.16:1

Table 10.2
Algebraic predictions of a match. Metameric matches and absorption of light by M and L cone cells. The combinations of wavelengths in the second and third rows will match the stimulus in the first row, producing the same number of absorptions in both the L and the M systems. Source: Clark 1993.

Wave-length (nm)	Quanta incident (count)	Percent absorbed by M	Quanta absorbed by M	Percent absorbed by L	Quanta absorbed by L
560	1576	19.7	310	16.5	260
515+	2100	13.1	275+	5.7	120+
615	1166	3.0	35	12.0	140
Total			310		310

system, or the color detection in a digital camera, would not endow the robot or the camera with a phenomenology; at least, it is not metaphysically necessary that they do so.) What we have here thus falls short of a reduction, in that it depends on something like contingent bridge laws between the neural state and the phenomenology of the percept. But it is still an extremely powerful form of explanation, which I have elsewhere called a "mixed explanation" (Horst 2005). The basic form of such an explanation requires two distinct components:

(ME1)   The qualitative properties in question are specially related to the activation of particular neural states.

(ME2)   The neural mechanisms leading to these states have the right properties to explain the formal shape of the problems to be explained. For example, the nature of the cone and ganglion system explains metamers, and (one projects) a full description of the visual system would result in a model of V4 state space isomorphic to the phenomenological color space.

ME1, of course, leaves a number of crucial questions unanswered: What is the nature of this "special relationship"? Is it one of causation, as Descartes would have it? Or is it better captured by type or token identity, supervenience, or property dualism, or even by some form of reduction that we do not yet have the conceptual machinery to work out? Or is it perhaps better cast in epistemic than metaphysical terms, as an artifact of our having (as theorists) to simply associate elements of two different models of the same processes without being able to reduce them to a single common denominator? We do not, at the moment, have a conclusive answer to such questions, and at present, at least, it does not appear that the science has supplied an answer, and thus the questions may be trans-empirical.

It seems to me, however, that having such philosophical puzzlement is not any kind of barrier to the science itself. A pragmatic association of elements from different models is not an unusual move in science. Sometimes such identifications later turn into something stronger, something more on the order of reductions or ontological identities. But the assumption that they will always do so (at least in the successful cases) seems more like a methodological principle to guide continuing inquiry than either an empirical discovery or a sound metaphysical principle. (That is, it is only by trying to find stronger links that we have any hope of settling whether or not they are there to be found, but the principle that we ought to try to find them does not entail that they are there to be found.)

It is worth distinguishing two "explanations" that fall out of models that have been discussed. On the one hand, we have a "mixed" explanation of properties of phenomenological space, and this explanation is incomplete in that ME1 leaves an explanatory gap. It is still a powerful explanation, but a part of it is epistemically opaque. On the other hand, we have a much fuller sort of explanation of the discriminative abilities of humans. The latter sort of explanation has a sort of epistemic transparency to it: given a description of the mechanisms in the retinal cells, certain discriminative properties simply "fall out"—that is, they can be deduced or constructed from the properties of the cells. This is an example of the type of explanation that was seized upon by seventeenth-century Rationalists and twentieth-century Positivists as the paradigmatic case of explanation: deduction and construction in mathematics or logic. I have characterized such explanations as conceptually adequate (Horst 1996): we can treat the explaining system as the definitions and axioms of a deductive system and demonstrate or construct the corresponding properties of the system to be explained without the addition of any new (non-formal) conceptual content. (We might sometimes need additional formal resources, such as the statistical machinery needed to derive the gas laws from classical interactions of gas molecules, or an independent math-functional description of a circuit that is not itself constructible from the physical properties of the circuit. However, these are presumably epistemically and ontologically innocuous, as they add nothing fundamentally new, at least on the assumption that we are entitled to help ourselves to formal resources.)

10.3.2   More Visual Modeling: Color Opponency

The three-color model underwritten by the cone system is also incomplete in a second way, in that it does not yet accommodate all the psychophysical data. A complication arises from Hering's (1878) discovery that there are pure phenomenological hues (ones not perceived as mixed) that are not accounted for by the three-color process model. There is, for example, a phenomenologically pure yellow, even though there is not a "yellow receptor" cone cell. That is, the data about the function C are not exactly isomorphic to what is produced by the Helmholtz three-color process model or to known properties of the cone system. Helmholtz's model is thus a kind of distorting idealization of the data. But it is in fact a fertile idealization with probative value: it does not account for all the data points, but it is a good match with what were later found to be properties of one stage of visual processing. In failing to capture some aspects of the "shape" of the dataset, it has latched on to a much more accurate description of one stage of the processing that produces that dataset. The three-color model is thus not falsified by its distorting idealizations. Indeed, in this case at least, the distorting idealizations lead us to something real about the underlying mechanisms. The three-color process model is not the whole story about color vision, but it describes important causal contributors to that story. In getting the output of the outer psychophysics wrong, it gets a stage of early psychophysics right.

This was, moreover, the way Hering interpreted the discovery of "pure" hues not predicted by Helmholtz's model. Hering postulated that, in addition to the three-color process, there is a second process of "color opponency." This too has a neural basis, in the retinal ganglion cells, which interact competitively on data received from the cones, yielding a blue-yellow and red-green opponency, based in different ganglion cells (figure 10.8).

Ganglion cells, although closer to the surface of the retina than cone cells, are neurally "downstream" from them, and process information passed on by the cone system. Ganglion cells are an example of a common type of neural processor, called a center-surround architecture. (See figures 10.9 and 10.10.) In such an architecture, cells in one layer (in this case the ganglion cells) have inputs from a number of cells in another layer (in this case, cone cells). One set of inputs comes from the center of the receptive field, the other from cells lying around the center in a particular spatial pattern. These are generally organized in a *competitive network*: e.g., activity of cells in the center of the receptive field in L1 excites the cell in L2 while activity of cells in the periphery inhibits it, or vice versa. Center-surround

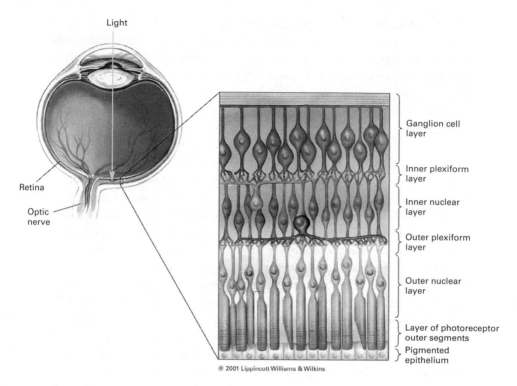

@ 2001 Lippincott Williams & Wilkins

Figure 10.8

Layers of cells in the retina. Signals from groups of rod and cone cells (bottom of diagram) are sampled by bipolar cells, which are in turn sampled by ganglion cells. Note that light enters the retina from the top of the diagram, passing through the front layers before reaching the phototransducers (rods and cones), but the flow of visual information in the nervous system begins with the transducers and proceeds "upward" as represented in this diagram. (Based on figure 9.2 of CD-ROM accompanying second edition of Mark F. Bear, Barry W. Connors, and Michael A. Paradiso, *Neuroscience: Exploring the Brain* (Lippincott Williams & Wilkins, 2001.)

(a)   (b)

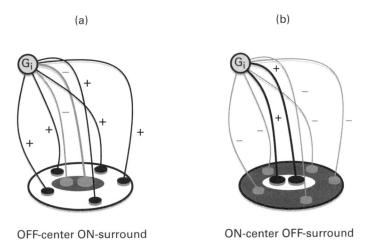

OFF-center ON-surround   ON-center OFF-surround

Figure 10.9
Center-surround architecture. Ganglion cell (G) has inputs from cells of another neural layer. In an OFF-center ON-surround architecture (a), inputs from the center of the receptive field are inhibitory and those from the surround are excitatory. In an ON-center OFF-surround architecture (b), inputs from the center are excitatory and inputs from the surround are inhibitory.

architectures are particularly useful for processing *contrasts* between activity in the center and the periphery. They are, among other things, the basis for detecting the contrasts of light and dark that signal edges and boundaries. Here, however, they are used to compare information from the different kinds of cone cells, here designated by the wavelengths they respond to: S(hort), M(edium), and L(ong). The center-surround cells are of three types, only two of which are shown in figure 10.11. The first type involves opponency between the M and L cones. The greater number of such cells have excitatory centers, either in the M or L systems, though some also have inhibitory centers. Such cells have peaks for both excitatory and inhibitory responses and are called "red-green opponent" cells. The second type of cell compares the S and the combination of the M and L functions. This process is called "yellow-blue opponent." A third type of ganglion cell does not appear to make chromatic distinctions, but follows the photopic luminosity function, and hence seems to code brightness and darkness. (See figure 10.12.) In these first two types of cells we have a neurological basis for the color opponency called for by Hering. Again, a number of psychophysical data can be predicted from the model, such as the fact that there is a phenomenologically pure yellow but not, say, a phenomenologi-

Response of
ganglion cell G_i

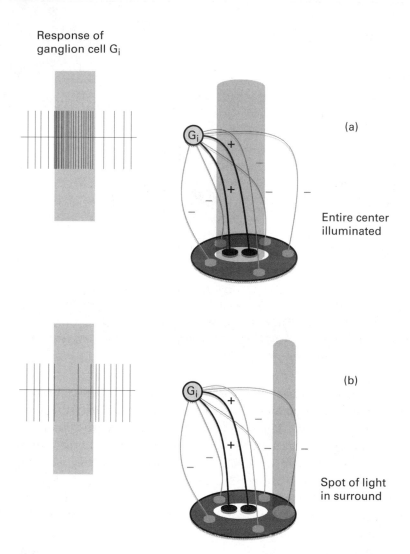

(a)

Entire center
illuminated

(b)

Spot of light
in surround

Figure 10.10
Activity of a ganglion cell with an ON-center OFF-surround architecture to stimulation in different parts of its receptive field. (a) Light stimulating the center but not the periphery causes increased spiking frequency in G_i upon onset of stimulus, which ends with the termination of the stimulus. (b) Light stimulating only the surround causes decreased spiking frequency in G_i during the stimulus.

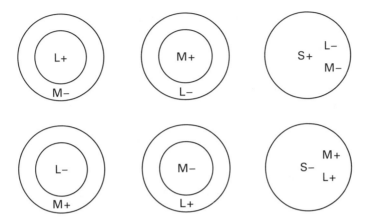

Figure 10.11
Spatial structure and frequency of incidences of the six most common varieties of color-opponent ganglion cells.

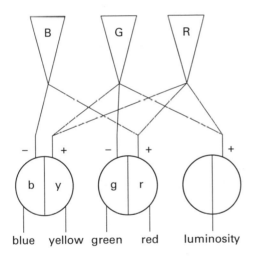

Figure 10.12
Color opponency in the ganglion cells. Inputs from the three types of cone cells interact competitively to activate ganglion cells, producing four chromatic channels (blue, yellow, red, green) and one channel for luminosity.

cally pure orange. The spectral luminance contrast sensitivities of the antagonist architectures also produce a curve that approximates the data for human chromatic sensitivity for test spots on a white background.

Hering's color-opponency model, like Helmholtz's three-color process model, was initially posed as a theoretical model, decades before a neural substrate was discovered. As a theoretical model, it both captures a set of robust psychophysical data and provides an abstract model of how the outer psychophysical transformations might be accomplished in early psychophysics. Color opponency was first proposed in the abstract, long before it was possible to find a neural correlate. The discovery of a neural correlate for the color-opponency model in retinal cells reveals that the transformations are performed *very* early in visual processing—before information passes from eye to brain.

The combination of these two models into a macrocircuit model yields a more adequate description of the outer psychophysical data, as it accommodates such facts as the presence of a phenomenologically pure yellow. However, it still does not allow us to capture all the data for color vision perfectly. For example, as Land (1974) and others noted, there are "mixed" colors (e.g. brown) that are not generated from these models alone. The models are thus still idealized in a way that fails to capture some of the psychophysical data. This has driven vision scientists to pursue more complex models in ensuing decades.

10.3.3   Local vs. Global Dynamics and the Importance of Neural Feedback

The two models also stand in an important relationship to one another. Color antagonism in the ganglion cells takes its inputs from the outputs of the processing described by the Helmholtz three-color-process model. The models can thus be connected to one another as a one-way causal sequence: the cones are transducers whose output is a function of the array of light they are exposed to and the photoreceptivity curve of each particular type of cone cell. These outputs (in spiking frequencies) are then the inputs of the ganglion system, which extracts information from the activities of combinations of cone cells lying near one another. (This is represented schematically in figure 10.13.) Because the system is local and feedforward, one can combine the models smoothly to obtain a function from the curve of spectral input in a given portion of the visual field to the activity of the ganglion cells operating on that portion of the field, given the distribution of different types of cone cells responding to that portion of the field (figure 10.14).

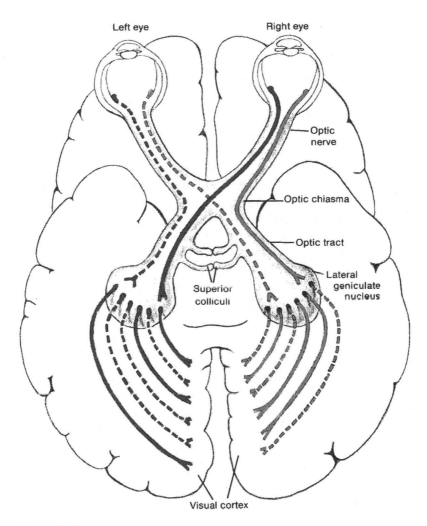

Figure 10.13
Visual pathways from retina to cortex. (Source: www.skidmore.edu.)

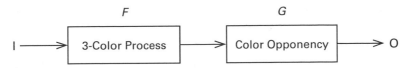

Figure 10.14
Feedforward processes as functions. The three-color process is a function F that operates on an input I to produce an output $F(I)$, which is in turn the input for color opponency, a function G. The output O is thus a function of input, namely $G(F(I))$.

The straightforward relationship between these two models is strikingly different from what one finds in later stages of visual processing, where processes increasingly involve feedback as well as feedforward interactions and operate at a level involving the dynamics of large regions of the brain rather than simple, anatomically localized cells or groups of cells. Among the more surprising twentieth-century discoveries about color vision was Edwin Land's claim (1974) that there are color-vision effects that depend not simply on the properties of the stimulus or the pattern of light on the retina but also on whether patches of color are interpreted as objects. This strongly suggests that there is feedback from whatever system(s) in the brain play a role in object groupings to some point in the causal stream that eventuates in color perception. And since there is no such feedback to the retina, it appears that we must look further into the brain before we are done with our localization of color sensation.

The ganglion cells in the retina are connected to the brain by the optic nerve. (Indeed, some neuroscientists are inclined to view the retina as a part of the brain that happens to extend into the eye, but the difference is not important for our purposes.) The signal passes through the optical chiasm, where signals from the left side of the visual field in both eyes are routed to the right side of the brain and signals from the right side of both visual fields are routed to the left side. These connections project (i.e., provide input to) a small body called the lateral geniculate nucleus (LGN), and from there to the visual cortex (located at the back of the brain). There are also feedback projections from parts of the cortex to the LGN, and indeed it seems to be the general rule that when there is a projection from one part of the brain A to another part B there are usually feedback channels from B to A too.

The visual cortex is an area of brain in which much of our visual processing takes place. It is divided into areas V1–V5, and each of these areas is divided internally into layers. Projections from the LGN enter V1 in the middle layers. Past that point, visual information seems to divide itself into three different streams: one for color, one for shape, and one for movement, location, and spatial relations. The visual cortex also projects to other parts of the cortex that are involved in yet more complex functions. Studies by Mishkin and associates (see, e.g., Ungerleider and Mishkin 1982) suggest that information from the visual cortex splits into two further streams. A dorsal stream (one projecting to the top of the brain) goes into the parietal lobe and seems to be responsible for perception of location of and orientation to objects (figure 10.15). This is sometimes called the "where stream" or the "how stream." Patients who have had damage to

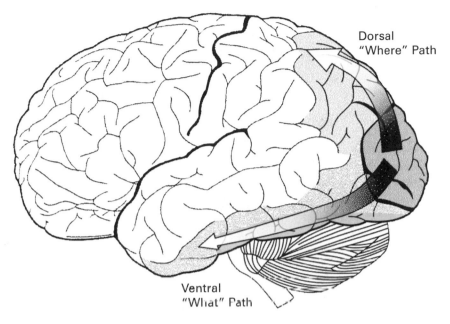

Dorsal
"Where" Path

Ventral
"What" Path

Figure 10.15
Information from the visual cortex splits into a dorsal "where" stream (top) and a ventral "what" stream (bottom). (Based on en.wikipedia.org/wiki/File:Ventral-dorsal streams.svg, gnu licensing.)

these parts of the brain are often able to identify objects, but unable to grasp them properly or to report on their spatial relations. A second, ventral stream (one that projects to the underside of the brain) goes to the temporal lobe and seems to be responsible for various sorts of recognition of objects. This is sometimes called the "what stream." One sub-area of the temporal lobe, in both monkeys and humans, seems to have the highly specialized function of recognizing faces of conspecifics.

The simplified diagram shown here as figure 10.16 involves a simplifying idealization that is ultimately distorting. It depicts the several streams of visual information as though they were all feedforward, from the retina to the various levels of the LGN to several areas and layers of the visual cortex and from there to other cortical areas. But in fact in most cases in which there is a feedforward connection between two cortical areas C1 and C2 there are also feed*back* connections from C2 to C1. Moreover, each of these areas has inputs from a number of other cortical areas, and also from areas of the thalamus.

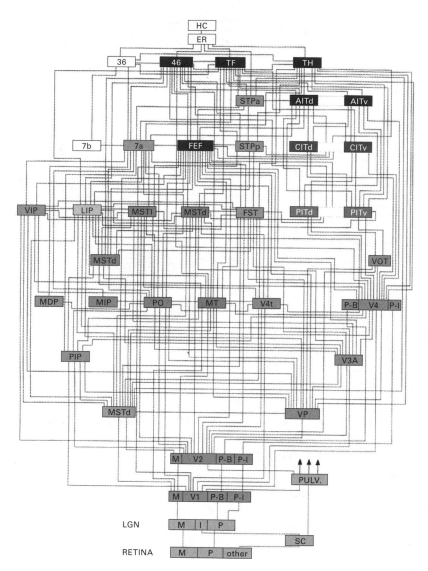

Figure 10.16
Circuit diagram of the macaque visual system. (Based on figure 2 on page 421 of Anderson and van Essen 1990.)

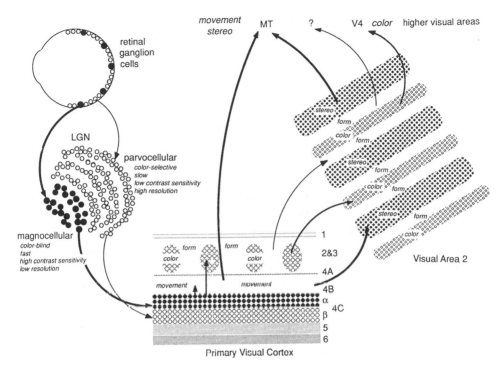

Figure 10.17
Schematic diagram of the flow of visual information through layers of LGN and
visual cortex (figure 23 on page 195 of Spillman 1990).

As a result, when we pass beyond the optic chiasm, our explanations
begin to change in kind and in quality. We know, for example, that there
is a color pathway that passes through the parvocellular areas of the LGN
into the blob cells in V1, and from there into the thin stripes of V2, which
then project to V4. (See figure 10.17.) But models of the processing done
in these areas is not so simple as a feedforward function between two
microcircuits. There are more complicated relations between color areas,
and there are also relations between some of these areas and areas outside
the color stream, and even outside the cortex, as cortico-thalamic loops
are involved.

And there are, indeed, difficult methodological difficulties in proceeding
further here. Whereas the explanations of psychophysical data that could
be read from the responses of cones and retinal ganglion cells could be
determined from examinations of single cells (or at their most complicated
from the feedforward behavior of single cells and their projections), higher

cortical activity seems to be typified by more global behavior, involving complicated feedback relations, both in the form of competition between cells at a single level and in the form of resonance phenomena between populations of cells in different systems (say, the LGN and particular areas of the visual cortex) (cf. articles in Grossberg 1987a, discussed in chapter 11). Moreover, in many useful models the cortical encoding of information does not take place in single cells but rather occurs in activity patterns distributed over groups of cells, or in the connection strengths between them. Indeed, Land's discoveries suggest that there is interaction between the color system and systems for shape and object recognition, so that it may not be possible to model color vision adequately just by understanding the so-called color pathways. Because of the complexity of cortical structures and the feedback relations among them, it is unlikely that the explanation of psychological phenomena residing in the cortex will be as closely linked to local cell physiology as it was in the retina. Because of these complications, the distance between our formal models and our neurophysiology is far greater in the cortex than it is in the retina. As a result, it is far more difficult to test the neural plausibility of rival models. Likewise, because of the distributed, somewhat opaque nature of the coding of neural networks, it is difficult to guess or verify what functional task a cortical module is performing when we do not even know the units of the "code."

Here we have an important issue for the philosophy of neuroscience. In early vision (processing within retinal cells), the units that figure in explanation of the psychophysical data are localized in specific cells that can be studied in isolation, much as one might study a particular mechanical structure or a simple electronic circuit. And indeed, it is the structural, chemical, and electrical properties of individual cells that do much of the explaining. But once we get past the retina, it is less clear just what the relevant units are. It is possible that in some cases individual cells really do perform functions that can be directly linked to the psychophysical data. But it seems likely that in many cases the relevant units are patterns of activity distributed across fields of cells (e.g., layers of the LGN, or cortical areas such as V4), or even in complicated feedback patterns relating several areas (e.g., feedback relations among the LGN, V4, and V2).

This creates complications of at least two sorts. First, the modeling techniques we need here are different from and more complicated than those we need for understanding circuit-like behavior in cone cells. Hence, network modeling techniques such as Grossberg's (1987a) Adaptive Resonance Theory have taken on a life of their own in exploring cortical dynamics. (Parts of this project will be discussed in the next chapter.) Second, it is not currently possible to sample all the cells in a region of the brain as a subject performs a perceptual or cognitive task. Imaging technology does not provide the necessary level of temporal or spatial resolution. Single-cell sampling cannot be performed on millions of cells at once and in any case would be too invasive in a human subject. And electroencephalograms, which provide good global information with a high degree of temporal resolution, do not provide the spatial resolution necessary to distinguish spatially distributed patterns of activity within a particular region. These limitations of current experimental technology may or may not prove insuperable. Moreover, on at least some possible scenarios—such as the possibility patterns of activity distributed across cortical areas, rather than single-cell activations, are the significant units—these limitations might keep us from being able to discern the physical properties that correspond to the significant units. As a result, for at least some types of problems, modeling of cortical dynamics must often proceed at a fairly global level, in abstraction from the details of the implementing system. Nor is this really comparable to the distinction between software-level and hardware-level descriptions of a digital computer. In considering the representation of numbers in a computer, we might know that a number is represented by some pattern of bits in some discrete location, even if we do not know whether it is represented by 8, 16, or 32 bits, or whether these are implemented in vacuum tubes, transistors, or integrated circuit boards, or in a Pentium 3 or G4 chip. In the brain, we do not know whether the significant units are localized in discrete areas or are patterns distributed over a population of cells. (For example, the encoding of two perceptual data or two concepts may be implemented in the very same population of cells, and may be factorable through some kind of vector algebra rather than stored in separate cells.)

10.4 Conclusion

This chapter has explored the relations among psychophysics, modeling, and localization in two areas of vision science: brightness and color vision. The outer psychophysical data do indeed yield to systematization in the form of laws, such as the Weber-Fechner laws. These laws resemble other scientific laws both in their form (i.e., they are mathematical equations relating empirical variables) and in their empirical robustness. Like most or all scientific laws, they are not exact predictors of real-world behavior. They say something true about causal processes that are normally going on in vision, but they also bracket many other things that can also be causal contributors to any particular instance of vision, and the list of things bracketed is always essentially open-ended. Moreover, the use of 'normally' indicates a kind of pragmatic decision to treat some cases as normal and others as abnormal. It is a good decision, and the resulting laws are apt, insofar as the generalizations bought are worth the price—that is, when the generalizations capture genuine regularities over populations, license (approximate) predictions, and point to new directions for research that would not be made available by more exacting models of the real-world behavior of particular individuals under particular conditions.

But to go further, vision science will have to bring psychophysics into closer connection with theoretical modeling and neural localization. The models produced there are *not* lawlike in form—they are not equations— but they are (often) mathematically exact formal models. This is, of course, by no means unusual in the sciences. Laws are either a special case of exact formal models or a special element sometimes present in such models. And the non-lawlike models thus produced are an improvement over the Weber-Fechner laws in a number of ways. First, they do a better job of capturing the subtleties of the data, and under a wider range of circumstances. Second, they do so without loss of appropriate degree of generality. A model of the three-color process realized in the cone system is not merely an inelegant kludge designed to accommodate some isolated abnormal data in particular individuals. It is itself an elegant model of a process that is normal in human vision. Third, such models are potential and partial *explainers* of regularities of outer psychophysics, as are the Weber-Fechner laws. And fourth, they supply explanations that go beyond merely nomic explanation by pointing to empirically tractable mechanisms whose known behavior *generates and predicts* approximations of those laws. Retinal mechanisms alone allow us to give conceptually adequate explanations of some of the discriminative abilities of creatures that have those mechanisms. And they yield powerful mixed explanations of aspects of visual phenomenology.

The models of early vision, moreover, are particularly tractable in that they are localized in anatomically identifiable neurons and groups of neurons that can be experimented on both *in vivo* and *in vitro* and in that their architecture is feedforward. There is thus a very close connection between model and neuroanatomy, which in turn yields a close relation between models and predictions despite the many idealizations involved (many of which, including saturation effects, can themselves be explained by appeal to lower-level mechanisms, such as depletion of neurotransmitters within the cells in question). It is not clear that models of later stages of visual processing (still within the bounds of early psychophysics—i.e., brain mechanisms, without concerns about phenomenology) share these features, as we shall see in the next chapter.

11   Modeling Cortical Dynamics

Whereas the preceding chapter concentrated on psychophysical laws and the circuit-like feedforward models appropriate to retinal processing, this chapter will examine models of visual processes located in regions of the visual cortex and their feedback relations with one another, with other cortical areas, and with the thalamus. Such models are dynamic rather than linear: the things they model are not arranged in a simple feedforward architecture, but involve complicated feedback connections between different areas. As a result, they proceed on different principles, and they involve an additional type of idealization significantly different from those types observed in models of early vision.

11.1   Subjective Contours

The visual psychophysical laws discussed in chapter 10 describe a function from objective luminance to perceptual brightness. One might naturally expect, on this basis, that under normal lighting conditions the subjective brightness of any patch of the visual field would be a simple function of the intensity of light on the corresponding portion of the retina. Likewise, one would expect that two portions of the visual field would seem equally bright if their corresponding areas on the retina (and the stimulus) were of equal luminosity, and that one portion would look darker than the other just in case the corresponding portion of the stimulus casts less light on the corresponding part of the retina. That is, one would extrapolate a logarithmic function from the luminance profile of the stimulus to the brightness profile of the percept.

However, there are well-known visual illusions in which the visual system does not behave in this fashion. I shall consider two of these here: the Craik-Cornsweet-O'Brien effect and subjective contour figures. There are numerous other examples that could serve the same function, but examining more than a few would make this chapter disproportionately long. I have thus chosen examples in which the effects themselves are easily conveyed, and which played a particular role in the development and presentation of the theoretical models to be discussed later in the chapter.

11.1.1 The Craik-Cornsweet-O'Brien Effect

The Craik-O'Brien-Cornsweet effect (COCE) involves two adjacent figures that are identical in luminance profile (i.e., in distributions of absolute measurements of reflected light) but differ in brightness (i.e., in the subjective perception of lightness and darkness). There are several ways of inducing this effect. One way (figure 11.1) is for the figures to be of a constant level of luminance everywhere except very close to their border, where there is a cusp (a slight increase in luminance on one side of the border and a slight decrease on the other). A second way (figure 11.2) is to have a small steady increase in luminance in each figure from side to side, so that there is a difference in luminance at the border between the figures (Craik 1940; O'Brien 1958; Cornsweet 1970). The resulting percept is one of two figures of different subjective brightness, each of which appears to be of constant brightness internally. The percept is, indeed, much the same as what would be produced by setting two figures of different luminance levels side by side so that the luminance profile would be step-shaped.

Such illusions violate our extrapolations from the Weber-Fechner laws in that areas with identical luminance profiles are sometimes perceived as being of different brightness. In lay terms, the two regions are identical in terms of the objective property of luminance profile, but one looks darker than the other. The difference in brightness between rectangles depends on the difference in luminance at the borders. This is demonstrated by occluding the border, which causes the difference in brightness to disappear. Removing the occlusion allows the difference to reappear, though only after a brief interval. This effect is sensitive to a number of factors, including viewing distance (Békésy 1972), average luminance level (Heggelund 1976), luminance contrast and extent of flanking gradients (Dooley 1977; Isono 1979; Growney 1986), and gradient polarity (Hamada 1982, 1985).

The COCE presents problems which it is the business of theoretical work in vision to solve. The problem, in this case, is a mismatch between the stimulus and the percept: local differences in brightness in the percept do not correspond to differences in luminance in the stimulus. Thus this type of effect provides a kind of black-box description of a function from a stimulus (in terms of a pattern of luminance that stimulates the retina) to

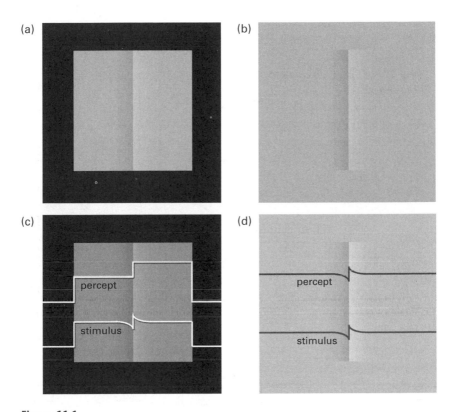

Figure 11.1
The Craik-O'Brien-Cornsweet Effect (COCE). (a) The figure presented against a contrasting background. The two areas are of equal luminance except for a cusp at the
border, but appear as two figures of internally even but contrasting brightness. (b)
The effect does not occur when the contrasting surround is removed. The objective
luminance profile of the stimulus and the subjective brightness profile of the percept
are shown for the illusory figures against a dark surround (c) and for the non-illusory
image without a dark surround (d). (Images based on slide 16 on page 8 of Grossberg
and Mingolla 2005. Adapted with authors' permission.)

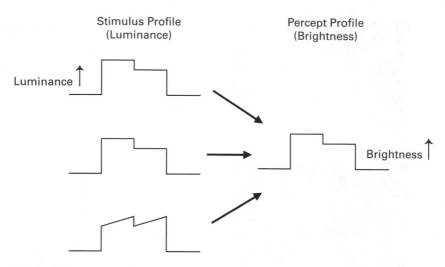

Figure 11.2.
Variations on the COCE. A step-shaped percept profile (right) can be induced by several distinct luminance patterns, including step-shaped, cusped, and ramp-shaped (left).

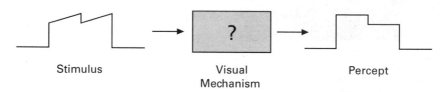

Figure 11.3
Psychophysics places constraints on visual theory by requiring that the model produced be able to account for the transformation from stimulus profile to percept profile.

a percept (in terms of an image that has contrasts in perceived brightness) (figure 11.3). Any viable model of the human visual system should be constrained by such data, in the sense that its output should correspond to the percept when its input corresponds to the stimulus.

11.1.2 Subjective Contour Figures
A second class of visual effects that seem to violate the predictions of the Weber-Fechner laws consists of subjective contour figures, such as the Kanizsa square (figure 11.4) (Kanizsa 1979). When viewing this figure, normal subjects report seeing a square that is slightly brighter than the

Figure 11.4
The Kanizsa square, a subjective contour figure.

background. The subject thus "perceives" boundaries corresponding to the sides of a square—boundaries that are not "really there," in the sense that there is no discontinuity in luminance to be found at the portions of the stimulus where boundaries are perceived. Normal perceivers also perceive the interior of the square as slightly brighter than the background, though in fact there is no difference in luminance between interior and background regions. Here the visual system is somehow "filling in" boundaries that are not there to be seen and producing an interpretation of the brightness of the interior region of the figure it supposes to be there. In lay terms, we "see a figure that isn't there" and see it as "brighter than it should be."

Here, again, there is a well-defined difference between the phenomenology of the percept and the gross physical properties of the stimulus. The constraint such an effect places on theoretical work in vision is, again, that a successful model of the visual system ought to reproduce the psychophysical phenomena observed in human subjects. A model whose output represents the interior of the "square" and the background as of the same brightness, or a model that does not represent boundaries along the "sides" of the "square" or does not pick out a square at all, is not an adequate explanation of the psychophysical data, because the output of the model does not correspond to the percept.

11.2   Illusions, Percepts, and Interpretations

Both the COCE and subjective contour figures reveal features of the visual system that cannot be understood simply in terms of mathematical functions from the intensity of the stimulus to the intensity of the percept. One way of summarizing what they reveal would be to say that they show that "seeing" is not simply a matter of faithfully reproducing the array of visible light present in the stimulus. And in particular, they seem to suggest that how the visual system perceives the brightness of a stimulus, or of portions of a stimulus, depends on whether the visual system interprets it as involving shapes and boundaries. In the COCE, the visual system detects real boundaries in luminance between the two squares and proceeds (inaccurately) to interpret each of the squares as being of an even internal brightness, one darker than the other. The visual system interprets the Kanizsa figure as a square and fills in boundaries that are not present in the stimulus (the sides of the square), even registering an illusory difference in brightness between the interior of the illusory square and its "background."

This is puzzling, because it suggests that the "detection" of shapes or boundaries (real or illusory) can also affect subjective brightness. It is puzzling because any interpretation of the stimulus as involving shapes or boundaries must be a result of processing that takes place after more accurate information about luminance is already present in the visual system. Unless the system is somehow prescient, this means that we cannot be dealing with simple feedforward processing from an array of representations of brightness to the extraction of cues about boundaries and shapes. Indeed, it seems as though the brain is editing its representation of the intensities of various portions of the stimulus on the basis of its imposition of interpretations of boundary and shape.

There is no reason to suppose that anything miraculous is going on here. The problem, rather, is one of finding an appropriate type of model to explain the psychophysical data in question: a model that can allow interpretations about boundaries, shapes, and figures to have an effect on experienced brightness in the right range of cases despite the presence of more accurate information about objective luminance distributions already encoded in early visual processing. And in particular, we seem to need a model that allows representations of information about luminance distributions to be inputs to the systems that detect contours and shapes while also allowing systems that detect contours and shapes to influence the representation of information about luminance distributions in the form of brightness contours.

11.3   A Brief Detour: Isomorphist and Non-Isomorphist Approaches to Modeling

Before we examine a set of models that address the above-mentioned visual illusions, a methodological excursion is in order. In the preceding section

I made an implicit methodological claim to the effect that modeling is problematic or at least incomplete until the model produces output curves that are isomorphic to those of the percept profiles identified through outer psychophysics. This was in fact a point of debate among discussants of the COCE in the 1970s and the 1980s. Some researchers (Cornsweet 1970; Ratliff 1978; Ratliff and Sirovich 1978; Campbell 1978) pointed to the firing profiles of cortical cells in a center-surround architecture that detect differences in luminance. These are often construed as "boundary detectors." Their firing patterns are characterized by a cusp. (See figure 11.7 below.) These models of boundary processing reproduce the cusp-shaped neural responses known to occur in relatively early visual processing. Moreover, similar cusp-shaped responses are produced by the range of stimuli that are perceived as having the step-shaped profile characteristic of the COCE. So clearly the models of Cornsweet, Campbell, Ratliff, and Sirovich are detecting, in *some* fashion, *some* feature that is common to the relevant stimuli. But their models do *not* produce the step-shaped profile of the percept. (One does not *see* a cusp in the COCE figures; one perceives the stimulus as two adjacent squares of different internal brightness.) Cornsweet, Campbell, Ratliff, and Sirovich suggested that the effect is explained by the fact that luminance profiles of steps and cusps have similar abstract properties. Todorovic (1987, p. 547) summarizes:

In terms of Fourier analysis, the two distributions have similar high frequency content but different low frequency components. However, the visual system is relatively insensitive to low-spatial-frequency stimulation (Campbell and Robson 1968). According to Cornsweet (1970), Campbell et al. (1978), Ratliff (1978), and Ratliff and Sirovich (1978), these facts amount to an explanation of the COCE. The cusp-shaped and step-shaped distributions looks similar because their effects are similar: the visual system suppresses the aspects of these stimuli that differ (shallow spatial variation of luminance), and transmits more faithfully the attribute they have in common (abrupt change).

An accompanying diagram identifies this shared feature with neural activity. (See figure 11.5.)

Todorovic goes on to criticize the theories cited on the ground that they do not account for the appearances:

However, it can be argued that this explanation is incomplete, since it does not seem to account for the structure of the *appearance* of the stimulus. The problem is that there is a mismatch between the shape of the brightness profile of the percept and its presumed neural counterpart (see Arend 1973; Cohen and Grossberg 1984; Cornsweet 1970; Davidson and Whiteside 1971). The luminance cusp distribution [figure 11.1b] gives rise to a percept that has the shape of a step [figure 11.1f]. However, the presumed physiological foundation of the percept, according to the

Craik-O'Brien-Cornsweet Effect
Isomorphist and Non-Isomorphic Theories

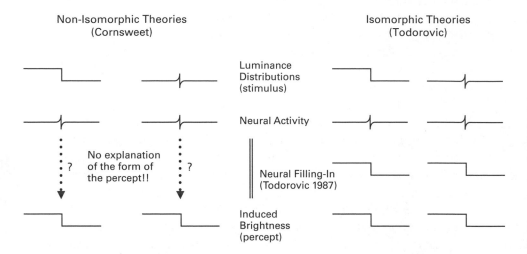

Figure 11.5

Isomorphist and non-isomorphist theories. Non-isomorphist models (left) do not have an internal stage whose activity matches (is isomorphic to) the profile of the percept. Isomorphist theorists (right) take the production of an isomorphic profile as a constraint on the success of the model. (Adapted from figure 1 on page 546 of Todorovic 1987.)

preceding analysis, has a quite different profile [figure 11.1d], one that is more similar to the cusp-shaped profile of the underlying luminance distribution. (ibid., p. 547, emphasis added)

What is really at issue here between Todorovic and his opponents? One possibility is that they disagree about the nature of the phenomenological data. Todorovic sees the outer phenomenological data, as I do, as ending in phenomenological percepts; his opponents see it as indicating capacities to discriminate boundaries. On the latter view, there may be no need for the model to reproduce something isomorphic to the percept profile, as outer psychophysics is claimed to be only in the business of accounting for detection and discrimination capacities, and this is accomplished by the fact that the models show cusp-shaped behavior in the same range of cases as their neural correlates. But even if one allows that there is such a project of accounting for data about boundary detection, those are not *all* the relevant outer psychophysical data. For example, there is the fact that subjects *see* one square as being brighter than the other, and this difference is not captured by the non-isomorphist models. The issue is even clearer with subjective contour figures: the non-isomorphist models account neither for the fact that subjects perceive an illusory figure nor for the fact that the figure is perceived as being brighter than its surround.

A second possibility would be that non-isomorphists might implicitly be taking a line similar to that which Laming took on some aspects of the outer psychophysics of stimulus intensity. (See the preceding chapter.) Laming suggested that the data might include artifacts of the experimental setup, as the subjects were not merely registering a fact about visual intensity but were making judgments about it, and the form of the subjective reports might be derivative, not from anything truly visual, but from the mechanism involved in sampling the truly visual representations and turning them into judgments. Similarly, one might think that the reports given by subjects exposed to the COCE or to subjective contour figures involve not only a report about intensities but also a judgment that involves the application of concepts such as 'square'. If one follows Kant in distinguishing the faculty for sensations from the faculty for applying concepts and judgments, Laming's concern might seem even more appropriate in this instance than in his criticisms of Stevens and Fechner.

Part of this interpretation is correct, and part of it is not. It is both correct and important to note that subjective contour figures (and arguably the COCE) involve an element of perceptual *intentionality* (in the technical philosophical sense of that term, in which it indicates the class of thoughts that are *about* something, in contrast with the sense of 'intentional' that means "purposeful"). They involve seeing the percept *as* a figure; this goes beyond what is present in the psychophysics of *intensity*, and *seeing-as* is intentional in nature. Moreover, it also bears a feature of intentionality emphasized by Brentano (1874) and Chisholm (1957): there is an "intentional object" (the percept of a square) *to which nothing objective need correspond.* (And indeed in this case there is no square that corresponds to the percept.) But this intentional interpretation of the stimulus *as* a figure of a certain kind *is* both visual and phenomenological. There is something it is like to see a square that appears slightly brighter than its background, and it is different from what it is like to see a triangle, or to see a square that is darker than its background. Moreover, the squareness is something that is *seen* and not merely abstractly *judged*. And indeed, if we follow Descartes in holding that judgment requires assent, the illusion does *not* require judgment: a person who understands that the figure is illusory can experience the illusion vividly and still deny that there is any square *really there.* The figure is *presented* as a square brighter than its background, but it is in our power to withhold our assent to any proposition about what is really true of the stimulus. (Indeed, were we unable to do so, we would be incapable of recognizing such effects as illusory.) The unavoidable conclusion would seem to be that *perception itself* involves at least a primitive form of intentionality, prior to any question of *judgment*. (This might be accommodated philosophically by following Brentano and Husserl in positing a base intentional modality of *presentation* of an object-seen-as-such-and-such.)

It would thus be *correct* to infer that the reports involved in these illusory perceptions involve the operation of mechanisms over and above those involved in differential sensitivity to light. But it would be *erroneous* to draw the further conclusion that they are non-perceptual or that they are not among the outer psychophysical data that are in need of explanation. Rather, we must reconceive perception itself as involving figure-constituting mechanisms that (a) have a phenomenology of their own and (b) affect the perceived phenomenological brightness of the illusory figures in question.

11.4   The Grossberg Group's Models

The research group at Boston University headed by Stephen Grossberg, one of the principal luminaries in neural network modeling of perception, has produced a family of models that offer explanations of a wide variety of psychophysical data, including the COCE and subjective contour illusions—models that meet the constraints of the isomorphist methodology. These models treat object perception as involving the recursive interaction of several cortical systems attuned to boundaries, to objects, and to visual features such as brightness and color. These systems, moreover, do not all stand in a linear feedforward relation to one another, as the cone and ganglion systems do; some operate through processes of mutual feedback that Grossberg describes as "adaptive resonance." Grossberg's Adaptive Resonance Theory (ART) is a model of the sort sometimes called *nonlinear dynamic* models. They are "nonlinear" not only in the simple sense of employing nonlinear functions (that is, ones involving second-order and higher-order equations) but also in the sense of involving cyclical causal processes: the state of each system at time t affects the state of the other system(s) at $t + \delta$, and the relevant dynamical equations describe a process through which the systems are brought into equilibrium with one another. We can see this more clearly by examining some details of the models.

11.4.1   The Macrocircuit Models

It is easiest to begin by looking at the schematic diagrams of the macro-circuits of the Grossberg models. I shall begin with the simplest of these, involving only monocular vision and preattentive perception, and then extend it to more complicated models.

In this first macrocircuit model (figure 11.6), monocular preprocessed signals (MP) are sent to two separate systems, identified as the Boundary Contour System (BCS) and the Feature Contour System (FCS). It is tempting to introduce these by way of a comparison with the home architectural rendering programs I have used. These tend to have multiple ways of viewing data. For example, one view shows only the borders of objects, and hence one sees a wall, for example, as a quadrilateral with nothing filling in the space between the lines, and a room as a kind of wire-frame cube. One can then change to a view that fills in the surfaces—the color of the walls, the wood-grain texture of the floors, and so on. The first view displays the boundaries that define surfaces and objects in the rendering; the latter fills in "features" such as brightness, color, and texture. In the Grossberg models, the BCS operates much as the wire-frame view of the rendering program does: it represents the (supposed) boundaries of objects. The "features" of brightness, color, and spatial pattern are represented in a separate module, the FCS. Grossberg and his associates have thus hypothesized that visual information initially acquired through the retinas is processed in two parallel streams, one representing boundaries without features and the other representing features without boundaries. It is only through the cooperation of these systems that one is able to experience percepts, which have both boundaries and features.

This simple circuit diagram involves two additional components. At the top of the diagram is an Object Recognition System (ORS). This box represents a system that can store "templates" of object types, including learned templates. The two-way arrows between it and the BCS indicate a feedback cycle: boundaries can activate the representation of a type of object—say, a square—through feedforward connections. But object templates also place constraints on what boundary contours are compatible with them—perhaps a rediscovery of what Kant called *schematism*. The interpretation of a percept *as* a percept *of* a particular type of object can influence how the object is perceived through feedback connections from the ORS to the BCS, either modifying the boundary contour representation or else (if there is a significant mismatch) inhibiting the object template in question so that the system can search for another object template that is a better match.

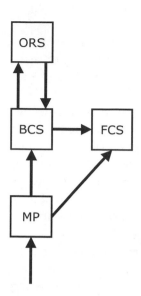

Figure 11.6

"A macrocircuit of processing stages: Monocular preprocessed signals (MP) are sent independently to both the Boundary Contour System (BCS) and the Feature Contour System (FCS). The BCS preattentively generates coherent boundary structures from these MP signals. These structures send outputs to both the FCS and the Object Recognition System (ORS). The ORS, in turn, rapidly sends top-down learned template signals to the BCS. These template signals can modify the preattentively completed boundary structures using learned information. The BCS passes these modifications along to the FCS. The signals from the BCS organize the FCS into perceptual regions wherein filling-in of visible brightnesses and colors can occur. This filling-in process is activated by signals from the MP stage." Source of figure and legend: Grossberg and Mingolla 1985, p. 143. A similar diagram in Grossberg 1987b also has feedforward and feedback connections between FCS and ORS. Grossberg 1987c includes a model for binocular processing.

The "preprocessing" in the lowest node indicates that what is passed along to both systems is not a raw array of topographically arranged pixel-like representations of intensities, but transformations of this raw retinal input through simple circuits such as the contrast-sensitive center-surround cells described briefly in the preceding chapter. These levels, further adumbrated in Grossberg 1988, are illustrated here in figure 11.7.

Level 5 in figure 11.7 corresponds to the BCS; level 6 corresponds to the FCS. Level 1 represents an array of brightness inputs (or chromatic inputs, depending on whether we are modeling a brightness-sensitive pathway or one fed by one of the color-opponency pathways). These are sampled by center-surround cells at level 2, which detect contrasts between the intensity at their receptive center and the average at their periphery. They are sensitive to contrasts, but they are not directionally sensitive. These, in turn, are sampled by cells in level 3, which extract information about contrast along particular orientations (for ease of discussion, we can use orientations from a clock face—12 o'clock, 1 o'clock, and so on) and across various distances. Cells at level 3 have elongated receptive fields in level 2 rather than the circular receptive fields characteristic of the projections of level 1 to level 2, allowing them to be sensitive to directional contrast information.

An important advance of the Grossberg models of the 1980s was that they invoked directionally sensitive contrast detectors operating on a variety of spatial scales. Two cells at level 3, cell L3a and cell L3b, might have the same orientation, and the center of their receptive field might be the same area of L2, but L3a might sample over a longer portion of that axis than L3b. L3 cells sampling the same area of L2 with different orientations are in competition with one another. L3 cells of the same position and orientation but different spatial scales are in a cooperative relationship: if L3a is firing, indicating an oriented contrast over a distance $d + \delta$, it makes it more likely that L3b, sensitive to contrast in subportion d in the same orientation, will also fire, and vice versa. As a result, the detection of oriented contrasts is inclined to cause boundaries to fill in and to propagate outward. (See figures 11.8–11.10.)

11.4.2 Veridical Perception with Noisy Information—An Evolutionary/ Adaptive Perspective

Why would such properties be adaptive? Why would the visual system be primed to fill in boundaries where there are gaps in the input? One answer is supplied by considerations of the physiology of the eye. In order to reach the rod cells and the cone cells, light must pass through the bodies of the

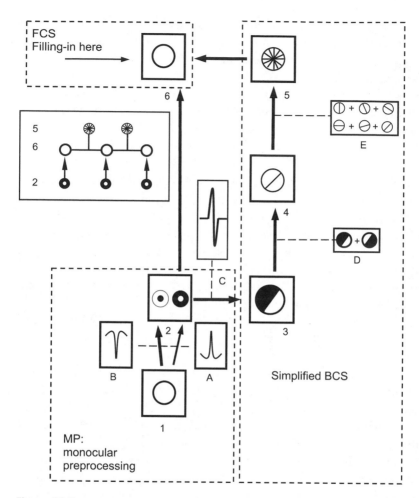

Figure 11.7

"Overview of the model. The thick-bordered rectangles numbered from 1 to 6 correspond to the levels of the system. The symbols inside the rectangles are graphical mnemonics for the types of computational units residing at the corresponding model level. The arrows depict the interconnections between the levels. The thin-bordered rectangles coded by letters A through E represent the type of processing between pairs of levels. Inset F illustrates how the activity at Level 6 is modulated by outputs from Level 2 and Level 5." Source of figure and legend: Grossberg and Todorovic 1988, figure 2.

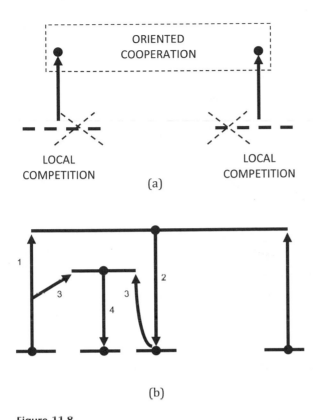

Figure 11.8

"Boundary completion. (a) Local competition occurs between different orientations at each spatial location. A cooperative boundary completion process can be activated by pairs of aligned orientations that survive their local competitions. (b) The pair of Pathways 1 activate the positive boundary completion feedback along Pathway 2. The pathways such as 3 activate positive feedback along pathways such as 4. Rapid completion of a sharp boundary between Pathways 1 can hereby be generated." Source of figure and legend: Grossberg and Mingolla 1985, p. 187, figure 11.

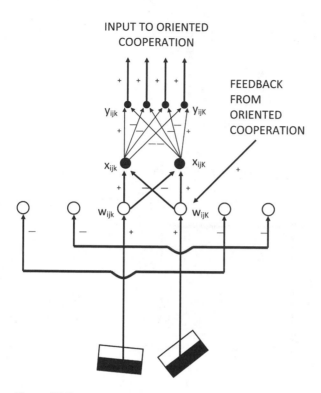

Figure 11.9
"Orientationally tuned competitive interactions. (A shunting on-center off-surround interaction within each orientation and between different positions is followed by a push-pull dipole competition between orientations and within each position. The different orientations also compete to normalize the total activity within each position before eliciting output signals to the cooperative boundary completion process that exists between positions whose orientations are approximately labeled.)" Source of figure and legend: Grossberg and Mingolla 1985, p. 195, figure 18.

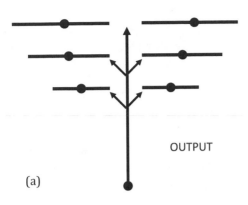

OUTPUT

(a)

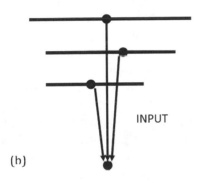

INPUT

(b)

Figure 11.10
"Interactions between an oriented line element and its boundary completion process. (a) Output from a single oriented competitive element subliminally excites several cooperative processes of like orientation but variable spatial scale. (b) Several cooperative processes of variable spatial scale can simultaneously excite a single oriented competitive element of like orientation." Source of figure and legend: Grossberg and Mingolla 1985b, p. 188, figure 12.

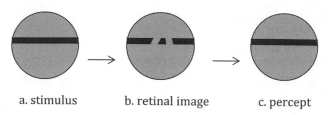

a. stimulus   b. retinal image   c. percept

Figure 11.11
Visual filling in. A solid line is presented as a stimulus (a). Owing to occlusions in the visual field, perhaps caused by veins in the eye, the retinal image (b) is not solid but broken. However, the visual system "fills" the gaps to generate a continuous percept (c).

ganglion and bipolar cells that lie closer to the surface of the eye, even though they are informationally downstream of the rods and the cones. In addition, there are veins in the eye that block light from reaching the rods and the cones, and each eye has a blind spot in which there are no rods or cones. The array of light that reaches the photoreceptors is thus noisy, and does not present an accurate projection of the array of light reflected from the distal stimulus. The array of light reaching the retina is interrupted by veins and cell bodies that block out parts of the visual array. If, for example, a boundary in the stimulus is intersected by one of these obstacles, the array of information reaching the photoreceptors will have gaps in its information (figure 11.11).

Experimental results make it very clear that we do not perceive the visible world as having such gaps or occlusions. The visual system seems to "fill in" the missing regions. If there is a line crossing the blind spot, one does not perceive an interrupted line, but an unbroken one. This is an adaptive feature of the visual system, as it prevents illusions that would occur as a result of occlusions of optical information before it reaches the photoreceptors. The cooperative interaction of oriented contrast detectors of various spatial scales allows the visual system to compensate for these gaps by filling in what is, in normal cases, missing information. But this architecture also opens the door to another type of illusion, caused by the filling in of (mis)information in abnormal cases where there really is no occlusion of real stimuli. This is arguably what happens in the filling in of illusory boundaries in subjective contour figures. Real oriented contrasts at the corners are detected (figure 11.12). But the situation at stage b is much like that of gappy information in perception of a real continuous boundary. The processes that fill in the

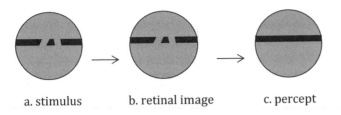

a. stimulus   b. retinal image   c. percept

Figure 11.12
Illusory filling in. A stimulus (a) presents an interrupted line, producing an interrupted retinal image (b). This approximates the retinal image in figure 11.11, produced by occlusions within the eye. The same filling-in mechanisms produce an unbroken percept (c), but in this case the percept is illusory.

(a)   (b)

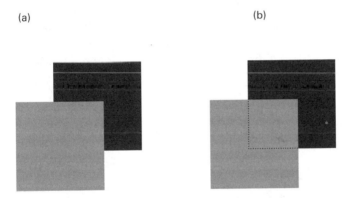

Figure 11.13
Occlusion and filling in. In (a), the square on the right is partially included by the square on the left. However, the brain fills in the occluded boundaries, as shown in (b).

missing bits of a boundary go into play and indicate a continuous boundary where in fact there is none.

The underpinnings of such a process are also adaptive in another context. Often parts of an object are occluded, not by parts of the eye itself, but by other distal objects (figure 11.13). In many such cases, we "see" the completion of the occluded figure—that is, we somehow represent the invisible boundaries even though there is no contrast information about them because they are occluded. Even in two-dimensional representations of such cases, such as figure 11.13, we are inclined to see depth in the scene, in that we construe it as two objects, one laid over the other and thus occluding a portion of it. The ability to complete the unseen boundaries of an object is absolutely essential if we are to represent partially occluded objects in a three-dimensional visual environment. For example, in the case of a subjective contour figure (figure 11.4) we "see" the illusory square as occluding portions of circles at the four corners, even though, on the paper of the page, there is really only one layer, and there is no hidden layer containing complete circles overlaid with a square.

11.5   Filling in the Features

Grossberg's models suggest that the FCS tends to "fill in" features through a process of *diffusive spreading* between nearby cells (figure 11.14). The hypothesis explored in these models is that there is a level of cells that form of "syncticum," or region at which activity of one cell can rapidly propagate to other nearby cells. Feature representations thus tend to spread. What constrains the extent of their spreading is the boundaries supplied by the BCS. The FCS thus requires two inputs: one containing feature information from preprocessed signals and one from the BCS "telling" it where to stop filling in a particular feature. Cells in the FCS

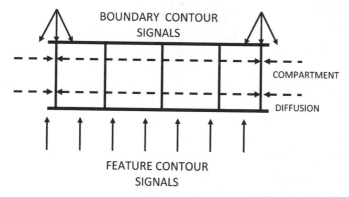

Figure 11.14
"Monocular brightness and color stage domain (MBC). (Monocular feature contour signals activate cell compartments that permit rapid lateral diffusion of activity, or potential, across their compartment boundaries, except at those compartment boundaries that receive boundary contour signals from the BCS stage. Consequently the feature contour signals are smoothed except at boundaries that are completed within the BCS stage.)" Source of figure and legend: Grossberg and Mingolla 1985b, p. 179, figure 3.

spread feature information until they are "told where to stop" by inputs from the BCS. Boundaries thus present barriers to feature diffusion. (See figure 11.8.)

Boundaries, by contrast, also "fill in," but by extending inward. In the Kanizsa square, for example, there are "real" boundaries (i.e., ones marked by real contrasts in luminance) at the corners of the squares that are registered by oriented contrast detectors. There are not "real" boundaries between these. But under the right conditions, the BCS "completes" these, registering boundaries where none are marked by contrasts in luminance. Grossberg describes such boundaries as being, *in themselves*, "invisible"— i.e., not marked by a perception of contrast. (Consider, for example, the boundaries that are assumed to be present in what appears to be an occluded object.) What happens in the Kanizsa square is that these (illusory) boundaries then mark limits for the diffusive spreading of a feature of brightness. The interior is seeded with information so that the interior is brighter as a result of the real contrasts in luminance at the corners. In the right conditions, this representation of differential brightness propagates throughout the region circumscribed by the (illusory) boundaries, so the figure is seen as having a greater brightness than its entire surround, including the parts where there are no "real" boundaries and no difference in luminance. This process is reproduced by computer models. (See, for example, Grossberg and Mingolla 1985.)

11.6   More Complicated Models

The models thus far presented represent work done in the 1980s. Since then, descendents of these models have been tooled to explain a larger number of psychophysical phenomena (increasing the explanatory and predictive power of the models) and have been integrated with the ever-increasing information available about the nervous system (helping to verify the neural realism of the models).

The ART (Adaptive Resonance Theory) and ARTMAP families of models (figure 11.15) provide explanations of the pattern matching thought to take place through interactions of the Object Recognition system with representations of features and contours (Carpenter et al. 1992). ART-EMAP (Carpenter and Ross 1995) expands on ART by adding models of systems where evidence accumulates in medium-term memory, adds an unsupervised learning process, and also accounts for ambiguous figure perception (figure 11.16). FACADE (Grossberg 1994) (see figures 11.17 and 11.18)

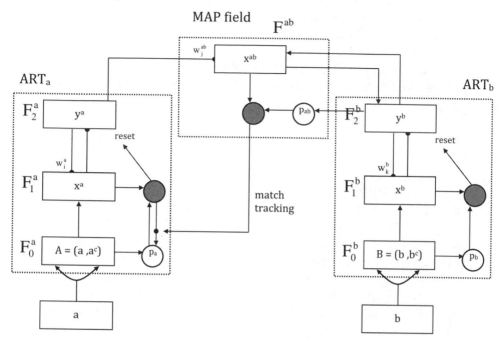

Figure 11.15

"Fuzzy ARTMAP architecture. The ART_a complement coding pre-processor trans-
forms the vector a into the vector A = (a,a^c) at the ART_a field F_1^a. Similarly, in the
supervised mode, the input to the ART_b field F_1^b is the vector (b,b^c). When a prediction by ART_a is disconfirmed at ART_b, inhibition of the map field F^{ab} induces the
match tracking process. Match tracking raises the ART_a vigilance (ρ_a) to just above
the F_1^a-to-F_0^a match ratio $|x_a|/|A|$. This triggers an ART_a search, which leads to activa-
tion of either an ART_a category that correctly predicts b or to a previously uncom-
mitted ART_a category node." Source of figure and legend: Carpenter and Ross 1995,
p. 805, figure 1.

accounts for depth-perception data, such as perception of occluded objects,
and VIEWNET (Bradsky and Grossberg 1995) provides a model of recognition of three-dimensional objects from multiple two-dimensional views.
(See figures 11.19–11.21.) These models continue the basic strategy of positing individual modules that represent different features of a scene, such as
forms and features of occluding and occluded objects, which are linked by
complex mechanisms that play roles both in integrating these separate
representations through resonance and refining them through feedback.

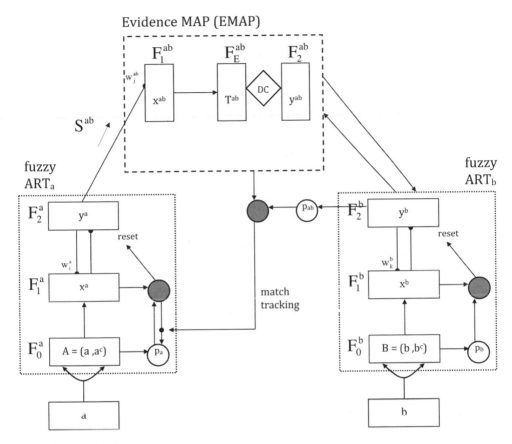

Figure 11.16
"ART-EMAP architecture. The ARTMAP field F^{ab} is replaced with a multi-field EMAP module. During testing, a distributed F_2^a output pattern y^a, resulting from partial contrast enhancement of $F_1^a \rightarrow F_2^a$ input T^a, is filtered through EMAP weights $w_{jk}^{a\,b}$ to determine the F_1^{ab} activity x^{ab}. If a predictive decision criterion is not met, additional input can be sought, until the decision criterion is met at F_2^{ab}." Source of figure and legend: Carpenter and Ross 1995, p. 809, figure 3.

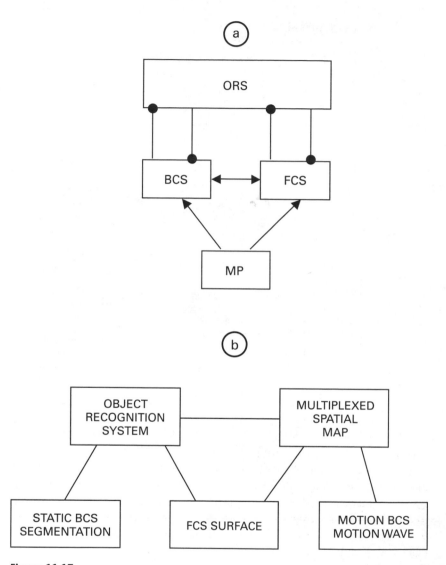

Figure 11.17
"Iterations of boundary perception macrocircuit to include motion and depth."
Source of figure and legend: Grossberg 1994, figure 7.

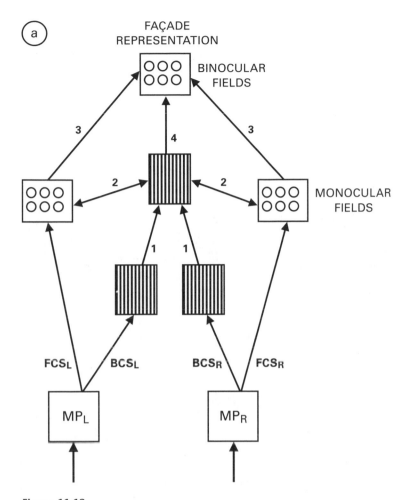

FAÇADE
REPRESENTATION

Figure 11.18

"(a) Macrocircuit of monocular and binocular interactions of the boundary contour system (BCS) and the feature contour system (FCS). Left eye and right eye monocular preprocessing stages (MP_L and MP_R) send parallel pathways to the BCS (boxes with vertical lines, designating oriented responses) and the FCS (boxes with three pairs of circles, designating opponent colors). The monocular signals BCS_L and BCS_R activate simple cells which, in turn, activate bottom-up pathways, labeled 1, to generate a binocular boundary segmentation using complex, hypercomplex, and bipole cell interactions. The binocular segmentation generates output signals to the monocular filling-in domains, or FIDOs, of the FCS via pathways labeled 2. This interaction selects binocularly consistent FCS signals, and suppresses the binocularly inconsistent FCS signals. Reciprocal FCS-BCS interactions enhance coherent boundaries and suppress boundaries corresponding to further surfaces. The surviving FCS signals activate the binocular FIDOs via pathway 3, where they interact with an augmented BCS segmentation to fill-in a multiple-scale surface representation of Form-And-Color-And-Depth, or FACADE. Processing stages MP_L and MP_R are compared with LGN data; the simple-complex cell interaction with V1 data; the hypercomplex-bipole interaction with V2 and (possibly) V4 data, notably about

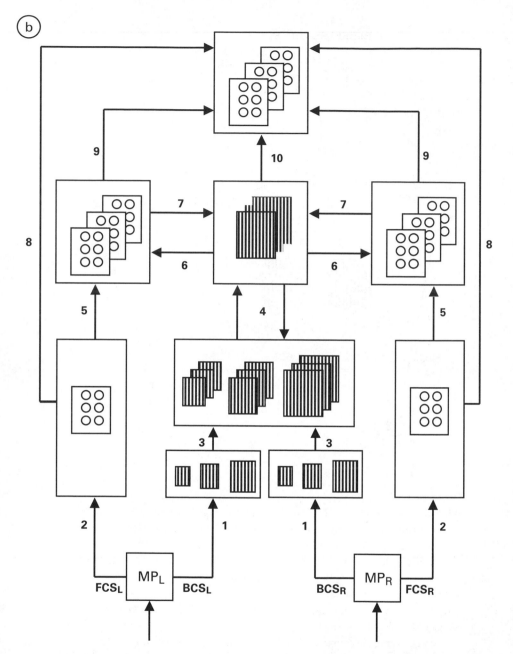

Figure 11.18

(continued)

interstripes; the monocular FCS interaction with the blob and thin stripe data; and the FACADE representation with V4 data. Additional interactions from FCS to BCS along pathways labeled 2, 3, and 4, and among FCS and BCS copies, are described in the text. (b) A finer representation of the FACADE interactions: Output signals from MPL and MPR activate BCS simple cells and multiple receptive-field sizes via pathways 1. MPL and MPR outputs are also transformed into opponent FCS signals

Figure 11.18
(continued)

via pathways 2. Pathways 3 generate multiple cell pools that are sensitive to multiple disparities and scales. BB intrascales are at work among the resultant cells, as are the first and second competitive stages. Pathways 4 combine the multiple scales that correspond to the same depth range into a single BCS copy via BB interscales. Multiple copies that correspond to different (but possibly overlapping) depth ranges exist. Pathways 5 are the monocular FF intercopies. Pathways 6 are the BF intracopies. Pathways 7 are the FB intercopies. Pathways 8 are the excitatory binocular FF intercopies. Pathways 9 are the inhibitory binocular FF intercopies. Pathways 10 are the BF intercopies." Source of figure and legend: Grossberg 1994, pp. 64, 65, figure 11.

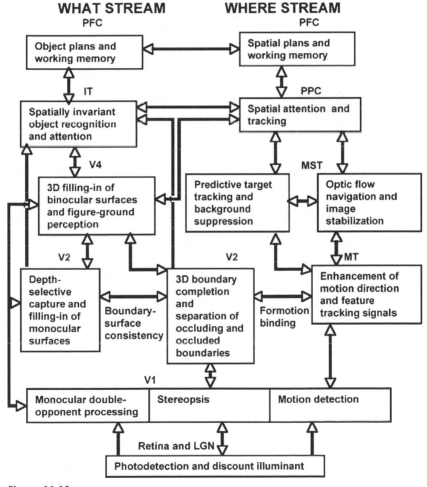

Figure 11.19

"Some visual processes and their anatomical substates that are being modeled as part of a unified vision system. LGN = Lateral Geniculate Nucleus; V1 = striate visual cortex; V2, V4, MT, MST = prestriate visual cortex; IT = inferotemporal cortex; PPC = posterior parietal cortex; PFC = prefrontal cortex." Source of figure and legend: Grossberg and Cisek 2005, p. 4, figure 1.

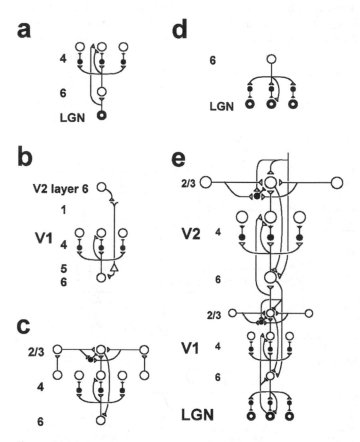

Figure 11.20

"How known cortical connections join the layer 6 → 4 and layer 2/3 circuits to form
an entire V1/V2 laminar model. Inhibitory interneurons are shown filled-in black.
(a) The LGN provides bottom-up activation to layer 4 via two routes. First, it makes
a strong connection directly into layer 4. Second, LGN axons send collaterals into
layer 6, and thereby also activate layer 4 via the 6 → 4 on-center off-surround path.
The combined effect of the bottom-up LGN pathways is to stimulate layer 4 via an
on-center off-surround, which provides divisive contrast normalization (Grossberg
1973, 1980; Heeger 1992) of layer 4 cell responses. (b) Folded feedback carries attentional signals from higher cortex into layer 4 of V1, via the modulatory 6 → 4 path.
Corticocortical feedback axons tend preferentially to originate in layer 6 of the
higher area and to terminate in layer 1 of the lower cortex (Salin and Bullier 1995,
p.110), where they can excite the apical dendrites of layer 5 pyramidal cells whose
axons send collaterals into layer 6. The triangle in the figure represents such a layer
5 pyramidal cell. Several other routes through which feedback can pass into V1 layer
6 exist (see Raizada and Grossberg 2001 for a review). Having arrived in layer 6, the

Figure 11.20

(continued)

feedback is then "folded" back up into the feedforward stream by passing through the 6 → 4 on-center off-surround path (Bullier et al. 1996). (c) Connecting the 6 → 4 on-center off-surround to the layer 2/3 grouping circuit: like-oriented layer 4 simple cells with opposite contrast polarities compete (not shown) before generating half-wave rectified outputs that converge onto layer 2/3 complex cells in the column above them. Just like attentional signals from higher cortex, as shown in (b), groupings that form within layer 2/3 also send activation into the folded feedback path, to enhance their own positions in layer 4 beneath them via the 6 → 4 on-center, and to suppress input to other groupings via the 6 → 4 off-surround. There exist direct layer 2/3 → 6 connections in macaque V1, as well as indirect routes via layer 5. (d) Top-down corticogeniculate feedback from V1 layer 6 to LGN also has an on-center off-surround anatomy, similar to the 6 → 4 path. The on-center feedback selectively enhances LGN cells that are consistent with the activation that they cause (Sillito et al. 1994), and the off-surround contributes to length-sensitive (endstopped) responses that facilitate grouping perpendicular to line ends. (e) The entire V1/V2 circuit. V2 repeats the laminar pattern of V1 circuitry, but at a larger spatial scale. In particular, the horizontal layer 2/3 connections have a longer range in V2, allowing above-threshold perceptual groupings between more widely spaced inducing stimuli to form (Amir, Harel, and Malach 1993). V1 layer 2/3 projects up to V2 layers 6 and 4, just as LGN projects to layers 6 an 4 of V1. Higher cortical areas send feedback into V2 which ultimately reaches layer 6, just as V2 feedback acts on layer 6 of V1 (Sandell and Schiller 1982). Feedback paths from higher cortical areas straight into V1 (not shown) can complement and enhance feedback from V2 into V1. Top-down attention can also modulate layer 2/3 pyramidal cells directly by activating both the pyramidal cells and inhibitory interneurons in that layer. The inhibition tends to balance the excitation, leading to a modulatory effect. These top-down attentional pathways tend to synapse in layer 1, as shown in figure 11.2b. Their synapses on apical dendrites in layer 1 are not shown, for simplicity." Original source of figure and legend: Grossberg and Cisek 2005. Reprinted, with permission, from Raizada and Grossberg 2001.).

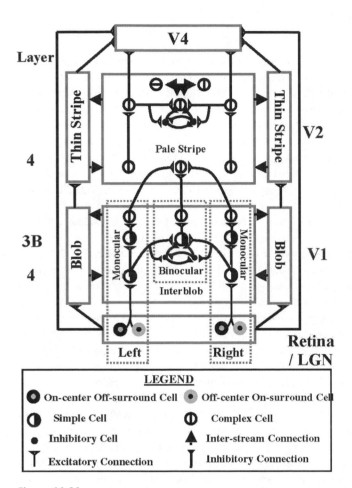

Figure 11.21

"Model circuit diagram. The full 3D LAMINART model consists of a boundary stream
that includes V1 interblobs, V2 pale stripes, and part of V4, and computes 3D perceptual groupings that are predicted to be amodal, or perceptually invisible, within
this stream; and a surface stream that includes V1 blobs, V2 thin stripes, and part
of V4, and computes 3D surfaces that are infused with visible color and lightness
in depth. These two streams both receive illuminant-discounted signals from Retina/
LGN cells, and interact with each other to overcome their complementary deficien-
cies to create consistent 3D boundary and surface percepts in cortical area V4. Also,
3D boundary and surface representations formed in the pale stripes and thin stripes
of cortical area V2, respectively, are amodally completed, and provide neural support
for the object recognition process in inferotemporal cortex. See Cao and Grossberg
2005 for additional discussion." Source of figure and legend: Grossberg and Cisek
2005, p. 23, figure 7.

During this same period, and through the first decade of the twenty-first century, the models came to be linked more closely with hypotheses about their neural realizations. Modules of the theory were localized anatomically, and the processing done by circuits given a physiological interpretation (figures 11.19–11.21). These last diagrams also incorporate an important addition to the earlier models: taking the laminar structure of the brain into account, as reflected by the name of the LAMINART model. Each of the anatomical regions of the brain, such as V1, comprises multiple layers of cells, arranged on top of one another in a laminar structure. There are processing circuits that connect cells in a single region and layer, between layers of a region, and between layers of different regions. Moreover, the circuits involved in processes identified at a functional level—the pathways for form, color, and motion, the what and where streams, or the boundary and feature systems—involve pathways passing through multiple anatomical regions, and through distinct layers of these regions. As a result, the "localization" of such functions is not simply a matter of correlating them with a single contiguous anatomical region. On the one hand, the localization is distributed across multiple anatomical regions; on the other hand, it involves only particular layers of the regions it utilizes.

Grosberg and Cisek (2007) deem the new features of this model to be deeply significant, and to explain the laminar structure of the cortex, as well as to confirm assumptions of earlier research:

A number of models have been proposed (Douglas et al. 1995; Stemmler et al. 1995; Li 1998; Somers et al. 1998; Yen and Finkel 1998) to simulate aspects of visual cortical dynamics, but these models have not articulated why cortex has a laminar architecture. Our own group's breakthrough on this problem (Grossberg et al. 1997; Grossberg 1999a) began with the suggestion that the laminar organization of visual cortex accomplishes at least three things: (1) the developmental and learning processes whereby the cortex shapes its circuits to match environmental constraints in a *stable* way through time; (2) the binding process whereby cortex groups distributed data into coherent object representations that remain sensitive to analog properties of the environment; and (3) the attentional process whereby cortex selectively processes important events.

These results further develop the proposal that even the earliest stages of visual cortex are not merely a bottom-up filtering device, as in the classical model of Hubel and Wiesel (1977). Instead, bottom-up filtering, horizontal grouping, and top-down attention are all joined together in laminar cortical circuits. Perceptual grouping, the process that binds spatially distributed and incomplete information into 3D object representations, starts at an early cortical stage; see figure 11.2c. These grouping interactions are often cited as the basis of "non-classical" receptive fields that are sensitive to the context in which individual features are found (von der Heydt et al. 1984; Peterhans and von der Heydt 1989; Knierim and van Essen 1992; Grosof et al. 1993; Kapadia et al. 1995; Sillito et al. 1995; Sheth et al. 1996; Bosking et al. 1997; Polat et al. 1998). Likewise, even early visual processing is modulated by system goals via top-down expectations and attention (Motter 1993; Sillito et al. 1994; Roelfsema et al. 1998; Watanabe et al. 1998; Somers et al. 1999). The model proposes how mechanisms governing (1) in the infant lead to properties (2) and (3) in the adult, and properties (2) and (3) interact together intimately as a result.

The laminar model proposes that there is no strict separation of pre-attentive data-driven bottom-up filtering and grouping, from attentive task-directed top-down processes. The model shows how these processes may come together at a shared circuit, or interface, that is called the *preattentive-attentive interface*, which exists between layers 6 and 4 (figures 11.2a–c, e). Significantly, by indicating how cortical mechanisms of stable development and learning impose key properties of adult visual information processing, the model begins to unify the fields of cortical development and adult vision. The model is called a LAMINART model (figure 2; Grossberg 1999a, Raizada and Grossberg 2003) because it clarifies how mechanisms of Adaptive Resonance Theory, or ART, which have previously been predicted to stabilize cortical development and learning of bottom-up adaptive filters and top-down attentive expectations (Grossberg 1980, 1999c; Carpenter and Grossberg 1993) can be joined together in laminar circuits to processes of perceptual grouping through long-range horizontal interactions (Grossberg and Mingolla 1985b). (Grossberg and Cisek 2007, pp. 4, 5)

The diagrams and prose descriptions employed thus far have glossed over a feature that is necessary to any attempt at modeling: the mathematical equations employed in computing interactions within each circuit. Such equations provide the models with formal exactitude, and are employed in computer simulations that are compared with both psychophysical data and data about the known behavior of cells (for example, the Hodgkin-Huxley equation) as constraints on the models' success. The models re-use a number of basic mechanisms of cellular and inter-cellular processing, which are incorporated into a somewhat larger number of functional modules, and a much larger number of architectures. Grossberg and Mingolla (2005, part 1, slide 6, used by permission of author) summarize it as follows:

A real *theory* can be had [from]

• **A small number of *mechanisms***

• short-term memory
• long-term memory

- habituation
- adaptive gain control—normalization
- local circuits with feedback—bottom up, top down,
- and lateral connections

- **A somewhat larger number of *functional modules***

- filters of various kinds
- center-surround networks
- gated dipoles—"nature's flip-flops"

- **A still larger number of *architectures***

- specialized combinations of **mechanisms** and **modules** for cognition, audition, **vision**, ...

11.7   Remarks on the Models

Several features of the Grossberg models immediately stand out from our examination of the early iterations:

1. The initial macrocircuit diagram included one explicit feedback relationship between the BCS and the OCS. This, in fact, explains an extremely important and robust set of data, originating from the work of Land (1974), who showed that psychophysical features of the percept often depend on whether it is interpreted as an object. This is quite provocative in two ways. First, it suggests that even sensory phenomenology is not totally independent of intentionality. Intentional states may, of course, have their own distinctive phenomenological dimension (cf. Horgan and Tienson 2002; Horst 1996); but it is quite telling that even qualitative phenomenology (such as that of brightness intensity) can be affected by intentional constitution of objects. Second, we now have a feature in our macrocircuit model that was absent in models we have considered in the preceding chapter: the presence of feedback as well as feedforward relationships. Indeed, feedback circuits have played an increasing and ubiquitous role in the more recent models. I will discuss the ways this complicates the nature of modeling later.
2. In the macrocircuit diagram, we see causal pathways that diverge and then reunite. The input to the system splits into multiple streams, going to the BCS and to the FCS. But the FCS also receives input from the BCS. (In some versions of the Grossberg models, there are also feedback connections between the FCS and the BCS or between the FCS and the ORS.) Again, this nonlinear network architecture has continued to play a role in subsequent models, and indeed the interactions between circuits have grown ever more complex.

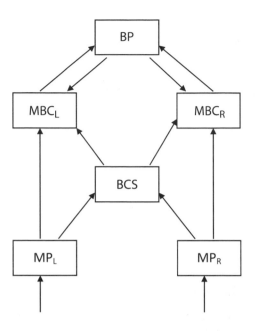

Summary of Neural Analogs

Abbreviation	Full name	Neural interpretation
MP$_L$	Left monocular preprocessing stage	Lateral geniculate nucleus
MP$_R$	Right monocular preprocessing stage	Lateral geniculate nucleus
BCS	Boundary contour synthesis stage	Interactions initiated by the hypercolumns in striate cortex—Area 17 (Hubel & Wiesel, 1977)
MBC$_L$	Left monocular brightness and color stage	Interactions initiated by the cytochrome oxydase staining blobs—Area 17; (Hendrickson, Hunt, & Wu, 1981; Horton & Hubel, 1981; Hubel & Livingstone, 1981; Livingstone & Hubel, 1981)
MBC$_R$	Right monocular brightness and color stage	Interactions initiated by the cytochrome oxydase staining blobs—Area 17
BP	Binocular percept stage	Area V4 of the prestriate cortex (Zeki, 1983a, 1983b)

Figure 11.22

In this diagram, BP seems to represent a single stage in which the entire percept comes together. The fact that this is given a neural interpretation evidences that the authors thought of this as a *place* where the percept is realized. Contrast with the figure reproduced in figure 11.6, in which there is no single stage where it "all comes together." Source: Grossberg and Mingolla 1985, pp. 179, 180.

3. The outer-psychophysical datum, the percept, is a result of processing through these multiple and interconnected pathways. In some versions of the Grossberg models, there is a "unit" that represents the percept in its entirety (figure 11.22). But in other versions the percept seems to be located in a dynamic relationship between multiple units—e.g., the systems that represent boundary contours, boundary features, and objects. It is, of course, an empirical question whether there is a physiological region of the brain in which these data streams come together and are integrated in a single representation of, say, a rectangle of a particular brightness. However, considerations of the binding problem (Minsky 1985; Dennett 1991; Crick 1993) have pointed to the real possibility that there is no single anatomical region corresponding to a Humean/Cartesian Theater in which object representations or scene representations take place.

11.7.1 Feedback

What is the difference between (exclusively) feedforward and feedback processes? At one level, the issue may be cast as one of the proper sort of model or representational system and of the types of mathematical machinery needed to model them. The kind of functional analysis appropriate to, say, simple logic circuits—that is, the kind of functional analysis philosophers have tended to apply in cognitive science—tends to model feedforward processes fairly adequately. For example, we saw in the preceding chapter that the information processed by the cone cells is fed forward to the ganglion cells. In such a case, each system can be modeled independently, with a rather innocuous idealization away from what comes before it and after it in the visual cascade. By contrast, with a feedback relationship between two systems, A and B, a model of either system on its own is incomplete in capturing its causal dynamics in an additional way. The function and the normal behavior of each system must be understood in terms of the unfolding dynamics of its relationship with the other. This requires an additional set of equations for the causal dynamics between systems. (In the Grossberg models, for example, it requires equations of dynamic equilibration.) As a result, a model of just one system, taken in isolation, is idealized, not only in bracketing features that are in some sense independent (because located at a different stage of the causal process), but also in bracketing feedback relations that are essential to its normal behavior. The equations describing the behavior of units *within* a module such as the BCS do, of course, pick out real invariants in its behavior. But these are not the only invariants governing its behavior. Its behavior is also governed by feedback processes by which it is related to other systems.

Thus, descriptions of the FCS or the BCS, taken in isolation, would significantly misdescribe and mispredict the real-world behavior of these systems, not because of the influence of separate and independent forces, but because they abstract away from the role of separate but interdependent processes.

It is useful to contrast the properties of this kind of dynamic system with the relation between dynamic and kinematic descriptions in basic physics. At one level, there is a distinct similarity. The behavior of a particle between times t and $t + \delta$ is a function of the summation of various forces acting on it at t—e.g., gravitational and electromagnetic forces. Likewise, the behavior of a cell in the BCS between t and $t + \delta$ is a function of the summation of inputs from earlier stages of processing and feedback from the ORS. But there is an important difference as well. Gravitational forces at t do not themselves affect electromagnetic forces at either t or $t + \delta$—the forces are independent—but the inputs to the BCS from earlier processing at t *do* affect the feedback from the ORS at $t + \delta$. The feedback dynamics must be captured by equations that describe the unfolding process (e.g., of resonance) going on between two units. Moreover, in an environment shielded from electromagnetic reactions, a particle would behave "normally" and even "ideally" according to the gravitational model: it would behave like an ideal gravitational body. But if the BCS were cut off from feedback from the ORS, its behavior would decidedly not be normal. Here we have an additional type of gap between a theoretical model of one system, taken in isolation, and real-world behavior. The equations for how the BCS interacts with the OCS describe an essential part of its normal operation, and hence we cannot view its operation simply as a function of its upstream inputs. When we are dealing with independent forces, an experimental situation in which an object is shielded from all forces but one will behave ideally as the model of that force predicts. But in a feedback system, this is not so. A portion of the brain, cut off from its normal interactions with other parts of the brain in which it is in feedback relations, does not behave normally, much less ideally. A monkey LGN in a Petri dish does not behave like an ideal LGN; it behaves like a morsel of monkey-brain sushi.

Depending on the nature of the inter-modular causal pathways, there can also be *emergent* behavior that is not predictable from the behavior of the units seen in isolation. One feature found in many of the Grossberg models, for example, is a relation of dynamic resonance between modules or levels: a level L1 sends signals representing input to a level L2, activating a template. This then results in sending feedback signals to L1. These

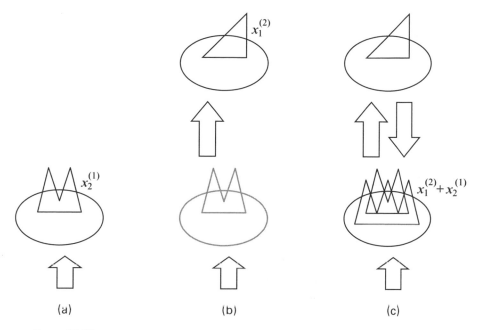

Figure 11.23
Schematic of resonant pattern matching from Grossberg 1980 (figure 7, p. 10). The stages (a), (b), and (c) schematize the rapid sequence of events whereby afferent data are filtered and activates a feedback expectancy that is matched against itself.

essentially involve "matching" the L1 input with the L1 patterns "expected" by L2, resulting in either reinforcement of the L1 pattern or a dissonance that causes the two systems to reset and attempt an alternative pattern match (figure 11.23). This is best understood, not in terms of simple circuit-like behavior of units within individual modules (even if it is emergent or resultant from such behavior), but as a higher-order equilibrium principle. There is no comparable equilibrative cycle between, for example, gravitational and electromagnetic models.

In this respect, models of systems such as the BCS and the ORS are radically different from models of gravitational and electromagnetic invariants, in that the factors modeled in each individual model are profoundly *open* to and *interactive* with exogenous forces for their normal operation. (This situation is, of course, not unique to neural dynamics; it is found in biological, chemical, and more complicated physical processes. The point is not that neural dynamics is unique, but that it has characteristics that one would not foresee if one were to take basic physics as one's only paradigm.)

11.7.2   Divergence and Convergence

It seems to be a basic design principle of the visual system, and perhaps of the brain as a whole, that information is separated into distinct process-ing pathways that sometimes later reconverge. At the most basic level, the visual system first employs separate pathways for form, color, and motion, and at a later stage, separates into a "what" stream for conceptual identi-fication of objects and a "where" stream employed for practical kinesthetic interaction with them. This has long been suggested by abnormal cases in which one system is damaged while the other is left intact. Sacks (1985) and Ramachandran (1999) have presented for the general public pathologi-cal cases in which a patient can, for example, identify and label objects but not reach out and grasp them effectively, or vice versa. Ungerleider and Mishkin (1982) have identified brain areas that provide plausible localizations of these streams. The Grossberg models suggest the possibility that such causal streams may nonetheless constrain one another; for example, the region in which brightness, color, and other features are "filled in" by the FCS seems to be constrained by boundaries produced by the BCS.

In this particular example, there is a one-way dependence of the dynam-ics of the FCS on the BCS, rather than a feedback relationship between them. But again, this is different from the situation of independent forces that can simply be summed. Moreover, it is an empirical question whether the way the FCS processes its separate input streams from pre-processing and the BCS is simply a summation of forces or something more compli-cated, involving such nonlinear, dynamic phenomena as equilibration relations over time, as suggested in some of the Grossberg models.

11.7.3   One Percept, Multiple Modules?

When presented with the COCE figure or a subjective contour figure, we have the impression of seeing a single percept—e.g., a gestalt in which we are presented with adjacent regions of different brightness or a brighter figure against a darker background. If the Grossberg models are correct, however, representations of figure and brightness are located in distinct modules in anatomically distinct portions of the brain. This raises interesting questions about the "neural correlate" of such percepts. It is natural to assume that there must be some *place* in the brain (a "gestalt module," as it were) that represents "brighter square"—i.e., that our taxonomy of percepts is neatly mapped onto a taxonomy of brain states, in the sense of activation states of particular brain modules. But it is not clear that this is so.

For one thing, not every model invokes such a module. For another, though there is good reason to think there are particular parts of the brain that can plausibly be assumed to represent boundaries and features, it is far less clear that there is a part that represents a combination of boundaries and features. This raises the so-called binding problem of how features represented in different parts of the brain get reconnected. (See figure 11.24.) If a subject is presented with a blue square and a red triangle, for example, there will be parts of the brain that represent "blue" and "red" and other parts that represent "square" and "triangle" (or at least represent boundaries of figures that can be described by these terms). But how does the brain know that "blue" is to be linked to "square" and "red" to "triangle"? At least one influential hypothesis, advanced by Francis Crick and Christof Koch (see Crick 1993), is that this does not take place in an additional area where color and shape data are recombined, but rather through the representations of the associated features being locked together through phase binding: the representation of "blue" fires in phase with that of "square" and that of "red" with "triangle."

It the Crick-Koch hypothesis is correct, the "representation" of "blue square" is very different from the constituent representations of "blue" and "square." Indeed, one is torn between two equally surprising ways of construing the situation. One way of construing it is to say that the unity of the percept (as a blue square) is not underwritten by a representational unity, in the form of a single unified representation, but by a kind of triangulation of the object in a perception through separate representations of form and feature through phase binding. What is a unity in phenomenological, cognitive, and behavioral terms is underwritten by a plurality of brain processes that cooperate rather than integrate into a single representational system. The alternative construal is to speak of "representations" of things like "blue square" in a fashion that does not require these "representations" to be things like symbols characterized by patterns of local activity in a region of the brain. "Representations" of boundaries and features may be local and symbol-like in this sense, but intentional representations of objects are characterized by global patterns of activity (or at least patterns distributed across multiple physiological areas) such as phase locking (Crick/Koch) or dynamic resonance (Grossberg et al.). In the abstract, such object representations might be seen as points in a vector space whose dimensions include the state spaces of the various constituent systems (the BCS, the FCS, the ORS, and so on). But this implies that a model of object representation would have to involve the dynamic interrelations between these systems, such as phase locking or dynamic resonance.

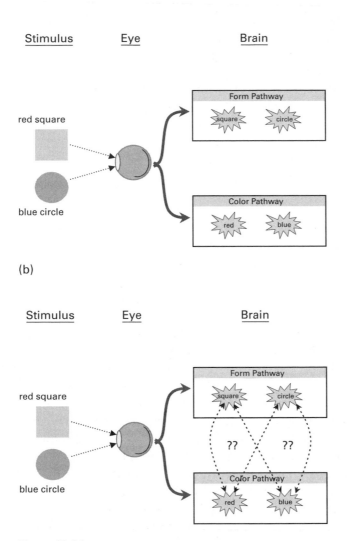

Figure 11.24

The binding problem. (a) Information from the retina is divided into separate processing streams for color and form (and also motion, not shown), which pass through the LGN and visual cortex. (b) The presence of colors and shapes are registered in different portions of the visual cortex. As a result, the binding problem arises: how does the brain know, when presented with a red square and a blue circle, that RED goes with SQUARE instead of with CIRCLE, or with nothing at all? (c) It is tempting to suppose that binding must be accomplished in some further unit where the different aspects of visual perception are all represented together. We experience a unified perceptual gestalt, but there does not seem to be an anatomical area that could count as such a "Cartesian Theater" (Dennett 1991) where it all comes together. (d) A more neurally realistic hypothesis is that the neural correlate of binding is neural synchrony or phase locking between the activities in different neural areas representing features that are bound together.

(c)

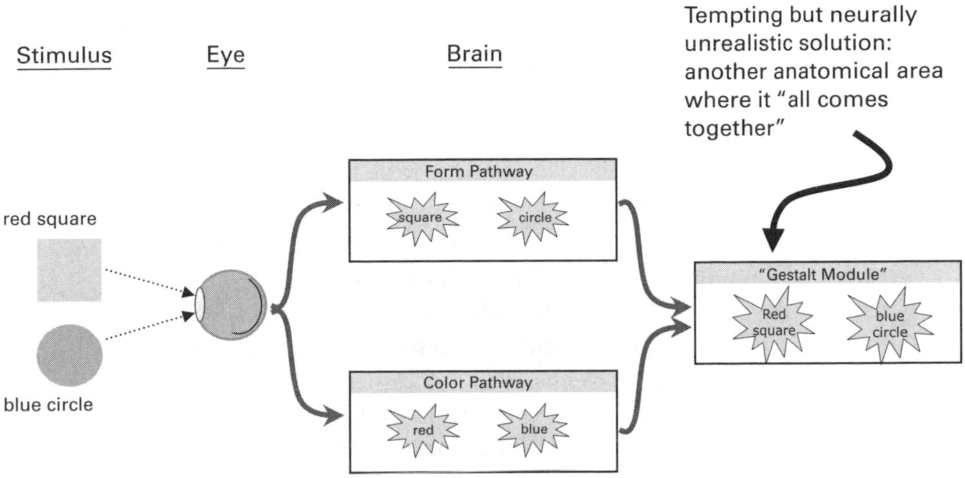

(d)

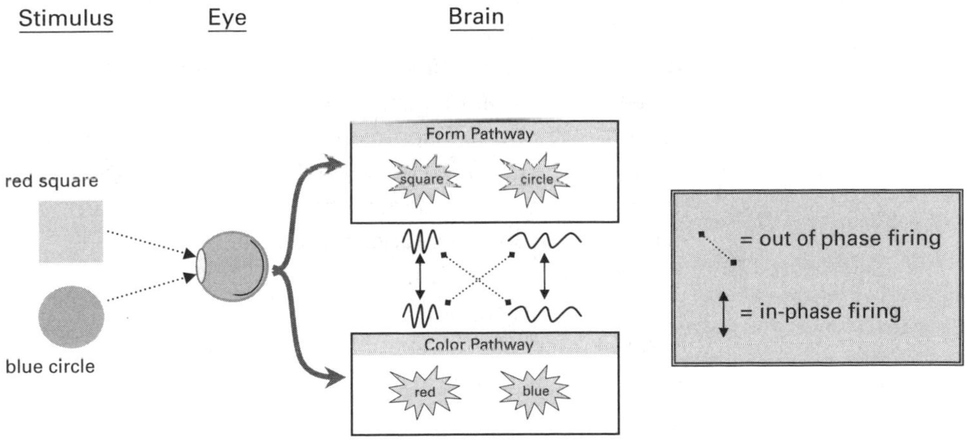

Figure 11.24
(continued)

11.8   Idealization in the Models

The family of models developed by the Grossberg group has thus moved toward models that are increasingly comprehensive and decreasingly idealized. The initial models were idealized in a number of ways. They tended to model particular hypothetical circuits in abstraction from their neural realization; but this idealization led to useful hypotheses and improvements, which in the long run facilitated the localization of components of the model that revealed the importance of pathways across anatomical regions and laminar structures. Early models were also more idealized in treating subsystems of the later models as single circuits, and in treating smaller circuits (e.g., of monocular processing) in abstraction from their embeddedness in larger systems. And the earlier models employed more informal (non-mathematized) explanations and approximations of aggregate activity not generated from lower-level hypotheses.

We should not, however, conclude from this that the more recent models are not still idealized. They clearly make idealized assumptions about low-level physiological factors, such as transmitter levels and individual differences in fine-grained details of the number, location, and connections of neurons. (As was discussed in chapter 10 with respect to psychophysics and the early visual system, such idealizations are necessary in order to formulate any generalizations about species-typical features.) The lowest-level equations are only an approximation of the Hodgkin-Huxley equation, which is itself in all likelihood only an approximation of real neural behavior *in vivo*. Moreover, the activity of individual neurons has a significant stochastic element. This raises the possibility of chaotic behavior. However, this may be less problematic in a normally functioning brain than in some physical systems, since the models suggest that the brain has internal feedback mechanisms for stabilization and normalization of behavior. Such self-regulating properties may have the effect of "enforcing" the "normal" higher-level behavior upon otherwise unruly components (an effect not seen in models that employ only feedforward mechanisms).

The models are also idealized in that they are largely models of *perceptual* systems, or in the case of some models not covered in this chapter, of perceptual-motor loops. Whatever modulation of behavior (and perhaps even of perception) is conferred by higher cognitive processes has thus been idealized away from, as the latter have not been modeled to the same degree. The "Object Recognition System" of the initial models, for example, might plausibly be thought to extend into conceptual and epistemic systems that are at least as complex as the perceptual processing mechanisms already explored. It is, of course, an empirical question just how much influence higher cognition can influence perception, and in what ways; but the neural modeling of such processes as there may be is still largely uncharted territory.

11.9 Comparisons with Other Models

The models from Grossberg's group are among the most sophisticated and neurally realistic models of vision. (This is, in large measure, the reason I have used them for my examples.) There is, however, insight to be gained from comparisons of different types of models of vision, and of neural networks generally.

For philosophers, the most familiar theory of vision is that proposed by David Marr (1981). That theory became widely known within cognitive science as much for Marr's division of levels of description into the computational, algorithmic, and implementation levels as for the details of the theory. Marr's typology has gained much currency in cognitive science and philosophy of mind, though some writers have substituted their own alternative labels for the levels.

Marr conceptualizes the visual process as consisting of a series of stages, beginning with retinal transduction and ending with a three-dimensional model of a visual scene. His model relies heavily on feedforward processing and does not accord the same role to "top-down expectations" and feedback loops as do the Grossberg models. It is also much less concerned with neural realism and connections to neuroscience. This is due in part to Marr's untimely death before the recent flood of research in the anatomy and physiology of the visual system. But it is arguably also a predictable consequence of Marr's doctrine of the independence of the algorithmic and computational levels from the implementation level. And many of Marr's followers have likewise concentrated on abstract algorithms for visual processing in a fashion disconnected from neuroscientific discoveries, and hence view idealization away from the particulars of the neural implementation not only as methodologically innocent but as a methodological canon.

The other modeling tradition that is likely to be familiar to philosophers is the "connectionist" lineage that emerged out of the PDP (Parallel Distributed Processing) group (Rumelhart and McClelland 1987). PDP models, unlike Marr's model, are built on the premise that the network architecture of the nervous system is crucial in the organization of cognition, particularly learning. However, the PDP paradigm has been developed as much as an alternative style of computation as an account of human or animal cognition. In particular, PDP models are generally framed very abstractly, with little or no connection to neurophysiology or neuroanatomy. PDP models of learning are also characterized by the very significant idealization that training is guided by an external "instructor" to provide feedback in the training period—a method notably different from how animals generally learn *in vivo*.

James Anderson and his associates have been pursuing more neurally realistic models over the same period as the Grossberg group. (See Anderson 1977, 1978, 1981, 1988, 1995; Guan, Anderson, and Sutton 1997.) I view the two groups as having similar research goals; however, I shall single out a difference that, though probably not significant in comparing the quality of the models, is of interest from the standpoint of a philosophical examination of modeling. In many cases, Anderson and Grossberg employ different mathematical tools in their models—for example, difference equations vs. differential equations. If we explore a larger class of models of neural processes, we will find still other mathematical tools employed heavily, such as stochastic methods and chaos theory. I suspect that all parties probably would agree that the test of a given mathematical tool is whether it does the job of predicting real-world behavior. And, much as Fechner's logarithmic law and Stevens's power law were equally good for many purposes in characterizing psychophysical data, different mathematizations of network behavior may in some cases be equally good for neural models. Sometimes, however, they may make an important difference in how rich a set of data they explain. Moreover, just as the "fit" between models of different cases in physics (e.g., models used for laminar vs. turbulent flow) is sometimes not as smooth as the introductory textbooks make it out to be, models of the dynamics of neural circuits may employ equations whose relationship to mathematical models of cells (such as the Hodgkin-Huxley equation) is often good enough for practical purposes, but is formally problematic.

11.10   Laws and Formal Models

Neural models such as those produced by Grossberg and his colleagues at Boston University contain law-like entities most clearly in the form of equations used to describe low-level processes such as gating between units and to describe aggregate activity such as "winner-take-all" competition. Indeed, when a model employs equations governing the dynamics of high-level circuits that are not derived from aggregate activity of low-level circuits, the model is more idealized than one in which the properties of the low-level circuits completely explain the higher-level behavior.

However, the *structure* of the Grossberg models we have examined—the enumeration of and relations between units—also has an important kind of formal exactitude. Such structural properties, and their contributions to system dynamics, tend to be represented, not in the form of algebraic equations, but either diagrammatically or in the form of a computer program used to make the model into a simulation. Both diagrammatic representations of structure and program-driven simulations of dynamics are, of course, found in the physical sciences too. Reconceptualizing the basic unit of scientific explanation as the model rather than the law allows us to see deep commonalities here that otherwise might be ignored.

In short, neural models provide "laws" in the narrow sense of equations describing the dynamics of neural and cognitive processes. Like the laws of most special sciences, these are closely tied to structural models of mechanisms within whose normal functioning the laws are apt. The assumptions of normal structure (e.g., abstraction from developmental and clinical abnormalities) and functioning (e.g., abstraction from variations in transmitter levels) involve a common and familiar type of idealization. The structural features of the models, and the mechanisms they describe, are made formally exact through diagrams and programming in ways analogous to models of dynamic processes in the natural sciences.

There is, however, an important difference between the idealizations involved in models of brain and cognition and most natural-scientific models. There is a standard of biological *normalcy* to cognitive and biological systems not found in physical or chemical systems. The "normal" functioning of any module in the brain must ultimately be understood in terms of its interactions with other systems in the brain, with non-neural aspects of the organism, and with the organism's evolutionary history and ecological embeddedness. On the one hand, what a module is for is tied to evolutionary and ecological facts about an organism and its ancestors. On the other hand, particularly with neural systems, the complex feedback system of the brain plays a causal role in regulating the normal behavior of each subsystem. Whereas models of physical systems (e.g., gravitational or thermodynamic models) may depart from accurate predictions of real-world behavior because of independent forces (e.g., electromagnetism) or exogenous forces (a model system is treated as closed, but no subset of the physical universe is truly closed), with neural and cognitive systems there is another element of complexity. A particular neural "unit" (e.g., a layer of a region of cortex), or even a circuit consisting of multiple "units" (e.g., the visual color pathway), operates properly after its kind only with the help of modulation by other parts of the brain (and often of the environment) that may be idealized away in the model. If we isolate a body from non-gravitational forces, it will indeed behave ideally as a model of gravitation predicts. But if we isolate a region of the brain from its accustomed connections, it does not perform ideally as a color module or a form module. Either it ceases to operate at all, or else it operates abnormally.

Each part of the brain plays its role within the larger economies of the whole brain and the entire organism, in that organism's adaptive interactions with its environment. Consequently, organism, brain, and brain module must all be understood as fundamentally open systems. The physical systems modeled by physicists, chemists, and engineers are, of course, open systems. And because of this, idealized dynamic models can break down as tools for explanation and prediction of real-world events. But the existence of non-gravitational forces does not make our gravitational model incomplete as a dynamic model, as the gravitational model can still capture, and describe exactly, the dynamic contribution of gravitational force to real-world kinematics. The model pays the price of kinematic idealization to purchase theoretical insight into dynamics. Neural models also lend theoretical insight into neural and cognitive dynamics. But because they are models of open systems, an individual model cannot fully capture the nature or dynamics of its target system the way that a model of gravitation can. In this respect, neural modeling must also be an open-ended endeavor, as it explores an ever-broader range of interactions between organism and environment. Grossberg (2005) puts the point this way: "A second important methodological constraint derives from the fact that no single step of theoretical derivation can derive a whole brain. One needs to have a method that can evolve with the complexity of the environmental challenges that the model is forced to face."

11.11   Neural Models and Cognitive Pluralism

The style of neural modeling we have described here lends a certain degree of indirect support to my general suggestion that the plurality of scientific models is best seen as a special case of the plurality of mental models employed quite generally in everyday cognition. It seems to be a basic design principle of the brain that our understanding of the world is accomplished through a kind of division of labor in which different modules of the brain represent different features, each in a self-contained and optimized representational system, and these separate models then cooperate (but do not necessarily recombine) to generate a more comprehensive understanding. It is, of course, perilous to extrapolate from what one finds in the retina, in the LGN, and in visual cortex to higher cognitive processes involved in scientific theorizing or even everyday interpretation of a world of objects. Among other things, it is highly unlikely that we would find portions of the brain that are, as a product of natural selection, assigned the tasks of representing relativistic mechanics or chess the way areas of the visual cortex may be products of selection for tasks such as representing boundaries and features. This, however, can be overcome if the more flexible parts of the brain employed in higher cognition can be shaped, through experience, into "soft modules"—i.e., modules that are produced by learning rather than by natural selection. Such soft modules could be partially isolated in employing their own (learned) representational systems for particular problem domains without being innate or even localized in a single anatomical region. Domain specific knowing might thus be implemented through brain processes that share some of the features of modularity of the hypothesized BCS and FCS at a functional level while being different in that there are not innately allotted portions of brain anatomy that serve these functions. And our ability to triangulate the world by moving between multiple models might be functionally like the feedback processes between modules in the visual cortex (say, in involving resonance phenomena) without being innate.

12 Belief-Desire Psychologies

The disciplines examined in the preceding two chapters—psychophysics, neural localization, and neural modeling—all fall squarely within the bounds of familiar forms of science. They proceed from experimentation and empirical data, and they aim toward the production of formally exact models, some of which are also quantified. Philosophers of science have discussed potential methodological problems for these disciplines, some of which we have now discussed; however, the criticisms that have been leveled at belief-desire psychology require a separate discussion.

The most basic difference lies in the difficulty of pinning down what it is that we are talking about when we speak of "belief-desire psychology." In the case of psychophysics, it was easy to identify both a standard set of data, and the laws that attempt to accommodate those data, because these are found in any textbook on the subject. Psychophysics is a fairly mature scientific discipline. There is less consensus on how modeling of neural systems should be pursued, and for that reason I undertook in the preceding chapter to concentrate on one particular research program in computational neuroscience. As that research program has a number of explicit models that employ mathematical equations to capture processes in the brain, it was again easy to identify the subject whose status we were examining.

There is not, in a similar way, a single scientific field called "belief-desire psychology." Cognitive and developmental psychology do indeed employ models of cognitive processes that appeal to beliefs and desires and to kindred intentional states. At the same time, philosophers (and some scientists) talk about something they call "folk psychology"—meaning something like a common-sense understanding of beliefs, desires, and actions—as though it were something on the order of a single theory, or a group of such theories employing common notions of belief and desire.

Curiously, it is this "folk psychology" that has most often been the target of philosophical attacks—for example, that common-sense truisms about how belief and desire lead to action are not really lawlike, or that they are lawlike in character but are such dismal failures at describing the real nature of the mind that they and their theoretical posits of "belief" and "desire" should be eliminated from our theoretical vocabulary.

I call this situation curious for several reasons. First, treating common-sense models of the mind—or, indeed, of anything—as though they were the same sorts of things as scientific theories strikes me as an unpromising beginning. I think that both scientific theory and common-sense under-standing are best understood in terms of mental modeling, so of course I agree that they have important features in common. But the features that they have in common are precisely those that are not distinctive of scien-tific theory as such. Second, finding fault with "folk" understandings of the mind and concluding that there cannot be good scientific models involving intentional notions such as "belief" and "desire" strikes me as equivalent to citing the shortcomings of "folk physics" as evidence against the existence of mechanical laws employing the notions "mass," "motion," and "gravity."

In this spirit, I shall devote the bulk of this chapter to an examination of several kinds of attempts to craft scientifically rigorous psychological theories that make use of the intentional notions "belief" and "desire." My own view is that common-sense belief-desire explanations of behavior may well be based on models that involve implicit or explicit generalizations, but that these (like most or all common-sense models) lack the special regimentation and rigor that are characteristic of scientific laws. After all, it can be argued that the notion of "natural laws" was not invented until the seventeenth century. And if "folk psychology" is supposed to be some-thing that is shared by scientific and pre-scientific humans, it cannot make use of a notion of "law" that is of such recent vintage. But even if the reader disagrees with me on this, it really does not matter. The question of whether there are laws at the level of intentional states can be settled only by looking, not at the most widespread form of intentional explana-tion, but at the best forms we can come up with.

12.1   Ground Clearing: Law Representations and Laws in Nature

In chapter 9, I made a distinction between two uses of the word 'law'. In one use, a law is a real regularity in the world. In the other use, a law is something cognitive and representational (e.g., the equation $F = ma$) that aims at tracking a real regularity in the world but may fail to do so. I disambiguated these uses as *laws in nature* and *law representations*, respectively, and cited Descartes' putative law of conservation of motion as an example of a law representation for which there is not a corresponding law in nature, as motion is in fact not conserved in mechanical interactions.

There are thus two distinct questions to be asked when assessing whether various sorts of intentional psychology "have laws." One is a question about whether they possess certain types of representational resources that aim at tracking regularities. A purely taxonomic science, for example, might lack law representations altogether, as might a subfield of natural history. The second question concerns whether generalizations cast in terms of intentional states can aptly track real-world regularities. These two issues are doubly dissociable. On the one hand, not all law representations (for example, Descartes' aforementioned conservation law) succeed at tracking real regularities. On the other hand, there are plenty of non-scientific generalizations that are not law representations, though some of these may nonetheless succeed at tracking regularities in ways that are apt for their non-scientific purposes.

In what follows, my primary concern will be to assess whether several variations on intentional psychology possess law representations, and to evaluate how these may be similar to or differ from those found in other scientific endeavors we have discussed. Most of these attempts to regiment a psychology of beliefs, desires, and other intentional states are of relatively recent vintage. As a result, such assessments as I shall venture to give regarding their aptness (that is, whether they track genuine laws in nature) are intended to be understood as quite tentative, much as I left questions about the aptness of particular models in psychophysics and cognitive neuroscience open in chapter 11.

12.2   More Ground Clearing: Dispositional and Occurrent States

A second bit of ground clearing is also in order. The terms 'belief' and 'desire' are used in multiple ways. Sometimes they are used to express explicit and conscious states. In thinking through an important decision, I may consciously engage in practical reasoning in which I explicitly formulate both what I want and the beliefs that are relevant to obtaining it. I may think, for example, "I'm out of Diet Coke and really need some caffeine to work on this chapter. What's the quickest way to get some? Shucks, it's after 9 p.m., so the deli is closed. Who is open this time of night? Ah, the convenience store at the gas station is open 24 hours. I'll get in the car and go there and buy some Diet Coke." If my goddaughter, learning her addition tables, asks me "What is 9 + 15?" I may think about it and give an answer based on arithmetic thoughts. These cases involve *occurrent mental states*—conscious mental events that occur at some specific time. These are episodes of my mental life.

But we also speak of "beliefs" and "desires" when we talk about things that do not involve occurrent thoughts, and even things a person may never have thought about. I sometimes ask my students a question like "Do you believe that 9 + 15 = 24?" To answer, they have to think about numbers and do a quick bit of arithmetic. I then ask them "Did you believe 9 + 15 = 24 five minutes ago?" Usually, a number of them answer "Yes" even though they were not thinking about arithmetic five minutes before. The astute students also immediately see that there is an interesting philosophical puzzle to put their minds to. This is because 'believe' is also used to report some sorts of mental states that are *not* conscious judgments. They may sometimes be occurrent but abiding and infraconscious states— there may be something like a stored episodic memory of an addition table learned in grammar school. But they may be something like capacities to quickly generate answers to addition problems.

Likewise, one may have other sorts of beliefs and desires that are never consciously entertained. Freud, for example, hypothesized that boys have a repressed desire to have their mothers to themselves and displace their fathers in order to do so. (As the Oedipus Complex predates genital sexuality, it is probably misleading to say it consists in a boy's desire to have sexual relations with his mother.) Freud conceived these as occurrent but unconscious beliefs and desires. But there may also be beliefs and desires that are never occurrently formulated: through therapy or Socratic dialectic, one may come to the conclusion that what one has most deeply wanted all along is to have a quiet and stable domestic life rather than a meteoric career, even if one has never thought of it explicitly or even formulated an unconscious state with this content. Likewise, we interpret other people's motives in ways that they have probably never formulated, and which they might well reject if they heard them. I recall one friend saying of another "He thinks he is entitled to at least fifty percent of the conversation space regardless of the number of people in the conversation." This may well have reported something true about the friend's conversational assertiveness—a kind of implicit maxim he could be described as following—but it probably is not anything that the friend ever explicitly represented, either consciously or unconsciously. (And if he did represent it consciously, he probably would either have rejected it as false or attempted to change his attitude toward conversational turn taking.) I sometimes continue the dialogue with my students by asking something like "Did you believe, yesterday, that at least three dogs have spleens?"—a belief with a content that presumably none of them had ever thought about before.

These states that do not seem to plausibly involve explicit representations of the content attributed as believed or desired are sometimes called "dispositional beliefs/desires" or "dispositions to believe/desire" (Audi 1993). I regard the mechanisms underlying such dispositions as open to debate, and I see such states as legitimately interpreted as theoretical entities—that is, as states that are hypothesized in order to explain explicit thoughts and behavior (Horst 1992). Their own ontological status is unknown, but they are called 'beliefs' and 'desires' by dint of the fact that they are the sorts of things that, if brought into conscious awareness (whatever such "bringing to awareness" might mean), would give rise to conscious beliefs and desires. Ontologically, the two sorts of states, occurrent and dispositional, might be very different, and it is a mistake (or at least a too-quick hypothesis) to simply suppose that dispositions to believe must themselves have either explicit content or the kind of grammatical and inferential structure of explicit thoughts. An adequate scientific theory of conscious reasoning might look very different from an adequate theory of the dynamics of unconscious and inexplicit motivations. The latter might in the end require something much more like the neural network models explored in the preceding chapter.

There may be an even greater variety to the ontological and evidential character of various sorts of intentional states. But for those we have surveyed, we might bring some order to them by representing them in the form of a table. (See table 12.1.)

12.3   Regimentations of Belief-Desire Psychology: An Abbreviated and Potted History

Let us now turn our attention to attempts to make a psychology that explains action in terms of intentional states into something more rigorous, such as a philosophical or scientific theory with laws. Belief-desire explanation has been a favorite topic of philosophers at least since Plato. In the *Gorgias*, Plato introduces the first version of this view that I am aware of. (I shall leave open the question of whether Plato, the author, ever *held* this view, or whether it was a view he put into a character's mouth.) In the dialogue, the character Socrates suggests that people always "will the

decision theory, reprising Plato's suggestion in the *Gorgias* that people actually do what they think is best for them.

Decision theory has been a popular and powerful tool in the social sciences (particularly economics), and decision theorists have developed a powerful mathematical apparatus that can be used as a mathematically exact model of the psychology that underlies action. In saying that it is a mathematically exact model, I do not mean to imply that the model is correct or psychologically realistic. In this case, 'exact' just means "quantified." Such a model is thought by many to be a useful *predictive* tool, especially when used in statistical averages over large populations, even though everyone knows that people are not really ideally rational agents. Indeed, its empirical utility may be independent of the question of whether it provides a realistic account of psychological *mechanisms* at all, just as it can be useful to think of biological adaptations as "solutions" to environmentally imposed "problems" even though evolutionary mechanisms are not themselves teleological or purposeful.

Belief-desire psychology has also been regimented as a model of actual psychodynamics in cognitive psychology and artificial intelligence. Decision-theoretic procedures have been modeled in computers. And research in knowledge representation has attempted to make explicit the kinds of representational structures that might underwrite practical decision making. Some of this goes beyond the belief-desire model.

Freudian psychology is also arguably in part an attempt to provide a psychologically realistic account of psychodynamics in which beliefs and desires play crucial causal roles. (See Grünbaum 1984. For a contrary interpretation of Freud, see Ricoeur 1970.) In one sense, Freudian psychology is a repudiation of the traditional ethical project with which intellectualist psychology was initially linked (Riker 1997). For Plato and Aristotle, the exploration of the cognitive underpinnings of action was in the service of moral improvement through rational self-understanding and a kind of therapy on one's own beliefs and desires. Arguably, this project is viable only to the extent that our beliefs and desires are accessible to us and are under our control. Freud rejected both of these assumptions, claiming that the real causes of behavior are largely unconscious, and hence not directly knowable, and are more powerful than our attempts at conscious intervention.

Freud's theory is radical in how it might threaten ethics as traditionally conceived. But Freud's strategy for accounting for this in an expanded psychodynamics of the unconscious is in other ways quite conservative. In his early work, Freud concentrated on unconscious beliefs and desires, which seem to have been understood as the same in kind as conscious beliefs and desires (e.g., as occurrent states with intentional content) but as repressed. To account for repression, Freud later postulated a number of more basic drives, mechanisms such as repression and sublimation, and faculties (the id, the ego, and the superego). But the dynamics of beliefs and desires continued to play a central explanatory role in Freudian psychology. The defense mechanisms, for example, are supposed to transform threatening unconscious beliefs and desires into ones with more innocuous content that can be entertained consciously.

Freudian theory has become notorious as a result of a criticism of one way in which it fails to be scientific: that it accommodates any possible data, and hence is untestable. Nevertheless, it is an important attempt to regiment belief-desire psychology into an explicit theory. It uses an expanded repertoire of beliefs and desires to explain both normal and abnormal behavior, and it strives for formal exactitude.

The purpose of these examples is to make it clear that, although common-sense psychology may not take the form of formally exact models, it is possible to develop and expand on it in the direction of models that look more like scientific models. I do not mean to commend any of them as an unmixed success. Indeed, I have already signaled reservations about the psychological realism of decision theory, and I regard the standard worry about the unfalsifiability of Freudian psychology as a blow to its status as science. The point, rather, is that the real and marked differences between common-sense belief-desire models and scientific models need not pose a barrier to the formulation of formally exact belief-desire models.

12.4   Decision Theory as Psychology

The human sciences, particularly economics, often employ a model of minds and behavior that is in some ways very close to common-sense belief-desire psychology. People's choices are explained and predicted in terms of beliefs and desires, but to this is added an account of how beliefs and desires lead to choices. In particular, desires (or preferences) are given a quantitative dimension in the form of subjective utility values. This, plus a second quantitative element in which subjects assign probability values to the alternative outcomes of prospective actions, provides the basis for a decision-theoretic calculus that allows subjects to calculate which actions stand the best chance of bringing about what they desire, given their assumptions about the probabilities of different outcomes.

In economics, decision theory tends to be applied in a very idealized way. In addition to the elements of the theory already mentioned, economists tend to make the idealizing assumption that individuals are ideally rational, in at least the senses that (a) they perform calculations accurately and (b) they always do what they calculate will be the strategy with the highest subjective utility value. Sometimes economists make the additional idealizing assumption that individuals are fully informed and estimate the probabilities accurately. Economists do not, of course, believe that every individual is ideally rational in these ways, and hence their theories do not involve a commitment to a Realist stance toward the psychological theories involved. The theories are thought to be instrumentally useful, however, on the assumption that departures from ideal rationality (at least in the first two senses) will cancel out over large enough populations.

But perhaps "strictly speaking false, but instrumentally useful" is not the best way of characterizing decision-theoretic accounts of action. There are several elements of such accounts, and they raise different issues. Such accounts clearly make distorting idealizations in treating individuals as ideally rational. People make mistakes in calculation, and they do not always do what they believe will maximize utility, know all the salient facts, or make correct judgments about the probabilities of different possible outcomes. The account also makes bracketing idealizations in ignoring other, non-decision-theoretic psychological and contextual factors that may influence our choices. But bracketing and distorting idealizations are common features of scientific models, and their presence does not, in itself, falsify the model or render it inapt. They do not falsify it, because models are neither true nor false but rather are apt or inapt. And aptness and inaptness are always relative to particular types of problems and contexts. A decision-theoretic psychology might be apt for some types of economic modeling, less apt for economic modeling of people who are in a "hot" emotional state, and quite inapt for the purposes of, say, moral psychology. There are, of course, questions about the merits of any particular macroeconomic model. But these lie beyond the scope of this discussion and outside my particular areas of professional competence. My point is simply that viewing decision-theoretic accounts as models rather than as quantified universal claims about how people actually think and act changes the way we must assess such accounts.

A separate question is whether such accounts can be viewed as apt models of actual psychological processes, even if those models are idealized and are apt for enterprises such as economic forecasting. That is, even if the decision-theoretic account leaves out other factors that may influence choices, and even if we often make calculations that depart from mathematical norms, do we nonetheless decide what to do by making calculations based on beliefs and desires? And the question is not whether *some* people *sometimes* do so, but whether this is a good general account of how we make decisions.

The answer to this question is, I think, complicated. "Making calculations based on beliefs and desires" invites a reading on which people actually assign quantitative utility values and probability estimates in deciding what to do. More fundamentally, if we actually apply a calculus of utility, this seems to require that we represent our beliefs, desires, and probability estimates in symbolic form. But many of our decisions do not involve conscious representations of this sort, and even with those that do, their conscious content does not seem to involve quantitative variables. (I might consciously desire a glass of water strongly, but not with a numerical value of 9.8. The theorist may have ways of imposing a numerical scale on my preferences, but I do not experience them as numerically valued.) And it is hard to see how one could have an algebraic calculus at work without such a quantitative element.

To make the account plausible, we would have to take one of two courses. The first would be to hypothesize that there are infra-conscious or unconscious representations involved (some of them quantitative), and likewise to hypothesize the infra-conscious or unconscious application of a rule-based calculus. This view might seem plausible to advocates of the view that the mind is a computer (to be explored in the next section), though I find it unconvincing. The second possibility would interpret the situation in a fashion something like the following: Much of our decision making involves *some type of states* that we *speak of as* (dispositional) beliefs and desires. The real nature of these states is unknown, but their dynamics are tolerably well reflected by modeling them *as though* they were symbolic representations that could be used in such a calculus. Until we have a more perspicuous story about those dynamics, we do not know to what extent treating these mental states and processes as though they were a symbolic calculus distorts their real nature and idealizes away from factors that may be relevant to their dynamics. There are advantages to the second approach, if only because it is the more cautious and because it leaves open the possibility that further research will verify either the first hypothesis or some alternative to it.

Now, lest the preceding few paragraphs sound like a defense of decision-theoretic psychology, let me clarify what I have been trying to do here. In point of fact, I am not much of a fan of decision theory as a psychology.

My greatest concerns are with its use in *moral* psychology, where the importance of non-rational influences such as virtues and passions is profound. But even with respect to non-moral decision making, decision theory (in my opinion) seems an apt model only for a subset of our choices. Perhaps this does not matter when it is used in economics to model behavior of large groups; aptness for one purpose is compatible with inaptness for another.

My intent, rather, has been to make a case for the following assertions: (1) Decision-theoretic psychology provides an example of a regimentation of common-sense belief-desire explanation into a model with formal exactitude, and indeed its calculus can be seen as a law representation. (2) The model probably does not predict individual behavior well much of the time, and involves assumptions about ideal rationality that are clearly empirically false. But these issues are of a type that we have seen to be found in scientific models generally. They do not prevent a model from being apt for some purposes. Nor do they entail that its principles do not track real causal regularities in nature, even when the model contains distorting idealizations and we are not sure of the real natures of the things it models. Decision-theoretic psychology, no matter what one thinks about its ultimate prospects for various explanatory and predictive projects, is thus an example of a belief-desire psychology that has law representations, and some of these might track laws in nature.

12.5 Computational Approaches to the Mind

One of the variations on decision-theoretic psychology discussed in the preceding section involved the further claim that the mind performs a great deal of genuine but not conscious calculation on mental representations. This, of course, is a familiar view of the mind that has gained a great deal of currency in recent decades: the view that the mind is a digital computer.

Alan Turing, the founder of the modern notion of the computing machine, clearly saw a close relation between computers and the mind. His initial (1936) article on computation developed the notion of a computing machine on the model of a human performing mathematical computations—that is, following rote algorithmic procedures to evaluate a function. (Indeed, in that article, the word 'computer' is used solely to denote a human being performing computations.) And Turing's famous article "Computing Machinery and Intelligence" (1950) suggested that questions about human intelligence and thinking might be "replaced" (his word) by questions about what computing machines can do. The metaphor of the mind as computer has since driven a number of enterprises, including computational approaches to psychology that model psychological processes as computational processes, the Computational Theory of Mind in philosophy, and projects in artificial intelligence that seek to replicate human-level (and above-human-level) competences in machines.

12.5.1 Artificial Intelligence, Computational Psychology, and the Computational Theory of Mind

In the 1940s and the 1950s, first-generation work in artificial intelligence concentrated on the automation of purely formal processes, such as programs that could prove theorems in logic and mathematics (Newell 1956). The programs were modeled on the algorithmic and heuristic processes performed by human mathematicians. Such programs could also be used as models of the actual performance of computation by humans—clearly a form of human thinking, albeit a very specialized one, limited to a very specific domain. Such models are testable to the extent that one can examine whether a given program can, in fact, generate all the results that a human mathematician or logician can produce, and whether they arrive at their conclusions through the same sorts of steps employed by human mathematicians. Negative results would call for the refinement of the program in the form of additional heuristics, which in turn could be compared with the heuristics humans report employing.

Such projects are pulled in two opposing directions. On the one hand, an AI researcher might well be concerned with the results a program could produce, whether or not they were achieved in the same fashion by which a human would arrive at them. (And indeed a computing machine might yield results that a human could not, as machines can perform computations more quickly and parse longer symbol strings than humans can.) On the other hand, a researcher interested in modeling how human cognition takes place might seek to develop programs that would approximate the procedures humans use and perhaps would even generate the same sorts of errors in reasoning that people are subject to. The field of artificial intelligence has largely been driven by the first goal, the field of computational psychology (or "cognitive science" in the narrow sense[1]) by the second.

Cognitive science was further shaped by the emergence of functionalism in psychology and philosophy of mind. One form of functionalism is the view that the types of mental states (such as beliefs and desires) that take propositional contents—variously called "intentional states" or "propositional attitudes"—can be characterized as functions from perceptual inputs and other (prior) intentional states to behaviors and other (resulting) intentional states. This was widely linked with a representationalist view of content: to believe that a box is on a table is to stand in a particular functional relation to an inner symbolic representation whose content is that that box is on the table, and to desire that the box be on the table is to stand in a different functional relation to the same sort of representation.

12.5.2 Computational Models of the Mind in Artificial Intelligence and in Cognitive Science

Such a picture suggests several ideas for how beliefs and desires might be understood on the model of symbolic representations in a computer. For example, beliefs might be seen as explicit representations stored in a particular region of attentive "workspace" or in memory (the "belief box," as it were), and desires as explicit representations stored in another region (the "desire box"). Alternatively, one might conceive belief and desire on the model of functional operators applied to symbol strings, such as BELIEF[box on table] or DESIRE[box on table]. The functional character of the attitudes of belief and desire would, in turn, be understood in terms of the program of the machine; for example, there might be a part of the program that has a rule of the following sort:

If (DESIRE[x] *and* BELIEF[not-x]) *then* TRY_TO_BRING_ABOUT[x].

TRY_TO_BRING_ABOUT[x] would then be a program routine that would cause the machine (or person) to try to find a way to make x so, and might be terminated, for example, under the condition that BELIEF[x] is tokened.

In the 1970s a number of researchers undertook the modeling of sentential-level inference. Robert Abelson's group, for example, developed models of "implication molecules" (Abelson and Reich 1969) and "conceptual dependency analysis" (Abelson 1973) in cognition generally, and Kenneth Colby (a psychiatrist by training) modeled the peculiar inference patterns of a paranoid personality in PARRY (Colby 1975). Already in the 1950s, Alan Newell and Herbert Simon had developed the GPS (General Problem Solver) model of means-ends analysis. (Newell and Simon 1956) And Barbara Hayes-Roth (1980) developed a model of opportunistic planning.

Other researchers concentrated on formalizing the *semantic* structure of beliefs and desires. M. Ross Quillian (1968) developed a model of semantic memory, involving a diagrammatic representation of semantic relations between elements of propositions (figure 12.1). Don Norman and co-workers (1976) developed the more elaborate MEMOD model (figures 12.2

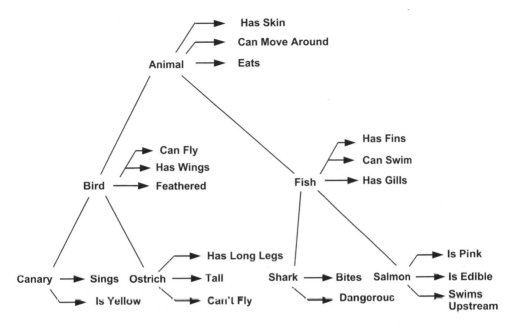

Figure 12.1
An example of a memory structure from Collins and Quillian 1969. Source: Cohen and Feigenbaum 1982, p. 40, figure E1-2.

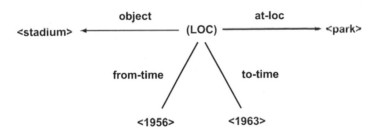

Figure 12.2
A representation from MEMOD: the LOC component of the verb 'located' in a sentence "A stadium was located in the park from 1956 to 1963." Source: Cohen and Feigenbaum 1982, p. 58, figure E4-1.

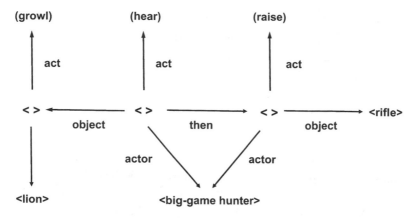

Figure 12.3
A representation from MEMOD of the episode "The big-time hunter heard the lion growl and raised his gun." Source: Cohen and Feigenbaum 1982, p. 61, figure E4-4.

and 12.3), which adds separate representations of episodes and events to Quillian's model, which represents only objects. John Anderson's group also developed semantic memory models, including HAM, in which relations are represented by a simplified English grammar, and ACT, which adds a procedural component to operate on the network knowledge base (Anderson and Bower 1973; Anderson 1980).

One can see the appeal of this research strategy by understanding it as an attempt to make explicit the kinds of structures and procedures that might underlie cognitive-level mental processes such as sentence understanding, memory, and inference, thereby conferring a kind of formal exactitude on belief-desire psychology. A computer program is a paradigmatic example of a type of formally exact modeling. It does not, or at least need not, employ laws, in the sense of algebraic equations. But programming languages and even pseudocode allow for formal exactitude even though they are not algebraic in form. As Newell and Simon write, "Theories of this type, which can be called information processing theories, are essentially non-quantitative (they may involve no numbers at all), although neither less precise nor less rigorous than classical mathematical theories." (1963, p. 366) Computational psychology is thus a strategy for turning insights of common-sense belief-desire psychology into respectable scientific models of mental processes.

Such a model is idealized in a number of ways. For example, if the same processes that go on in human cognition can be implemented in computers, the relevant generalizations must be framed at a level at which differences between circuit boards and neural networks do not matter. The relevant generalizations are thus conceived as abstract functional or program-level generalizations that can be implemented in a variety of physical substrates, much as two production-model computers can be functionally identical and run the same programs even though one is made of vacuum tubes and the other of silicon microchips. The independence of the functional and implementation levels has thus been treated as a central canon of computational psychology. Of course, no one believes that the implementation level is causally irrelevant in the explanation of real-world performance. One type of implementing system, for example, will be much faster than another. And each type of implementing system is subject to its own forms of breakdowns, which result in the machine or organism failing to perform as described by the functional description. This, however, is true of most or all models in the special sciences. Biology and biochemistry employ models of developmental and metabolic processes that can be undercut in a variety of ways resulting from abnormalities in an organism or events in its environment. Likewise, neurological and network models of brain processes will fail to apply in cases such as abnormal transmitter levels or strokes. Models in the special sciences generally idealize away from conditions that would prevent the system from functioning "normally," so in this respect the idealizations involved in computational psychology are on a par with those involved in biology and neuroscience.

Computational models often idealize away from other factors that fall within the realm of psychology as well. Computationalists are divided, for example, on whether to treat emotions and drives as additional computational and representational phenomena (the cognitive theory of emotion) or as non-computational and/or non-representational phenomena that also play a role in influencing behavior. Although this affects the generality of computationalist models, it is again a form of idealization that is widespread in the sciences. We saw in the preceding chapter that models of particular neural circuits idealize away from the contributions of other circuits. And even in basic physics, a gravitational theory idealizes away from the contributions of strong, weak, and electromagnetic forces.

A more vexed question concerns just how far down the parallels between human thought and machine computation are supposed to go. On the one hand, one might take computational models as specifying the abstract form of cognitive processes in humans without supposing that these are accomplished in the same ways (e.g., by syntactically based algorithmic operations on symbols) in both cases. If the computer requires explicit symbolic representations of the content of each belief, this need not entail that there are symbolic encodings of belief contents in the human brain. If the computer does what it does by *applying* formal rules, it need not follow that the mind does so too: it is enough if its operations are *describable* in terms of such rules. On the other hand, one might take the rule-governed symbol-manipulation of computers as a hypothesis about *how* the mind operates as well. The latter is the view developed in philosophy as the Computational Theory of Mind (CTM).

12.5.3 The Computational Theory of Mind

Fodor (1975, 1981, 1987) has argued influentially that viewing the mind as literally being a digital computer affords an important theoretical gain, in allowing us to see how rational processes can also be causal and how some causal processes can also be rational. The background for this discussion is an older and opposing philosophical orthodoxy that claims that reasons cannot be causes. To cite my desire for Diet Coke as a reason for my going to the refrigerator is to draw a semantic connection between that desire and other beliefs and desires. But it is hard to see how semantic properties can be causally efficacious. Semantic properties, as such, are available only to interpreting subjects. Thus, to causally explain my trip to the refrigerator in terms of the semantics of my belief, the explanation would have to appeal to an interpreting agent (either me or some homunculus in my brain that can know the semantic value of the belief), and hence interpreting agents would have to be included in our fundamental ontology. Though dualists and other supernaturalists might embrace such an implication, naturalists wish assiduously to avoid it, and to supply a more ordinary sort of causal mechanism to explain my action. However, one cannot simply ignore the semantically laden, reason-based account, because it is precisely this model that is employed in belief-desire psychology, which (Fodor argues) is the most powerful theory we have for predicting and explaining human behavior.

Viewing the mind as a computer supplies an ingenious way of handling this problem. In order to integrate the semantically laden, reason-based explanations of belief-desire psychology with underlying causal mechanisms, it is not necessary to suppose that reasons or semantic properties *be* causally efficacious; it is enough that the properties that are causally efficacious *track* the semantic properties by being linked to them in a lawlike way. Consider a computer simulation of human reasoning or rational action—say, a robot that has representations like DESIRE[Diet Coke] and BELIEF[There is Diet Coke in the refrigerator] and subprograms that take these representations as input and cause it to form further representations (e.g., DESIRE[go to the refrigerator]) and corresponding behaviors (e.g., going to the refrigerator and retrieving a can of Diet Coke). In the computer-driven robot, there is no understanding of semantic properties going on. At the physical level, there are only mechanical and electrical processes. At the functional or program level, there are computational processes that operate on symbols. These symbols *have* semantic properties (for *us*, not for the computer), but the computer does not operate on the basis of these. Rather, it operates on non-semantic, formal, syntactic properties of the symbols.[2] The genius of the program lies in the fact that one can design the representational systems and the program so that all the relevant semantic properties (to which the machine is not sensitive) are mirrored or "tracked" by the syntactic properties that cause its behavior.

All of this is derivative from the fundamental insight that Turing hit upon in proposing the notion of machine computation. One part of this insight was inherited from Peano, Frege, Boole, Hilbert, and other pioneers in the formalization of mathematics. Their insight was that many mathematical processes could be "formalized" in the sense that the inference rules could be stated in syntactic terms, independent of the mathematician's understanding of the meanings of the terms. In a formalized mathematical system, all the relevant semantic properties of the symbols are reflected in syntactic properties, on which the formal inference rules can operate. *Formalization revealed that syntax can be made to track semantics.* The second part of Turing's insight was original: that it is possible to create symbol-manipulating machines that are capable of performing all the syntactic operations needed for inference in any formalized system. *Computing machines reveal that causation can be made to track syntax.*

Together, formalization and computing machines provide a way of linking semantic properties to causation by way of the intermediate element of syntactic properties, as depicted in figure 12.4. A computing machine can do formalized mathematics, for example, generating sensible

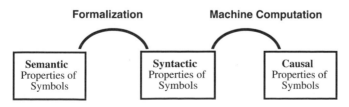

Figure 12.4
Connecting semantics with causation through syntax. Source: Horst 1996, p. 35.

solutions and theorems, but without understanding the symbols, because it is built so that its causal behavior is governed by the syntax of the symbols, and that syntax has been carefully crafted to reflect the semantics. Moreover, this is not just a revelation about mathematics. Many real-world systems can also be modeled in computer programs in the same way. A computer simulation of the weather, for example, requires no understanding on the part of the computer that, say, this bit of data represents a cold front. Rather, the program and data structures are designed so that the program and the syntactic properties of the symbols encode insights about the behavior of cold fronts. The computer thus generates results that are (for us) meaningful, but does so through garden-variety physical causation.

The application of all this to the mind is straightforward. If the mind is itself a digital computer, then we have an account of how the semantically laden processes described by belief-desire psychology can be underwritten by garden-variety physical causation. The causal processes in the computing brain are not sensitive to the semantic properties of the representations on which they operate; however, every semantic property is reflected in a non-semantic, "syntactic" property that is causally efficacious. Since we *want* an account of reasoning that links reasons to causes, CTM solves an important problem that we are committed to solving. And for those interested in naturalizing the mind—that is, exorcizing semantics and consciousness from fundamental ontology—the fact that the causal story turns out to be entirely physical means that it has the virtue of counting as a naturalization of reasoning. CTM thus provides an important sort of compatibility proof: If the mind is a digital computer, then a commitment to belief-desire psychology is compatible with a commitment to purely physical causation, and with a materialist ontology.

I have undertaken extensive critiques of CTM elsewhere (Horst 1996, 1999). One strand of that critique consists in the observation that what CTM supplies is largely a computational account of reasoning, and not an account of things like semantics or consciousness. Even if it is true that the mechanisms underlying human reasoning depend on "syntactic" properties of mental states that track their semantic properties, this does not amount to a wholesale naturalization of the mind, but only of how the mind makes transitions from one set of beliefs and desires to other beliefs and desires and to action. This itself would be a powerful result, and I leave it as an open question whether this line of research will pan out. But note that it does nothing to explain the meaningfulness of mental states or to explain why we (unlike the computer) are sensitive to those meanings *as* meanings. The account works by *assuming* that meanings are already in the picture, and that semantic differences are tracked by causally efficacious syntactic differences.

For the present discussion, I would point to the fact that these assumptions are a kind of idealization in the form of background assumptions. And indeed, to assimilate humans to computers one must bracket the differences in their relations to semantics. Even if it is only the non-semantic properties of mental states that are causally efficacious in humans, the semantic properties are present, and their status in us is arguably different from the sense in which semantic properties are rightly said to be present in representations in computers. Symbols in computers are meaningful to us, but not to the computer. The sense in which they are said to be "meaningful" is cashed out in terms of the conventions and the intentions of designers, programmers, and users. (For a detailed account, see the appendix to Horst 1996.) But if there are symbols in the brain that are involved in meaningful thought, their semantic properties do not depend on interpretive conventions or intentions. For a theory of *reasoning*, this idealization is arguably harmless. All one need do to embrace the theory is hold that the mind is, *among other things*, a computer, and that this explains how we reason. The success or failure of this theory will depend on things other than its inability to explain meaningfulness or our awareness of it. But it would be a mistake to think that this account of *reasoning* supplies an explanation of *meaning*, and thereby a naturalization of the mind in its entirety. That would, at very least, require independent naturalistic explanations of the meaningfulness of mental states and mental representations, and of our ability to be consciously cognizant of such meanings.

The theory is also idealized in other ways that affect its adequacy as an account of reasoning and behavior more directly. The theory is applicable only to knowledge domains that can be formalized. But even in mathematics, not all systems are formalizable, as Gödel showed. Some philosophers (e.g., Lucas 1961) and scientists (e.g., Penrose 1989) have used this result to argue that human mathematicians can grasp mathematical truths that cannot be derived in a formalized system. Others (Dreyfus 1979) have argued that there are types of human thought and agency, such as expert knowledge, that cannot be reduced to algorithmic procedures and hence cannot be executed by computational means.

I tend to think that these criticisms carry a good deal of *prima facie* plausibility, even though they are still argued in the literature. However, for our present purposes it is important to see how this does and does not compromise the theory. What the arguments of Lucas, Penrose, and

Dreyfus seek to establish is that *not all* human cognitive abilities can be explained in computational terms. This, however, is compatible with the claim that the mechanisms that enable *some* such abilities are computational in nature. They are objections to the scope of the theory, rather than to its aptness for some core domain. And this type of idealization is common in the sciences. The fact that temperature cannot be viewed as mean kinetic energy of molecules in the case of solids or plasma does not mean that it cannot be rightly viewed that way in the case of gases. And in the case of the brain there are many instances of redundancy—for example, information about depth can be gained from stereopsis, from motion, or from shadows. The fact that there are some cases in which depth information cannot be gained from shadow patterns (because in those cases there are none) does not imply that a model of the inference of depth from shadow is *never* apt. Likewise, even if *some* cognitive abilities cannot be algorithmic, this does not mean that none are.

CTM and computational psychology provide strategies for making models of belief-desire psychology more formally exact, and for connecting them with underlying causal mechanisms. They may or may not turn out to be psychologically realistic. My own bet would be that the verdict will, in the end, be largely against them. However, whether ultimately apt or inapt, they have many of the marks of respectable scientific models. They do not rely on algebraically formulated laws, but computer programs, pseudocode, and flowcharts are all formally exact in equally respectable ways.

12.6   Representation of Semantic Information in Artificial Intelligence and in Cognitive Science

First-generation AI concentrated on automating formal operations such as logical inference, and CTM likewise concentrates on how reasoning can be seen as a syntactically driven physical process. But much of our reasoning is not, at least on the face of it, in the form of formal inference, but involves use of our implicit grasp of semantic relations between terms. When we reason from "Lassie is a dog" to "Lassie is an animal," we do not characteristically do so by means of an additional major premise that claims that all dogs are animals. (At least we do not do so at a conscious level.) Rather, our semantic understanding seems to be structured in some inexplicit way—either by some concepts' containing others or through there being some non-argumentative links between concepts like DOG and ANIMAL. A second prong of the project of knowledge representation in second-

generation AI was concerned with making explicit such implicit connections through modeling structures of semantic understanding. I shall
explore two of these: semantic networks and the situated knowledge structures called frames and scripts.

12.6.1 Semantic Networks

W. V. O. Quine and Donald Davidson have claimed that words and concepts should be regarded neither as semantic atoms nor as items whose
semantic values are built up out of definitions from semantic atoms.
Rather, their semantics is best described by a network of semantic connections between terms. Indeed, these network connections are at least partially *constitutive* of the meaning of each term, and Quine and Davidson
even go so far as to say that these network connections are completely
global, so that all changes of associations between terms ramify to affect
the meanings of all terms in the network. Quine also famously denied that
we can fully separate semantics from epistemology: because semantic connections are understood in terms of inferential commitments, a change in
meaning is thereby a change in belief as well, and vice versa.

AI researchers of the 1970s began to explore ideas of this sort by creating
computer simulations of semantic and knowledge domains in the form of
semantic networks. The basic feature of semantic networks is that they
model semantic understanding by means of nodes (representing individual
lexical items or concepts) and links (representing various types of semantic
connections between nodes). For example, MEMOD used the "ISA" relation to represent the idea that an individual or type is a member of another
type (i.e., what is indicated by the phrase "is a"). Thus "Lassie is a dog"
might be represented as

LASSIE $\xrightarrow{\text{ISA}}$ DOG

and "dogs are animals" might be represented as

DOG $\xrightarrow{\text{ISA}}$ ANIMAL .

On this model, spelling out the complete semantics of a node would
involve mapping out all of its links to other nodes. As an example, consider
again the representation of semantic information in figure 12.1.

Network models are primarily concerned with mapping the formal
shape of relations between semantic nodes. They are themselves uncom-
mitted on the question of how these nodes and links might be implemented in computers or in the brain. They are thus more on a par with
the gas laws than with the mechanistic explanation of these in terms of

particle collisions. Even in computer models, such links might be implemented in different ways: for example, by a stock of conditional propositions (e.g., (x)(DOGx → ANIMALx)), or by a relational database in which the semantic relations are encoded in the data structure rather than in rules. Any such implementation might supply a candidate hypothesis for how semantic relations are realized in human minds, but the network structure itself is independent of any such hypothesis.

Semantic network theories might be viewed at two levels. At one level, they are very specific hypotheses about the semantic relations between nodes—e.g., that there is an ISA link between DOG and ANIMAL that is partly constitutive of the concept DOG. At another level, semantic network theory (in the singular) is a strategy for modeling semantic relations in general. A problem with a specific network model—say, that it leaves out specific implication relations—can be remedied within the general framework of semantic network modeling (e.g., by adding, deleting, or changing nodes and links). The general framework of semantic networks is also neutral on the question of the Quine-Davidson hypothesis that network relations ramify globally. There might be a global semantic network, or the representation of human semantic understanding (or that of any individual) might yield several disconnected networks. The semantic network hypothesis is likewise neutral on the question of whether the nodes and links in the model represent occurrent states and objects (say, explicit representations in the brain) or capacities.

Semantic network modeling is a strategy (to my mind, an attractive one) for providing formally exact representations of the semantic relations involved in understanding and underlying informal inference. (In addition, it might give greater clarity to what is going on when we say we "believed" propositions like "at least three dogs have spleens," even though we had never entertained them. The "belief" would turn out to be an implication relation implicit in the network structure.) The abstractness of such models is both a strength and a weakness. It is a strength in that it renders the models compatible with a variety of accounts of how such semantic structures might be realized in brains. It is a weakness in that it limits their ability to generate testable predictions. Indeed, in some ways the models might be subject to the same kind of criticism leveled at Freudian psychology: that any potential empirical data can be accommodated by postulating additional types of links or nodes. Moreover, in the case of these models, the obvious strategies for implementing such semantic networks in computers—e.g., representing links as rules or as structures in a relational database—seem to converge poorly with theories from neuroscience. This is not a deep objection to semantic network models, but it deprives them of one kind of role that advocates of CTM might hope AI models would play, as the machine analogies do not help unify computer science with human psychology and neuroscience.

12.6.2 Frames and Scripts

A second research program in knowledge representation was pioneered in this period by Roger Schank's lab. Schank's group focused on the fact that much of our understanding of the world cannot be accounted for by general *lexical* semantics, but requires understanding of specific *contexts*. Some of the more telling examples of this come from social contexts. Like most well-acculturated Americans, I know how to behave, and what to expect, at a restaurant. Indeed, I expect a particular stereotypic sequence of events: my party is seated, a waiter (or a waitress) brings menus, we are given time to order, the waiter returns to take our orders, the courses come in order, the plates are taken away when everyone has finished, we are given the bill, we pay the bill, we tip, and we depart. Deviations from this sequence are noted as violations of the implicit norms of restaurant behavior. For example, if the waiter brings desserts with appetizers (as once happened to me) it is noted as something done wrong. I do not have a similar understanding of how to behave at, say, a Japanese tea ceremony. I do not know what to expect (except that at some point tea is likely to be provided), or how to act at various stages of the ceremony, nor indeed will I necessarily recognize the stages in the ceremony as stages. There is some well-integrated knowledge that I possess with respect to the Western restaurant experience that I lack with respect to Japanese tea ceremonies.

Schank's group approached this problem by suggesting that, in addition to whatever generalized semantic knowledge we possess, we also have knowledge that is specific to particular situations, such as dining at a restaurant. These situations are called *frames*. For many a frame, there is a stylized *script* that outlines the basic possible moves within that frame. These are conceived as epistemic units—things of which we have some type of inner representation that is situation-specific. Schank's project was to make the structure of these frames and scripts explicit in the form of programs and data structures. For example, a portion of one version of the restaurant script was represented as in figure 12.5.

Like semantic network models, frames and scripts may be viewed at multiple levels. At one level, there are specific attempts to make explicit the moves available in a particular context. At another level, frames and scripts provide a general framework for modeling knowledge specific to

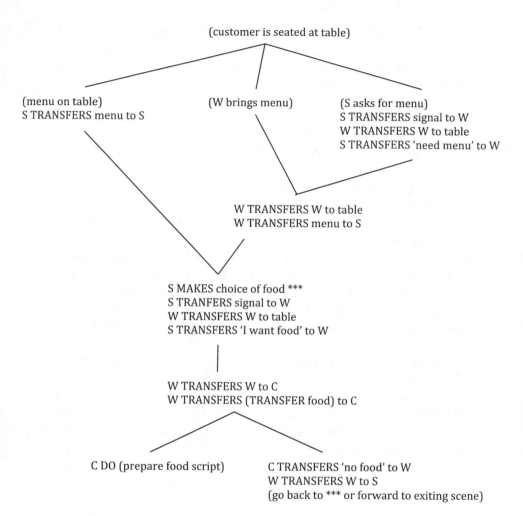

Figure 12.5
A version of the restaurant script. (Source: Schank and Abelson 1977.)

situational contexts. At a still greater level of abstraction, they represent a candidate strategy for addressing the more general insight that much of our understanding seems to be localized in situation-specific units that are plausibly underwritten by specific knowledge structures. (That is, they provide potential resources for making a Cognitive Pluralist account of understanding more exact.) And like the semantic network approach, the frame-based approach is largely neutral on the question of how such structures are implemented in humans or computers.

Frame-based models are also idealized in a number of other ways. They can be taken either as models of knowledge structures in particular individuals (e.g., I lack a tea-ceremony script, but presumably a well-acculturated Japanese person has one) or as social norms that cannot be located within a specific individual's mind. (Schank seems to have thought of them primarily in the first way—i.e., as psychological entities.) And they are idealized in a way that semantic network models are not. Whereas semantic network models are models of general features of cognition, and might additionally aspire to being united in a single all-encompassing network, frames and scripts are by definition partial and local, and hence of more limited use in predicting actual behavior. In particular, they do not tell us what to do when multiple frames are operative.

Suppose, for example, that someone walks through the door of the restaurant while I am dining. If the person is simply another customer, and is someone I do not know, this calls for no departures on my part from the restaurant script, and it calls upon the hostess to greet and seat the person. But if it is an armed person who intends to take hostages, a new script (if I possess one) for hostage situations immediately becomes operative. I probably will abandon the restaurant script and not expect the waiter to bring the rest of the meal in due course. But suppose someone with whom I must soon have an important business conversation enters. The restaurant script tells me how to continue with dinner. Some other relevant script would tell me to greet the person and have the necessary conversation. Nothing in either script tells me which frame should be treated as operative—whether I should "change gears" between operative frames, or how (if possible) to integrate the two scripts. Much of our social (and other practical) competence comes in the form of knowing how and when to move between frames and to weave them together. But nothing in a frame or a script tells us how we might do this. Each is an *idealized* model of how to behave in a particular context, and idealizes away any conflicts and interferences that might take place in real life. Nor do they tell us how to handle everything that might happen in real-world situations, such as when a waiter acts off script and brings dessert along with appetizers.

Dreyfus (1979) calls this problem the "Framing Problem." It is an important theoretical problem for AI, because its solution seems to resist the kind of algorithmic methods commonly employed in computer models. Unlike the steps of a script, the choices of what to do when scripts collide or go awry are poorly defined. Some, including Dreyfus (1979), would suggest that this calls for a kind of expert know-how that cannot be reduced to rules and which, as a consequence, classical AI techniques are poorly equipped to handle.

For our purposes, however, the Framing Problem presents no real difficulties. Our behavior in specific contexts, and our interpretation of those contexts, may be guided by knowledge structures corresponding to frames and scripts even if other behavior and other interpretations are not. Frames and scripts can provide apt models of one kind of cognitive process or structure without providing models of the entire mind. This is a way that these models are idealized, and it is parallel to knowing when to apply different types of models in physics or chemistry. The ability of the model to predict and explain real-world behavior will decrease as the idealization conditions of the model are violated, much as the correspondence of real-world behavior of projectiles will correspond better or worse to gravitational models depending on whether they fall in a vacuum, on a breezy day in the yard, or in a tornado.

12.7   The Idealization and Plurality of Mental Models

If we take seriously the idea that human cognition involves mechanisms that are tolerably well represented by frames and scripts, where does this idea lead us? Basically, it leads us precisely in the direction outlined in chapter 6: that the mind employs a plurality of mental models, that these are each idealized in form, and consequently that scientific models of any of these mental models must be viewed as partial and idealized.

Consider, for example, Schank's attempts at a representation of the knowledge involved in ordering at a restaurant. This is not simply a collection of individual beliefs, but an ordered structure that is specific to a situation. Even if there may be aspects of the representation of human action in the form of a rule-driven computer program that are psychologically unrealistic, something seems eminently right-headed about the idea that there are components of our knowledge that come in situation-specific chunks that are internally structured. If this is correct, then any given human being will have a large number of such "frames" and "scripts"—abstract models of the possibility space for action in different situations. The scientific modeling of such structures will have to take place piecemeal, in the form of making explicit the "scripts" for each such chunk of situation-specific understanding. Hence the overall representation of human psychology will require the (scientific) modeling of however many such (mental) models there may be. Frame theory is not so much a global theory of the types of processing underlying action as a style of explanation that must be fleshed out in the form of a number of specific scientific models.

The Framing Problem also has morals for philosophy of psychology. It shows that models posed at the level of frames and scripts cannot be the whole story about human psychology. We need, in addition, some type of account of how people know how to interweave and shift scripts. This is another way in which frame models or script models are idealized. They strive to tell us things about how people think in specific contexts, but not about how they identify contexts or how they choose to deploy one script or another. There is no question but that people know how to shift between frames and even to modify the behavior called for in one script to adjust for eventualities that the script does not address. (For example, a waiter with a cold knows how to behave while ill, and will, one hopes, integrate that knowledge into his job—e.g., making changes in the distance between himself and customers, and in how he handles utensils, how often he washes his hands, and so on. But the restaurant script does not tell him how to do this. Instead, he must make use of information from outside the restaurant script to adjust his script-based behavior to the situation.) This is arguably akin to feedback relations between modules, though to my knowledge it has not been formalized.

Frames and scripts also have implications for how we should understand people's modeling of other people. When we use a frame or a script, we do not predict or interpret behavior solely in terms of beliefs and desires. Much of our interpretation is based on the role a person is understood to occupy in the situation. We have a script for how waiters behave—a model that idealizes away from the vagaries of any given real-world waiter (who might, after all, be inept or obstreperous, or might be acting on the basis of other scripts by which he is related to the customer). I suspect that a great deal of our prediction and interpretation of other people is role-based and situation-based rather than involving the postulation of the other person's beliefs and desires (Doris 1998; Harman 1999). We revert to belief-desire interpretation only when our expectations are foiled (e.g., we need to question why the waiter acted "off-script") or when we are also pursuing other ends that require different approaches (e.g., we observe that the waiter seems despondent and decide to interrupt the dining experience to ask what ails him, or an action conspicuously off-script prompts us to ask what he is doing and why he is doing it).

In addition to situation-based and role-based interpretation, I think we also employ a great deal of characterological interpretation in our dealings with others. Often our predictions and interpretations of others are based, not on what we think they believe or desire, but on what kind of person we take someone to be. The readiest and best explanation of a person's actions is often that he or she is intrepid, or timid, or belligerent, or nurturing, or defensive. The fact that we often predict and explain behavior in such terms suggests that we have a variety of characterological scripts— models of how an intrepid person (or a timid person, etc.) acts. And the fact that such characterizations often result in strikingly good predictions of behavior suggests that such character traits may in fact be important invariants in individual psychology and hence apt candidates for scientific modeling of their own. They are not, of course, the sorts of things that result in true universal claims about how people will behave. But then the gravitation law does not yield true universal claims about how objects actually move.

Frame theory is thus a regimentation of common-sense psychology that confers on it tools for formally exact models such as are characteristic of the sciences. Its models are partial, plural, and idealized, as I have claimed scientific models in general to be. It also highlights the fact that common-sense psychology is not confined to belief-desire psychology. Scripts point to the fact—independently accessible to common sense and experimental verification—that our reasoning is often driven by models of situations and character types as well as by the imputation of beliefs and desires.

Frame theory is, of course, also an approach to psychology that is highly congenial to Cognitive Pluralism. Indeed, I would regard it as an example of how one might try to flesh out general psychological principles of a Cognitivist account of understanding of particular content domains—an account that also has pluralistic implications. The limitations I have pointed out would thus define important research agendas for a Cognitive Pluralist psychology.

12.8 Free Will (Again)

I conclude by once again returning to the topic of free will. As was suggested in part I, free will seems in some ways threatened, not only by the notion of a world governed by physical laws, but also by the idea of psychological and psychophysical laws. And here, indeed, the threat is even more direct. To the extent that psychological processes are governed by laws, or at least explained in terms of mechanisms that admit of rigorous formally exact models, they would also, as a consequence, seem in jeopardy of being deterministic. Indeed, the more mechanism-like our understanding of psychological processes, the less room seems to be left for free will. As a consequence, the general tenor of part III—that there are respectable models of the mind in the sciences of the mind that pick out real causal invariants in psychodynamics—would seem to raise anew questions about whether space is left for free will, which was defended in part II. To the extent that psychophysics, localization, neural modeling, and regimented versions of belief-desire psychology pin down real invariants in how the mind operates, there might seem to be correspondingly little room left for free will.

I agree that one is strongly drawn to such a conclusion. However, I think that, in light of previous observations, the pull toward it is really the pull of a kind of psychological illusion. In particular, it is an example of the type of fallacious reasoning that moves from a legitimate insight that a particular type of mechanism is real to the unsubstantiated conclusion that the *entire* story about the mind is mechanistic. To guard against this illusion, we must remind ourselves of the general story about models, and we must apply it to the particular cases at hand.

The general story about models is that they single out real invariants that are potential partial contributors to real-world behavior. Both the partiality and the potentiality need to be emphasized. The fact that a neural network model or a belief-desire model picks out real invariants does not mean that it supplies the whole story about psychodynamics. Rather, each model presents an incomplete and idealized story. And, among other things that may be idealized away, the story may idealize away from contributions of free agent causation. Of course, the fact that a model M idealizes away from some other possible causal contributor C does not in any way establish the reality of C. The gravitation law idealizes away from the actions of gremlins, but this by no means substantiates the existence of gremlins. Similarly, the fact that psychological, neural, and psychophysical models idealize away from free will does not itself establish that there are free actions. However, the idealization analysis does establish a kind of compatibility proof: nothing about our commitment to laws or other formally exact models is incompatible with there being, in addition, free will.

Let us look at this more concretely with respect to several of the cases discussed in earlier chapters. In chapters 10 and 11, psychophysical laws and their connection with explanations in terms of localization and mathematical models were examined. Psychophysical effects, however, are largely independent of any considerations about free will, because they are automatic and immune to voluntary interpretation. Psychophysical illusions, for example, cannot be dispelled either by knowledge of how the illusion works or by any act of will. Try as one might, the two areas of the Cornsweet illusion will look to be of different brightnesses, and the Kanizsa square will look brighter than the background. Regardless of whether there is free will in some domains of human experience and action, one does not find it here. Even the staunchest defender of free will ought not to think that one's perceptual gestalts are produced freely (except, of course, in the sense that one can choose where to look, or to close one's eyes).

The situation is rather different with respect to the belief-desire models discussed in the present chapter. Here, we have looked at such things as the mechanisms underlying reasoning processes, lexical-semantic connections as modeled by semantic networks, and structured semantic representations in the form of frames and scripts. Let us take each of these in order. First, let us assume that there are types of causal mechanisms that underlie reasoning processes and make such processes possible. Does this mean that reasoning is deterministic? Not entirely. Consider an analogy: There are mechanisms in my car that cause it to drive in the way it does—for example, mechanisms in the transmission convert revolutions of the engine into thrust in a deterministic way. But how fast the car moves depends on which gear I choose to put the car in and how far I depress the gas pedal. (This is more obvious with a manual transmission, but one can also force an automatic transmission to shift up or down.) The transmission works deterministically; however, which gear it is in is not determined by the (manual) transmission, but by the driver. Similarly, it could be that reasoning processes—i.e., processes of working through a theoretical or practical syllogism—are (in well-trained reasoners) fully deterministic and automatic, and yet there is another level of choice involved in whether to set these mechanisms to work, or to employ some other mechanisms, or merely to "put the clutch in" and abstain from inference.

Of course, this is, at best, a kind of compatibility proof. Moreover, the analogy is far from perfect. Descartes noted that the relationship between a person and his or her body is far more intimate than that between a pilot and a boat, and the same can be said for the transmission metaphor, though I happen to think the metaphor of "putting in the clutch" on one's thoughts and feelings is a very useful one for moral practice. I have surely not established that we have free control over when we make inferences from particular premises (and not from others). My point is far more modest: The assumption that the *reasoning* processes are mechanistic is not sufficient to establish that the *mind* is mechanistic *without remainder*, any more than the fact that a car's drive train operates mechanistically establishes that there is no driver who chooses when to shift gears.

With respect to semantic networks, there is also room for free will here. First and foremost, semantic networks are supposed to be descriptions of the relations between a person's concepts *at a single moment*, and hence are not themselves dynamic models at all. They can be supplemented with model of semantic inference that is program-like and hence appears mechanistic. But this is an idealized model of how one reasons *when one is content to stick with the inferential links one currently operates with*. But one can also change and refine the ways in which one understands one concept to be related to another. Indeed, we often do so *by choosing* to do so, and this at least appears to be a paradigmatic case of free action. On the one hand, one can choose to change the semantic links that are operative. One can, for example, choose to use a word in a new way, on a variety of grounds, ranging from empirical discoveries (e.g., that whales have more in common with mammals than with fish) to ideological grounds to pure obstreperousness. On the other hand, a semantic connection may depend on context, and may require a choice as to whether it is operative in the present context. The ability to rearrange semantic connections is needed in order to track other people's semantic links where they are different from one's own—what Brandom (1993) calls "scorekeeping." (I have to make myself remember that Smith the Aristotelian does not use the word 'matter' for a type of substance.)

Though reorganization of semantic networks is probably more the exception than the rule, frames and scripts seem to demand some kind of continual process of decision as to which frames and which scripts are treated as operative and relevant at the moment. And this raises the question of what kind of processes are at work here. The Framing Problem raises difficult issues about whether these processes can operate at the level of explicit representations and computational rules, and hence about whether one type of mechanism-like process can account for shifting frames. On the other hand, it is quite dubious, even by libertarian lights, that all such processes involve free will; no doubt many of them work automatically, even if at present we do not know the nature of the mechanisms by which they operate. However, at least some of the relevant situations seem to provide grist for the libertarian's mill.

Consider situations in which one experiences competing motivations. Suppose I am presented with an opportunity to gain profit under conditions that I deem to be unjust to some party or parties that will be exploited in the processes. Suppose that I have one frame (A) in which I pursue the opportunity in order to enjoy the profit and another frame (B) in which I decline the opportunity, and perhaps even expose it to public censure, out of an abhorrence of exploitation. I think we can appreciate the possibility of a situation in which I am truly tempted by both possibilities and remain for some time in a state of equipoise between them. Perhaps for the person who is sufficiently virtuous, or sufficiently wanton, the process is automatic. But when one is somewhere in between, this seems like a paradigmatic case in which we normally assume that a free choice is being made. For example, we hold a person particularly culpable if he first deliberates about whether to act justly and then chooses to act unjustly.

What will determine which course of action one chooses? At least four further answers suggest themselves. The first is that choices in such situations are determined by character. And if there are characterological models that allow us to predict and interpret action, these again might suggest a deterministic interpretation. Some philosophers have recently suggested, however, that experiments in social psychology suggest that character plays little or no statistically significant role in decision making, and that choices are better predicted by features of context (Doris 1998; Harman 1999). One might also combine these two alternatives into a theory that says that decisions are a function of character plus context. A third possibility, compatible with any of the others, is that decisions are determined by yet-unknown neural processes that are not like programs or like circuits. (The models would be compatible because they were framed at different levels.) However, nothing about any of these types of models *forces* a deterministic interpretation. The aptness of characterological, context-based, or neural models for explaining action requires only that they single out real partial and potential contributors to the dynamics of action, not that they provide a complete account. Indeed, experiments in social and cognitive psychology tend to produce data that require statistical rather than deterministic interpretations. Even a virtuous person sometimes acts against his or her own virtues. One doesn't act the same way every time one is in the same situation. And neural mechanisms, as we saw in chapter 11, are essentially open to influence from many exogenous factors.

Speaking of "laws" of the mind does indeed lead people to have doubts about the freedom of the will. But the explanation for this is to be found at a purely rhetorical level. To talk in terms of laws is sometimes to talk as though the processes had no element of freedom, but this is because we are dealing with idealized models. So long as we remember that fact, laws pose no direct threat to freedom. Laws can pick out *real* causal factors without picking out *all* the causal factors. It is only when we forget the ways our models are idealized that we are led illegitimately to infer that laws preclude freedom.

12.9 Conclusion

Common-sense psychology is to be understood in terms of a plurality of mental models of people's actions, thoughts, characters, and situations. These mental models probably lack the regimentation and formal exactitude of scientific models, though they share other features (plurality, partiality, idealization). However, common-sense psychology may contain core insights into how people think and come to behave—insights that can then be made into more exact and scientific theories through the use of more exacting tools, such as those of decision theory or information-theoretic knowledge representation. There are important questions about the psychological realism of all such theories. And each of them is highly partial and idealized, probably to a much greater extent and in more fundamental ways than the models employed in fundamental physics. Within a Cognitive Pluralist framework, however, we can see these as variations on a theme rather than as essential differences. All models are plural, partial, idealized, and cast in some particular representational system. Scientific models are particularly regimented and formally exact. And within the class of scientific models we find different types of idealization conditions that result in closer or more distant relationships between models and the real-world behavior that they are invoked to explain.

Moreover, the plausibility of structures such as frames and scripts points to a need to postulate localized and semi-autonomous knowledge domains that employ proprietary representational structures, even though they are not plausibly products of natural selection. It is exceedingly unlikely that evolution has selected modules for restaurant behavior or tea ceremonies. It is similarly unlikely that when restaurant behavior or tea ceremonies are learned there is a particular anatomical unit in the brain that is devoted to them in a species-constant fashion. Mental models are *like* "hard-wired" modules in behaving semi-autonomously and having their proprietary representational systems, but many of them are acquired through learning. This, in turn, lends greater credence to my suggestion, in part I, that scientific models are themselves a special case of a more ecumenical phenomenon of local and semi-autonomous models employed for dealing with the world in everyday life. Presumably one could explore frames and scripts for various experimental and theoretical contexts as cognitivist models of how people think in doing science. And presumably these would share the need to postulate separate frames and scripts for separate contexts, even though in this case all the contexts would be scientific.

Parts I and III of this book have thus woven together several mutually supporting strands of a general picture of the nature of human cognition and its specially regimented development in the sciences. Chapter 6 suggested a Cognitive Pluralist account of the mind in the service of examining several problems in philosophy of mind. On that account, both science and ordinary thought employ multiple specialized models of features and portions of the world, each idealized in various ways and employing a representational system that is apt for its own domain. In part III, this cognitive pluralist account has been brought into dialogue with case studies in several areas of the sciences of cognition. The general account and the case studies support and mutually inform one another in both directions. On the one hand, the general account is useful in revealing the similarities and differences between particular sciences of the mind and other sciences, cashed out in large measure in terms of the types of idealizations they employ. On the other hand, the case studies help support the general account in two ways. They do so first by dint of the fertility of the Cognitive Pluralist framework in highlighting features of the models examined. Second, they provide independent evidence, arising from neural modeling, cognitive psychology, and artificial intelligence, for the view that it may be necessary quite generally to postulate that the mind understands the world through a variety of special-purpose units, both hardwired and learned, through which it triangulates an objective world.

Notes

Chapter 2

1. I should note two things about this example. First, we have built the example as though all of the "other things" that need to be "equal" can be explicitly enumerated. It is tempting, however, to view the character of such claims as really open-ended. Open-ended conditions do not submit themselves readily to first-order logic, and so *ceteris paribus* laws are often formulated as "*Ceteris paribus*, ψ" or as "Other things being equal, ψ." Such a formulation, taken out of a particular logical formulation, can encompass both the cases in which the conditions C are enumerable and those in which they are open-ended. It is my understanding that the expressions "*ceteris paribus* laws" and "*ceteris paribus* clauses" have been used for both enumerable and open-ended claims. If there is ever a need to differentiate them, we might call them "enumerable *ceteris paribus* laws" and "open-ended *ceteris paribus* laws," recalling that only the former has been given a reconstruction in first-order predicate logic. Second, it is slightly controversial whether *ceteris paribus* laws are to be understood as equivalent to the Logical Empiricist notion of laws with boundary conditions. The Empiricists saw that, even within the physical sciences, their reconstructed laws often had to be restricted in scope. For example, the identification of temperature with mean kinetic energy works when one is talking about gases, but not when one is talking about solids or plasmas, in which there are not collisions of gas molecules. Such laws were thus understood to be hedged by boundary conditions specifying the cases in which the laws did or did not apply. (It is indifferent whether the conditions specify what is inside the boundaries or what is outside of them.) So if a strict law takes the form $\forall x(Lx)$, a law requiring boundary conditions takes the form not-B $\supset \forall x(Lx)$, where B is the list of conditions under which L does not hold. This is, of course, equivalent in form to what we have called a natural interpretation of *ceteris paribus* laws, and hence it is reasonable to think that the opposition between "strict and exceptionless" laws and "*ceteris paribus*" laws is to be understood as paralleling the Positivist analysis of laws *simpliciter* as universally quantified claims ranging over objects and events, and the *ceteris paribus* laws as involving laws of the same form, embedded within boundary conditions spelled out by the *ceteris paribus* clause.

2. I have not seen Kim address this issue in print. However, I brought it up with him in personal conversation during his visit to the 1993 NEH Summer Institute on Naturalism at the University of Nebraska, and to the best of my recollection he seemed to endorse this consequence.

Chapter 3

1. Functionalism is sometimes taken to provide a kind of definition of mental states in functional terms. If this means that it provides necessary *and sufficient* conditions for mental states, it is dubious that any such theory could prove adequate. Among other things, the functional description does not account for the intentional and phenomenological properties of mental states (cf. Horst 1996; Chalmers 1996). However, functionalism can also be taken, in a weaker sense, as claiming only that mental states have functional descriptions. These abstract descriptions may provide necessary conditions for a mental state to be of a certain type, but will not generally provide sufficient conditions. (Compare Horst 1996.)

Chapter 4

1. *Ceteris paribus* laws can be formulated with either a positive embedding clause (specifying the conditions under which they hold good) or a negative embedding clause (specifying the conditions under which they fail to hold). I have opted for the negative formulation, as it seems more accurate to view boundary conditions as an open-ended list of states of affairs under which a stated generalization fails to hold.

2. Similar points have also been argued by Lange (1993), Lipton (1999), and Morreau (1999).

3. Here is Cartwright's formulation: "*If* there are no forces other than gravitational forces at work, *then* two bodies exert a force between each other which varies inversely as the square of the distance between them, and varies directly as the product of their masses." (1983, p. 58) I think this is not the move one needs to make to generate a *ceteris paribus* law about actual behavior. Rather, the talk of forces seems to be a construal of the law that emphasizes the other prong of the ambiguity Cartwright has uncovered: causal capacities.

4. The notion that laws apply to ideal(ized) worlds rather than the real world was explored within the Logical Empiricist movement, and more recently, with respect to the current problem, by Horgan and Tienson (1996).

Chapter 6

1. One might well speculate that the capacity for models that allow prediction and description is phylogenetically much older than the capacity for theoretical modeling.

2. There is a story to the effect that the great mathematician Gauss was among the first to conceive of the idea of non-Euclidean geometries, in the early 1830s, but abandoned the idea because he was a devotee of Kant and thought Kant had proved the *a priori* truth of Euclidean geometry. He thus deferred to Kant in this, becoming, as it were, the father of "deferential geometry."

3. As paradigmatic examples of how this might be done in philosophy of the sciences of the mind, I recommend Simon 1977, Bechtel and Richardson 1983, Bechtel 1984 and 1993, and Bickle 1998 and 2002.

Chapter 9

1. Of course, Descartes, an interactionist dualist, did not really believe the physical world to be causally closed.

Chapter 12

1. 'Cognitive science' is sometimes used as a blanket term for all the disciplines studying the mind, regardless of their methodologies. But it is also used in a narrower sense to apply only to disciplines that employ information-processing or computational metaphors, thereby excluding neuroscience, network theories, and ethology.

2. Though see Horst 1996 for a criticism of the view that computers are sensitive to truly *syntactic* properties. There it is argued that syntax too is conventional.

Bibliography

Abelson, R. P. 1973. The structure of belief systems. In *Computer Models of Thought and Language*, ed. R. Schank and K. Colby. Freeman.

Abelson, R. P., and C. M. Reich. 1969. Implicational molecules: A method for extracting meaning from input sentences. *International Joint Conferences on AI* 1: 647–748.

Anderson, J. A. 1977. Neural models with cognitive implications. In *Basic Processes in Reading. Perception and Comprehension*, ed. D. LaBerge and S. Samuels. Erlbaum.

Anderson, J. A. 1995. *Introduction to Neural Networks*. MIT Press.

Anderson, J. A., and G. Hinton, eds. 1981. *Parallel Models for Associative Memory*. Erlbaum.

Anderson, J. A., and E. Rosenfeld, eds. 1988. *Neurocomputing*. MIT Press.

Anderson, J. A., J. Silverstein, S. Ritz, and R. Jones. 1978. Distinctive features, categorical perception and probability learning: some applications of a neural model. *Psychological Review* 85: 597–603.

Anderson, J. R. 1980. On the merits of ACT and information-processing psychology: A response to Wexler's review. *Cognition* 8: 73–88.

Anderson, J. R., and G. H. Bower. 1973. *Human Associative Memory*. Winston.

Antony, Louise. 1989. Anomalous monism and the problem of explanatory force. *Philosophical Review* 98, April: 153–187.

Arend, L. E. 1973. Spatial differential and integral operations in human vision: Implications of stabilized retinal image fading. *Psychological Review* 80: 347–395.

Audi, Robert. 1993. *The Structure of Justification*. Cambridge University Press.

Ayer, A. J. 1954. *Philosophical Essays*. Macmillan.

Békésy, G. von 1972. Compensation method to measure the contrast produced by contours. *Journal of the Optical Society of America* 62: 1247–1251.

Bradski, Gary, and Stephen Grossberg. 1995. Fast-learning VIEWNET architectures for recognizing three-dimensional objects from multiple two-dimensional views. *Neural Networks* 8 (7/8): 1053–1080.

Brentano, Franz. 1874. *Psychologie vom empirischen Standpunkt*. Duncker & Humblot.

Campbell, F. W., E. R. Howell, and J. R. Johnstone. 1978. A comparison of threshold and suprathreshold appearance of gratings with components in the low and high spatial frequency range. *Journal of Physiology* 284: 193–201.

Carpenter, Gail A., Stephen Grossberg, Natalya Markuzon, John N. Reynolds, and David B. Rosen. 1992. Fuzzy ARTMAP: A neural network architecture for incremental supervised learning of analog multidimensional maps. *IEEE Transactions on Neural Networks* 3 (5): 698–713.

Carpenter, Gail A., and William D. Ross. 1995. ART-EMAP: A neural network architecture for object recognition by evidence accumulation. *IEEE Transactions on Neural Networks* 6 (4): 805–818.

Cartwright, Nancy. 1983. *How the Laws of Physics Lie*. Oxford University Press.

Cartwright, Nancy. 1989. *Nature's Capacities and Their Measurement*. Clarendon.

Cartwright, Nancy. 1999. *The Dappled World: A Study of the Boundaries of Science*. Cambridge University Press.

Cat, Jordi, Nancy Cartwright, and Hasok Chang. 1996. Otto Neurath: Politics and the unity of science. In *The Disunity of Science: Boundaries, Contexts, and Power*, ed. P. Galison and D. Stump. Stanford University Press.

Chalmers, David. 1996. *The Conscious Mind: In Search of a Fundamental Theory*. Oxford University Press.

Chisholm, Roderick. 1957. Intentional inexistence. In R. Chisholm, *Perceiving: A Philosophical Study*. Cornell University Press.

Chomsky, Noam. 1965. *Aspects of the Theory of Syntax*. MIT Press.

Chomsky, Noam. 1966. *Cartesian Linguistics*. Harper and Row.

Chomsky, Noam. 1988. *Language and Problems of Knowledge*. MIT Press.

Clark, Austen. 1993. *Sensory Qualities*. Clarendon.

Cohen, Michael A., and Stephen Grossberg. 1984. Neural dynamics of boundary perception: Features, boundaries, diffusion and resonance. *Perception & Psychophysics* 36 (5): 428–456.

Cohen, Paul R., and Edward A. Feigenbaum. 1982. *The Handbook of Artificial Intelligence*, volume 3. William Kaufman.

Colby, Kenneth M. 1975. *Artificial Paranoia*. Pergamon.

Cornsweet, T. N. 1970. *Visual Perception*. Academic Press.

Craik, J. J. W. 1940. *Visual Adaptation*. Cambridge University.

Crick, Francis. 1993. *The Astonishing Hypothesis: The Scientific Search for the Soul*. Scribner.

Crick, Francis, and Christof Koch. 1993. A framework for consciousness. *Nature Neuroscience* 6 (2): 119–126.

Davidson, Donald. 1970/1980. Mental events. In *Essays on Actions and Events*. Oxford University Press.

Davidson, Donald. 1973/1980. The material mind. In *Essays on Actions and Events*. Oxford University Press.

Davidson, Donald. 1974. Philosophy as psychology. In *Philosophy of Psychology*. Macmillan.

Davidson, M., and J. A. Whiteside. 1971. Human brightness perception near sharp contours. *Journal of the Optical Society of America* 61: 530–536.

Dennett, Daniel. 1984. *Elbow Room. The Varieties of Free Will Worth Wanting*. MIT Press.

Dennett, Daniel. 1987. *The Intentional Stance*. MIT Press.

Dennett, Daniel. 1991. *Consciousness Explained*. Little, Brown.

DeWitt, B. 1970. Quantum mechanics and reality. *Physics Today* 23 (9): 30–40.

Dooley, R. P., and M. I. Greenfield. 1977. Measurements of edge-induced visual contrast and a spatial-frequency interaction of the Cornsweet illusion. *Journal of the Optical Society of America* 67: 761–765.

Doris, John. 1998. Persons, situations and virtue ethics. *Nous* 32 (4): 281–530.

Dray, William. 1957. *Laws and Explanations in History*. Clarendon.

Dreyfus, Hubert. 1979. *What Computers Can't Do*. Harper and Row.

Dupré, John. 1993. *The Disorder of Things: Metaphysical Foundations of the Disunity of Science*. Harvard University Press.

Earman, John, John Roberts, and Sheldon Smith. 2002. *Ceteris paribus* lost. *Erkenntnis* 57: 281–301.

Fechner, Gustav Theodor. 1877. *Sachen der Psychophysik*. Breitkopf & Hartel.

Flanagan, Owen J. 2002. *The Problem of the Soul: Two Visions of Mind and How to Reconcile Them*. Basic Books.

Fodor, Jerry. 1974. Special sciences (or: the distunity of science as a working hypothesis). *Synthese* 28: 97–115.

Fodor, Jerry. 1975. *The Language of Thought*. Crowell.

Fodor, Jerry. 1981. *RePresentations*. MIT Press.

Fodor, Jerry. 1987. *Psychosemantics*. MIT Press.

Fodor, Jerry. 1990. Making mind matter more. In *A Theory of Content*. MIT Press.

Gibson, J. J. 1966. *The Senses Considered as Perceptual Systems*. Houghton Mifflin.

Giere, Ronald. 1999. *Science Without Laws*. University of Chicago Press.

Gillett, Carl, and Barry Loewer. 2001. *Physicalism and Its Discontents*. Cambridge University Press.

Gopnik, Alison, and H. M. Welman. 1994. The theory theory. In *Mapping the Mind: Domain Specificity in Cognition and Culture*, ed. L. Hirschfeld and S. Gelman. Cambridge University Press.

Grossberg, Stephen. 1980. How does the brain build a cognitive code? *Psychological Review* 87: 1–51.

Grossberg, Stephen. 1983. The quantized geometry of visual space. *Behavioral and Brain Sciences* 6: 625–692.

Grossberg, Stephen. 1987a. *The Adaptive Brain*. North-Holland.

Grossberg, Stephen. 1987b. Cortical dynamics of three-dimensional form, color, and brightness perception, I: Monocular theory. *Perception & Psychophysics* 41: 87–116.

Grossberg, Stephen. 1987c. Cortical dynamics of three-dimensional form, color and brightness perception, II: Binocular theory. *Perception & Psychophysics* 41: 117–158.

Grossberg, Stephen. 1988. Nonlinear neural networks: Principles, mechanisms and architectures. *Neural Networks* 1: 17–61.

Grossberg, Stephen. 1994. 3-D vision and figure-ground separation by visual cortex. *Perception & Psychophysics* 55 (1): 48–120.

Grossberg, Stephen. 1998. *The Complementary Brain: Unifying Brain Dynamics and Modularity*. Boston University.

Grossberg, Stephen, and Ennio Mingolla. 1985a. Neural dynamics of perceptual grouping: textures, boundaries, and emergent segmentations. *Perception & Psychophysics* 38: 141–171.

Grossberg, Stephen, and Ennio Mingolla. 1985b. Neural dynamics of form perception: Boundary completion, illusory figures and neon color spreading. *Psychological Review* 92: 173–211.

Grossberg, Stephen, and D. Todorovic. 1988. Neural dynamics of 1-D and 2-D brightness perception: A unified model of classical and recent phenomena. *Perception & Psychophysics* 43: 241–277.

Growney, R. L., and D. F. Neri. 1986. The appearance of the Cornsweet illusion: Measures of perceived contrast and evenness of brightness. *Perception & Psychophysics* 39: 81–86.

Grünbaum, Adolph. 1984. *The Foundations of Psychoanalysis: A Philosophical Critique.* University of California Press.

Guan, L., J. A. Anderson, and J. P. Sutton. 1997. A network of networks processing model for image regularization. *IEEE Transactions on Neural Networks* 8: 1–6.

Hacking, Ian. 1996. The disunities of the sciences. In *The Disunity of Science: Boundaries, Contexts, and Power,* ed. P. Gallison and D. Stump. Stanford University Press.

Hadot, Pierre. 2002. *What Is Ancient Philosophy?* Belknap.

Hamada, J. 1982. The contour-enhancement effects produced by darkening effects. In *Psychophysical Judgment and the Process of Perception,* ed. H. G. Geissler and P. Petzold. North-Holland.

Hamada, J. 1985. Asymmetric lightness cancellation in Craik-O'Brien patterns of negative and positive contrast. *Biological Cybernetics* 52: 117–122.

Harman, Gilbert. 1999. Moral philosophy meets social psychology: Virtue ethics and the fundamental attribution error. *Proceedings of the Aristotelian Society* 99: 315–331.

Hayes-Roth, B. 1980. *Human Planning Processes.* Rand Corporation.

Heggelund, P., and S. Kreklink. 1976. Edge dependent lightness distributions at different adaptation levels. *Vision Research* 16: 493–496.

Helmholtz, Hermann von. 1867. *Handbuch der Physiologischen Optik.* Voss.

Hering, E. 1878. *Zur Lehre von Lichtsinn.* Gerald.

Honderich, Ted. 1982. The argument for anomalous monism. *Analysis* 42: 59–64.

Horgan, Terrence, and John Tienson. 1996. *Connectionism and the Philosophy of Psychology.* MIT Press.

Horgan, Terry, and John Tienson. 2002. The intentionality of phenomenology and the phenomenology of intentionality. In *Philosophy of Mind: Classical and Contemporary Readings,* ed. D. Chalmers. Oxford University Press.

Horst, Steven. 1992. Notions of 'representation' and the ambiguity of 'belief'. *Synthese* 104: 123–145.

Horst, Steven. 1996. *Symbols, Computation and Intentionality: A Critique of the Computational Theory of Mind.* University of California Press.

Horst, Steven. 1998. The computational theory of mind. In *The MIT Encyclopedia of the Cognitive Sciences,* ed. R. Wilson and F. Keil. MIT Press.

Horst, Steven. 1999. Symbols and computation. *Minds and Machines* 9 (3): 347–381.

Horst, Steven. 2003. Computational theory of mind. In Stanford Encyclopedia of Philosophy (http://plato.stanford.edu/entries/computational-mind/).

Horst, Steven. 2005. Modeling, localization and the explanation of phenomenal properties. *Synthese* 147 (3): 477–513.

Horst, Steven. 2007. *Beyond Reduction: Philosophy of Mind and Post-Reductionist Philosophy of Science.* Oxford University Press.

Hurvich, L. M. 1981. *Color Vision.* Sinauer.

Isono, H. 1979. Measurement of Edge-Induced Visual Contrast. NHK Laboratories.

Kanizsa, G. 1979. *Organization in Vision.* Praeger.

Kant, Immanuel. 1998. *Critique of Pure Reason.* Cambridge University Press.

Kim, Jaegwon. 1993. *Supervenience and Mind: Selected Philosophical Essays.* Cambridge University Press.

Kim, Jaegwon. 2003. Philosophy of mind and psychology. In *Donald Davidson,* ed. K. Ludwig. Cambridge University Press.

Laming, Donald. 1997. *The Measurement of Sensation.* Oxford University Press.

Land, Edwin H. 1974. The retinex theory of colour vision. *Proceedings of the Royal Institution of Great Britain* 47: 23–58.

Lange, Marc. 1993. Natural laws and the problem of provisos. *Erkenntnis* 38: 233–248.

Lepore, Ernest, and Barry Loewer. 1987. Mind matters. *Journal of Philosophy* 84: 630–642.

Levine, Joseph. 1983. Materialism and qualia: The explanatory gap. *Pacific Philosophical Quarterly* 64: 354–361.

Lipton, Peter. 1999. All else being equal. *Philosophy* 74: 155–168.

Lucas, J. R. 1961. Minds, machines and Gödel. *Philosophy* 36: 112–127.

Macintyre, Alisdair. 1957. Determinism. *Mind* 66: 28–41.

Minsky, Marvin. 1985. *The Society of Mind.* Simon & Schuster.

Morreau, Michael. 1999. Other things being equal. *Philosophical Studies* 96: 163–182.

Newell, Alan, and Herbert Simon. 1956. The logic theory machine. *I.R.E. Transactions on Information Theory* 2: 61–79.

Newell, Alan, and Herbert Simon. 1963. Computers in psychology. In *Handbook of Mathematical Psychology*, ed. R. Luce, R. Bush, and E. Galanter. Wiley.

Noë, Alva. 2004. *Action in Perception*. MIT Press.

Norman, D. A., and D. E. Rumelhart, and the The LNR Research Group. 1976. *Explorations in Cognition*. Freeman.

O'Brien, V. 1958. Contour Perception, Illusion, and Reality. *Journal of the Optical Society of America* 48: 112–119.

O'Connor, Timothy. 2000. *Persons and Causes: The Metaphysics of Free Will*. Oxford University Press.

Papineau, David. 2001. The rise of physicalism. In *Physicalism and Its Discontents*, ed. C. Gillett and B. Loewer. Cambridge University Press.

Papineau, David. 2002. *Thinking about Consciousness*. Oxford University Press.

Penrose, Roger. 1989. *The Emperor's New Mind*. Oxford University Press.

Pereboom, Derek. 2001. *Living Without Free Will*. Cambridge University Press.

Piaget, Jean. 1957. *Construction of Reality in the Child*. Routledge & Kegan Paul.

Pinker, Stephen. 1994. *The Language Instinct*. Penguin.

Polkinghorne, John. 1989. *Science and Providence: God's Interaction with the World*. Shambhala.

Quillian, M. R. 1968. Semantic memory. In *Semantic Information Processing*, ed. M. Minsky. MIT Press.

Ramachandran, V. S. 1999. *Phantoms in the Brain: Probing the Mysteries of the Human Mind*. Harper.

Ratliff, F. 1978. A discourse on edges. In *Visual Psychophysics and Physiology*, ed. J. Armington, J. Krauskopf, and B. Wooten. Academic Press.

Ratliff, F., and L. Sirovich. 1978. Equivalence classes of visual stimuli. *Vision Research* 18: 845–851.

Ricoeur, Paul. 1970. *Freud and Philosophy: An Essay on Interpretation. Translated by D. Savage*. Yale University Press.

Riker, John Hanwell. 1997. *Ethics and the Discovery of the Unconscious*. SUNY Press.

Rumelhart, David E., James L. McClelland, and PDP Research Group. 1987. *Parallel Distributed Processing*. MIT Press.

Sacks, Oliver. 1985. *The Man Who Mistook His Wife for a Hat and Other Clinical Tales*. Simon and Schuster/Summit.

Simon, Herbert. 1977. *Models of Discovery and Other Topics in the Methods of Science.* Reidel.

Skinner, Burrhus F. 1971. *Beyond Freedom and Dignity.* Knopf.

Smith, Sheldon. 2002. Violated laws, *ceteris paribus* clauses, and capacities. *Synthese* 130: 235–264.

Spillman, Lothar, and John S. Werner, eds. 1990. *Visual Perception: The Neurophysiological Foundations.* Academic Press.

Stevens, S. S. 1951. *Handbook of Experimental Psychology.* Wiley.

Suppe, Frederick. 1989. *The Semantic Conception of Theories and Scientific Realism.* University of Illinois Press.

Todorovic, D. 1987. The Craik-O'Brien-Cornsweet effect: New varieties and their theoretical implications. *Perception & Psychophysics* 42: 545–560.

Turing, Alan. 1936. On computable numbers. *Proceedings of the London Mathematical Society* 24: 230–265.

Turing, Alan. 1950. Computing machinery and intelligence. *Mind* 49: 433–460.

Ungerleider, L. G., and M. Mishkin. 1982. Two cortical visual systems. In *Analysis of Visual Behavior*, ed. D. Ingle. MIT Press.

Van Essen, David C., Charles H. Anderson, and Daniel J. Felleman. 1990. Information processing in the primate visual system: An integrated systems perspective. *Science* 255 (5043): 419–423.

van Inwagen, Peter. 1983. *An Essay on Free Will.* Clarendon.

Varela, Francisco J., Evan Thompson, and Eleanor Rosch. 1991. *The Embodied Mind.* MIT Press.

Vihvelin, Kadri. 2007. Arguments for Incompatiblism. In Stanford Encyclopedia of Philosophy (http:plato.stanford.edu/entries/incompatibilism-arguments/).

Weber, Ernst Heinrich. 1834. *Du pulsu, resorptione, audiu et tactu. Annotationes anatomicae et physiologicae.* Koehler.

Wellman, H. M. 1990. *The Child's Theory of Mind.* MIT Press.

Wigner, Eugene P. 1970. *Symmetries and Reflections: Scientific Essays.* MIT Press.

Winch, Peter. 1958. *The Idea of a Social Science.* Humanities Press.

Woodward, Jim. 2002. There is no such thing as a *ceteris paribus* law. *Erkenntnis* 57: 303–328.

Index